This is the story of Seattle during its first hundred years, seen through the lives of the gusty and vigorous personalities of its settlers and early citizens. Along with tales of the gamblers, sawdust women and fancy men who made the first and original Skid Road as famous as San Francisco's Barbary Coast, there are marvelous accounts of Doc Maynard and Chief Sealth (or Seattle), Asa Mercer and John Considine, Judge Thomas Burke, Mayor Gill, and the fabulous Dave Beck.

Informal and picturesque, SKID ROAD is also a sound history of Seattle: pioneering, Indian warfare, lumber, railroads, the great fire of 1889, the Alaska gold rush, the amusement business, newspapers, the general strike of 1919, and the tumultuous politics of city and state that have made history in the Northwest.

SKID ROAD

An Informal Portrait of Seattle

Murray Morgan

Revised Edition

BALLANTINE BOOKS • NEW YORK

Library of Congress Catalog Card Number: 60-9775

SBN 345-24310-2-150

This edition published by arrangement with
The Viking Press, Inc.

First Printing: April 1971
Second Printing: May 1971
Third Printing: March 1972
Fourth Printing: May 1973
Fifth Printing: October 1974

Cover photograph by Art Holt, Seattle, Washington.

Printed in the United States of America

BALLANTINE BOOKS
A Division of Random House, Inc.
201 East 50th Street, New York, N.Y. 10022

This book is for

Howard and Judith Daniel

SKID ROAD

One Man's Seattle

The hills are so steep in downtown Seattle that some of the sidewalks have cleats. They used to be steeper. Less than fifty years ago Seattle seemed to have reached the physical limit of its growth; it had climbed the hills as far as a town could go. The streets were so steep that members of the Seattle Symphony, who had to climb three blocks to reach their practice hall from the place where they stored their instruments, arrived winded, and sometimes rehearsals were over before all the horn players caught their breath. The musicians rigged a pulley to carry the instruments uphill, so that strangers in town were sometimes startled to have a cello or a tuba swoop past them on the street. The rest of Seattle's residents couldn't solve their problems with pulleys, and they called in engineers to take the tops off the worst of the hills.

By washing nearly as much dirt from the downtown hills as was moved during the digging of the Panama Canal, the engineers made it possible for a modern metropolis to be built on the half drowned mountain that lies between Puget Sound and Lake Washington. Seattle has continued to spread out over the hills, and the hills are still steep. A three-block walk through the business district may leave a visitor from flat country panting. If, after making the ascent from Second Avenue to Fifth Avenue, he gasps some depreciation of hills in general and, say, Madison Street in particular, he is unlikely to receive sympathy from a resident. "Oh, they aren't bad," a Seattleite will say about his hills. Or else, "Sure they're steep. But look at the view."

Since most of the city clings to the sides of hills that rise from lake and bay and river, there is always a view. Lake Washington is to the east, at Seattle's back door. It makes a good back yard. It is a long and lovely lake, still marked with the wilderness though highways encircle it and a floating bridge of concrete spans it. The racing shells of the University of Washington practice on it, and estates and mills and small homes and a naval air station stand on the shore. "A mountain lake at sea level," a visitor called it sixty years ago, when most of the shore was still outside the city limits. It still feels like a mountain lake.

The real mountains are thirty miles farther east. The Cascades run north and south across the state of Washington, and the wet winds from the Pacific drop their moisture as they sweep over the mile-high barrier, so that the western slope is dark with evergreens for half the year and for the other half deep with snow. The Cascades shut Seattle off from the eastern part of the state, psychologically as well as physically. Seattleites don't think in the same terms as the people who live across the mountains, where the climate is dry and the trees shed their leaves and wealth is fruit and wheat; Seattle thinks in terms of lumber and deep water. Puget Sound is the town's front yard. The first settlers came there in canoes.

The business district faces west by south. From the office buildings that have grown where the Douglas fir and western cedar stood as tall as skyscrapers, businessmen look westward across the water at another mountain range, the Olympics, wilder and wetter than the Cascades —the Last Wilderness, some call them—a timbered world to be conquered and cut. From their downtown offices executives can watch the streamlined ferries that carry commuters to and from the Olympic Peninsula and the islands of the Sound; but they forget the ferries when a freighter glides into Elliott Bay and nudges one of the piers. The freighter reminds them that beyond the mountains is the Pacific, and beyond the Pacific is a continent to trade with and grow rich on. The first settlers called the town "New York-Alki," meaning in Indian jargon "New York by-

and-by," and Seattle still hopes to be for Asia what the port of New York is for Europe.

Sometimes war or politics shuts off that continent, but there is always Alaska. The half-million people in Seattle tend to look on Alaska as their very own. "We're the only city in the world that owns a territory," a booster once remarked, and the 128,643 Alaskans agree, though they are not happy about it. Seattle stores display sub-arctic clothing, though Puget Sound winters are usually mild; Seattle curio shops feature totem poles, though no Puget Sound Indian ever carved one; Seattle radio stations carry programs especially for Alaska, though Seattle is as far from the territory as New York is from Hudson Bay.

At the foot of the hills, between the office buildings and the bay, lies a narrow strip of low land: here on the waterfront Seattle's history and Seattle's future meet and merge.

To know Seattle one must know its waterfront. It is a good waterfront, not as busy as New York's, not as self-consciously colorful as San Francisco's, not as exotic as New Orleans, but a good, honest, working waterfront with big gray warehouses and trim fishing boats and docks that smell of creosote, and sea gulls and tugs and seafood restaurants and beer joints and fish stores—a waterfront where you can hear foreign languages and buy shrunken heads and genuine stuffed mermaids, where you can watch the seamen follow the streetwalkers and the shore patrol follow the sailors, where you can stand at an open-air bar and drink clam nectar, or sit on a deadhead and watch the water, or go to an aquarium and look at an octopus.

The trucks and trains rattle past behind you, but there are sea sounds too, the cries of the gulls, the creak of the lines as the moored ships gently move, the slap-slap of small waves against the sea walls, the splash of a leaping salmon. These have not changed since the day, nearly a hundred years ago, when a young physician and poet named Harry Smith got thoroughly lost while walking the three miles from his cabin on the cove that now bears his name to Doc Maynard's general store, the Seattle Exchange, which was located on the low land where the hills

flatten out and run into the tideflats near the mouth of the
Duwamish River, an area then called the Sag. At low tide
it was possible to walk along the beach from the cove to
the Sag, but when the tide came in the water lapped
against the clay bluffs and it was necessary to climb the
hill and walk through the forest. The trees grew to the
edge of the bluff, a thick stand of giant evergreens rising
out of a tangle of underbrush—ferns and wild rose bushes
and salal and Oregon grape. From a few yards back in the
woods it was impossible to see the water; in the deep
forest even the sun was hidden from sight. So it was that
young Doctor Smith walking south through the woods
that covered the hill now called Queen Anne, lost his way
and instead of coming out at the Sag discovered a cabin in
a clearing by the water where he was sure no cabin or
clearing or water should be, a cabin that proved upon investigation to be his own.

It would be difficult to get lost between Smith Cove and
the Skid Road today. From the hill, logged by the pioneers and lowered by the engineers, the city spreads out
before you. Seattle is located on the eastern shore of Puget
Sound on Elliott Bay. From the top of Queen Anne, the
highest of all the Seattle hills, you look down on the harbor; piers slant out into the bay from Smith Cove to the
mouth of the Duwamish River; the eastern shoreline is
jagged as a sawblade. Beyond the Duwamish the land
sweeps back to the northwest. Elliott Bay, which lies
within this horseshoe curve, opens onto the Sound, and
across the Sound you see the islands—Vashon, which was
named by Vancouver for a British naval captain, and
Bainbridge, named for the captain of Old Ironsides. Beyond the islands lie the Olympic Mountains. Looking to
the east, you see three lakes. The first, Lake Union, is an
industrial lagoon bordered by shipyards, boatworks, and
the city gas plant. Hundreds of houseboats, built on floats
of cedar logs, are moored to the bank, some of them
clammy, one-room shacks, others with as many as six
rooms, radiant heat, and specially designed lightweight
fireplaces. Green Lake, the city's favorite swimming hole,

is surrounded by a small park; and the third is the long lovely stretch of Lake Washington. A canal connects Lake Washington and Lake Union with the Sound; the second largest locks in the world raise ships from salt to fresh water.

The skyscrapers of the business district rise from the western slope of the narrow waist of land that separates Elliott Bay from Lake Washington. Dirt sluiced from the hills has covered the clam beaches along the salt water; even at high tide you can follow the waterfront all the way from the Cove to South First and Washington Streets, where Doc Maynard's store once stood.

As you walk south along Alaskan Way, the city on your left, the water on your right, you pass over the anchorage where in the old days the brigs and the clippers and the lumber schooners dropped their hooks and waited their turn to load lumber at the docks. The *Beaver* anchored here too, the first steamer on the coast, flagship of the Hudson's Bay Company fleet. And the *Major Tomkins*, which was wrecked; the *Traveller*, which sprang a leak and sank; the *Fairy*, which exploded; and the *Water Lily*, which was auctioned off as junk. And there were the great paddlewheelers like the *Eliza Anderson*, which for years served as highway and newspaper and post office to the people of the Sound. You can still see paddlewheelers here. The tan-colored sternwheeler *Skagit Chief* lies up from time to time at Pier 66, and sometimes the *Skookum Chief* comes down from the upper Sound. On rare occasions a sailing vessel, a veritable white-winger, enters the harbor. But most of the vessels are American freighters or Scandinavian cargo-passenger ships, sharp-prowed and fresh-painted, so large that when you lean against the waterfront rail to admire them you have to look up to see the anchors at their bows and to read their names.

On the bluff to your left are the public market, where the descendants of the Indians who once possessed the bay now sell vegetables; the neon-marked headquarters of the International Longshoremen's and Warehousemen's Union, where the lieutenants of Harry Bridges plan their unending war with Dave Beck; the tall white building named Dexter Horton, in honor of a sawmill hand who became the town's first banker; and the block-long red-brick building that James Colman built after the tide and the engineers had covered with dirt the beached clipper bark he used as a home. Most impressive of all is the forty-two-story Smith Tower (named for the typewriter, not the pioneer poet), which towers over the site of the main battleground in Seattle's two-day Indian War.

This is the oldest Seattle. Standing by the Alaska Pier, you look up a street that climbs straight over the hill toward Lake Washington. You walk up it, and two short blocks from the waterfront come to First Avenue, which was called Front Street in the days when it ran along the bluff above the beach. Here stood the mill that, in the fifties, meant Seattle was really a town, not just a hope; and here in the doldrum era of the seventies Val Wildman sold Seattle's first stein of nickel beer.

This is Yesler Way. Once it was called Mill Street, and before that it was simply the skid road, the route along which the ox-teams skidded logs to Yesler's Mill in the Sag. It is a dividing line. A hundred years ago it divided the land claimed by Doc Maynard from that claimed by Carson Dobbins Boren; it marked the center of the narrow strip of land that Boren and Maynard gave to Henry Yesler so that he could build his mill where he wanted to. Fifty years ago Yesler Way was the Deadline, the northern limit of what Seattleites called "our great restricted district"; bawdyhouses and low theaters were expected to stay south of the Line. Today Yesler Way is still a dividing line of sorts: to your left as you climb the steep street are the big new buildings, symbols of Seattle's dominance over a state and a territory and its dreams of controlling the trade of a distant continent; to your right, in the red-brick buildings untopped by neon, along the unswept sidewalks where the rejected men stand and stare, are the symbols of the past, the monuments to men who dreamed the wrong dreams or, like Doc Maynard, the right dreams too soon.

This region south of Yesler Way has been known by many names. For a time it was called Maynardtown, after

Doc Maynard; later, when Yesler's Mill had been running long enough for its debris to fill the tidal inlets, the area was known simply as Down on the Sawdust. After its character became established during the seventies it was called variously the Lava Beds, the Tenderloin, White Chapel, and the Great Restricted District. For a while it was referred to as Wappyville, in honor of a chief of police who distinguished himself by the amount of graft he collected there. But the first name, the functional name, has outlasted all the others. When the pioneers rolled logs by hand down to the waterfront, when the ox-teams plodded over the hill dragging logs for Yesler's steam mill, this was the skid road, and it is the Skid Road today. This district south of Yesler Way, this land below the Deadline, has helped fix the word on the American language. The Skid Road: the place of dead dreams.

You see here the things you see on other skid roads in America: men sitting on curbs and sleeping in doorways, doors padlocked for non-payment of rent, condemned buildings, signs that read: "Beds, twenty cents." "Oatmeal, five cents. With sugar, seven cents. With cream, nine cents." "Be Saved by Sister Faye." "A charge of three cents will be made for packages stored more than two days." "Indians who want wine must show documents they are not wards of the government." The *People's World* is sold on the street corners, and secondhand nudist magazines are on sale in cigar stores. There are missions and taverns and wine shops and stores where you can buy a suit for $3.75.

And there are things peculiar to Seattle: a totem pole; cafés with Indian names; a manifesto posted on the wall, which recalls the days when this was a stronghold of the IWW and the One Big Union promised an eight-hour day. "Fellow Workers! Unite for the 4-hour day and the 4-day week. No cut in pay."

Once the people here did find a short cut to riches. From a red-brick hotel down the street, Swiftwater Bill Gates, the Dawson plunger, showered nuggets on the Seattleites who gathered in the streets below. Still earlier Doc Maynard tried to get rich and instead brought wealth to others. Doc was the first of the dreamers along the Skid Road. He was Seattle's first booster, the man who was sure greatness could come; he owned a tract of land worth, city officials guess, a hundred million dollars. Wrapped in his dream of making Seattle grow, he gave it bit by bit to anyone whose presence might help the town expand. Seattle grew, but by the time it was big Maynard was dead and the government had taken most of the property he left to his wife. He died poor, but he was a great man.

This book is the story of Maynard and of the men like him, the ones who weren't quite respectable but helped build the great city of the Northwest. The formal history of Seattle has been written many times over, sometimes well; the sons and daughters of the men who moved north of the Skid Road have lovingly told the story of the folk who dreamed the right dreams at the appropriate times. This is the story of the others, of some who tried and failed and of some who achieved success without becoming respectable, of the life that centered on the mills and on the wharves. That is Seattle from the bottom up.

I

Doc Maynard and
the Indians, 1852-1873

1.

In 1850 Dr. David Swinson Maynard was living in Lorain County, Ohio; he was forty-two years old and in debt. On the morning of April 9 he shook hands with his wife Lydia, whom in twenty years of marriage he had come to dislike, kissed his two children, mounted his gray mule, and rode off toward California, where he hoped to recoup his fortunes. Maynard intended to join another Ohioan, Colonel John B. Weller, in the gold fields, but kindness and cholera sidetracked him. Instead of panning for nuggets he became one of the founding fathers of Seattle and in some ways the most influential figure of the early days on Elliott Bay.

Maynard was a man of parts, a warm human being whose worst faults grew out of his greatest virtue, his desire to be helpful; and few people ever got into more trouble trying to help others. He went broke being helpful in Ohio, where during the 1830s he ran a medical school. There is no record that the Vermont-born doctor ever dunned a patient, and he not only extended unlimited credit but signed his patients' promissory notes. His school went under during the panic of 1837, and so did the projects of a number of friends he had sponsored; he found himself saddled with more than thirty thousand dollars of other people's debts. For twelve years he labored to pay off his creditors and feed his family; but

9

when his children were old enough to look after themselves, Maynard found irresistible the appeal of California, where a man might unearth a fortune. The fact that
the new El Dorado lay half a continent away from his
wife made it no less attractive. The first entry in his travel
diary expressed the intention of many another man who
eventually settled in Seattle: "Left here for California."

Maynard was still intent on California when he reached
St. Joseph on the Missouri. He was traveling light. He
had a mule, a buffalo robe, a few books, a box of surgical
instruments and some medicines; he had almost no cash
and he relied on his profession to pay his way. At St.
Joseph he attached himself to a caravan of wagons bound
for the West. They crossed the river on May 16. Four
days later the doctor scribbled in his journal: "Passed some
new graves."

Death was part of the pioneer experience. Day after
day, as the wagons rolled west across prairies green with
spring, Maynard counted the graves beside the trail:

May 21. Passed the grave of A. Powers, of Peoria County,
Illinois, died on the 20th inst. about sixty-five miles west of
St. Joseph. Traveled about eighteen miles. Was called to visit
three cases of cholera. One died, a man, leaving a wife and
child, from Illinois, poor. He lived seven hours after being
taken.
May 22. Rainy. Fleming and Curtis taken with the cholera.
Wake all night. Called upon just before we stopped to see
a man with cholera, who died soon after.
May 23. Curtis and Fleming better but not able to start in
the morning.
May 24. Camped at Blue River. One grave, child eleven years
old. Forded the stream. Raised our loading. Got my medicine
wet.

The doctor himself was touched with the disease. He
said nothing, not wanting to worry his companions, but he
confided his trouble to the journal:

May 29. Started at six o'clock, going about eighteen miles.

Water scarce and poor. Curtis gave the milk away. Went
without dinner. A drove of buffaloes were seen by a company
ahead. Left the team and went on ahead. Saw one buffalo
and one antelope. Took sick with the cholera. No one med-
dled or took any notice of it but George Moon.
May 30. Feel better. Start on foot. Continue to get better.
Travel up the Little Blue twenty miles. Wood, water, and
feed tolerable.

That week they passed Forth Kearney, a low, wood-and-
mud building on a sandy plain that rose into sandhills.
Maynard wrote with wonder of the tame buffalo grazing
near the fort. A spring cloudburst caught them on the
Platte and for two days the party shivered, unable to get a
fire going; there was more cholera.

June 4. A man died with the cholera in sight of us. He was
a Mason. I was called to see him but too late.
June 5. Have a bad headache; take a blue pill.
June 6. Unship our load and cross a creek. One death, a
Missourian, from cholera. Go eighteen miles. Pass four graves
in one place. Two more of the same train are ready to die.
Got a pint and a half of brandy. Earn $2.20.

The next day cholera changed Maynard's life. But at
the time Maynard was most impressed by the fact that he
earned nearly nine dollars, doctoring.

June 7. Start late. Find plenty of doctoring to do. Stop at
noon to attend some persons sick with cholera. One was
dead before I got there and two died before the next morning. They paid me $8.75. Deceased were Israel Broshears and
Mrs. Morton, the last being mother to the bereaved widow
of Israel Broshears. We are eighty-five or ninety miles west
of Fort Kearney.
June 8. Left the camp of distress on the open prairie at half-
past four in the morning. The widow was ill both in body
and mind. I gave them slight encouragement by promising
to return and assist them along. I overtook our company at
noon twenty miles away. Went back and met the others in

trouble enough. I traveled with them until night. Again overtook our company three miles ahead. Made arrangements to
be ready to shift my duds to the widow's wagon when they
come up in the morning.

The Broshears' train was headed for Tumwater at the
extreme southern tip of Puget Sound, where the widow
Broshears' brother, Michael T. Simmons, had settled five
years earlier, in 1845—the first American to homestead
on the Sound. Maynard agreed to stay with her until she
reached there. The doctor, who had never so much as
switched an ox, now found himself in charge of a team
with five yoke of oxen and two yoke of cows. He was also
physician to a group that was deathly ill; even with his
ministrations, the party had seven deaths from cholera in
two weeks. And he was the newcome leader of a group
split by dissension; several members wanted to turn back.
For two weeks after shifting his duds to the widow's
wagon the doctor was too busy even to write in his
journal—the only lapse in his record—but by the Fourth
of July things were in good enough order for him to note:
"We celebrated a little."

They kept moving. For two months the Broshears' train
edged westward, four miles, ten miles, occasionally twenty
miles a day. Maynard experienced the routine hardships
of the Trail and knew too the occasional joys of good
water, of fresh fish, or a day without petty disaster. He
underwent the ordeal that gave the settlers of the Pacific
Northwest a hard core of mutual understanding. Nearly
every family that came to Seattle during the early days
had passed through the trials by dust and dysentery that
Maynard, writing by firelight or in the early dawn, pen-
ciled in his little journal:

Dragged the team through sand eight miles to Devil's Gate.
. . . Oxen sick; vomiting like dogs. . . . Discovered a party of
Indians coming upon us. We heard that they had just robbed
one train. Prepared for an attack. When within half a mile
they sent two of their number to see how strong we were.

After viewing us carefully left us for good. . . . Kept guard for fear of Mormons. . . .

Traveled in sand all day, and camped without water or feed. . . . I was well worn out, as well as the team, from watching at night. A miserable company for help. . . .

Traveled all day and night. Dust from one to twelve inches deep on the ground and above the wagon a perfect cloud. Crossed a plain twelve miles, and then went over a tremendous mountain. . . .

Team falling behind. Found them too weak to travel. . . . Left camp at six-thirty, after throwing Lion and doctoring his foot, which Mrs. Broshears, George and myself did alone. . . .

Indians are plenty. . . . Was called to see a sick pappoose. . . . Got to Fort Hall. Found the mosquitoes so bad that it was impossible to keep the oxen or ourselves on that spot. Oh, God! the mosquitoes.

Sick all day and under the influence of calomel pills. . . . Started late on Lion's account. Drove two and a half miles, and he gave up the ghost. We then harnessed Nigger on the lead. . . .

Lost our water keg. Sixteen miles to water. Road very stony. . . . Traveled six miles to Salmon Falls . . . bought salmon of the Indians. This place is delightful. The stream is alive with fish of the first quality, and wild geese are about as tame as the natives. . . . Watched team all night. Am nearly sick but no one knows it but myself. . . .

Crossed creek and climbed the worst of all hills. Went up three times to get our load up. . . . Geared the wagon shorter. Threw overboard some of our load. . . . Cut off the wagon bed and again overhauled. . . . Left this morning a distressed family who were without team or money and nearly sick from trouble. . . . Left Brandy and Polly to die on the road. . . .

Here we began climbing the Blue Mountains, and if they don't beat the devil. . . . Came over the mountains and through dense forest of pine, twenty miles. Traded for a mare and colt and Indian dress. Paid for the things a brass kettle, two blankets, a shirt, etc. . . .

Bought a fine spotted horse, which cost me $55. . . . Came

to the Columbia River twenty miles through sand all the way. This night I had my horse stolen. I was taken about sunset with dysentry, which prostrated me very much.

Drove to the Dalles. Sold the cattle to a Mr. Wilson for $110 and prepared to start for Portland down the river. Sat up nearly all night and watched the goods.

Loaded up our boat and left. Came down about fifteen miles and landed for the night. We buried a child which we found upon the bank of the river, drowned. . . . Hired a team and got our goods down below the rapids. Engaged Chenoweth to start out with us immediately, but he, being a scoundrel, did not do as he agreed.

Hired an Indian to carry us down in his canoe to Fort Vancouver. We had a hard time, in consequence of the Indian being so damned lazy. By rowing all the way myself we got to the fort at 1 in the morning as wet as the devil. . . .

Left the fort with two Indians who took us down the Columbia thirty-eight miles to the mouth of the Cowalitz, which is a very hard stream to ascend. . . . Came to Plomondon's landing about noon. Obtained horses and started out ten miles to Mr. J. R. Jackson's. . . .

Made our way twenty miles through dense forest and uneven plain twenty-five miles to M. T. Simmons's, our place of destination, where we were received with that degree of brotherly kindness which seemed to rest our weary limbs, and promise an asylum for us in our worn-out pilgrimage.

2.

Maynard, of course, was in love with the widow Broshears, and he quickly fell in love with the Puget Sound country. The weather was wet but mild; after the dust and heat of the plains, after the cold of the mountains, after the alkali water of the plains, Maynard did not mind the rain. He liked the gray, overcast days when the firs and hemlocks on the near-by hills combed the bottom of the heavy clouds that pulsed in from the Pacific. The salt water fascinated him: the Sound stretched northward for more than a hundred miles from the Simmons' homestead, a quiet inland sea, its shoreline charted but its surrounding hills almost unexplored. It was good too, after the weeks on the trail, to relax in a house with windproof walls, to listen to rain on the cedar shakes, to sleep in a bed, to eat white bread and fresh vegetables, to talk to Catherine Broshears, who was beautiful, or even to her sister-in-law Elizabeth Simmons, who was not.

The brotherly kindness shown by Simmons on the party's arrival did not extend to Maynard after Simmons detected that his sister's interest in the doctor exceeded that of an employer for her ox-team driver. It did not matter to Simmons that Maynard was a doctor and a fellow Democrat—he was also a married man. Simmons suggested that Maynard move on to California before the other fellows dug all the gold.

Maynard stalled. He had heard rumors that coal had been discovered on the lower Sound and he wanted to investigate. In mid-November he hired some Indians to paddle him north on a prospecting trip. The Sound stretches south between the Olympic Mountains and the Cascades. To the west the Olympics sheer up from the water "big and abrupt as a cow in a bathtub," as one early traveler put it; they were almost black with fir and hemlock, and though explorers had located several good anchorages along the western shore, the absence of any extensive farm lands discouraged settlement. Like the Hudson's Bay people who had covered this territory before him, Maynard skirted the eastern shore as he paddled north. The Cascades stood well back from the water; a plain nearly thirty miles wide stretched between the salt water and the rugged foothills. The plain was forested and useless for farming, but mountain streams flowing from the glaciers on Mount Rainier and Mount Baker had cut several valleys, which offered broad acres of rich, volcanic soil—the Nisqually, already cultivated by the Hudson's Bay Company; the Puyallup, twenty miles to the north, and just beyond the Puyallup, the Duwamish.

Maynard was headed still farther north, to the Stilquamish, a swift stream that enters the Sound at a point due east of the Strait of Juan de Fuca, the channel to the

Pacific Ocean. His journal of the trip is matter-of-fact, but it is not hard to imagine the feelings of a man from the plains as he rode in the black-painted cedar dugout over the gentle waters of the Sound, the islands dark with Douglas fir, the wind sharp with salt and sweet with the scent of red cedar. The great mountain rose in the east, its white cone streaked with blue-black ridges, and to the west stood the Olympics, white with the early snow. Seals bobbed up to stare round-eyed at the black canoe, and porpoises curved through the waters ahead. Just below the surface floated translucent jellyfish, and when the Indians paddled close to shore Maynard could see giant starfish clinging to the rocks, and anemones, pink and green and gold, moving in the currents. Even the barnacles were open and waved pale tentacles in search of food. And fish! When the canoe drifted through the Narrows on the outgoing tide Maynard could look down and see salmon lying head to current in the deep water below the clay cliffs. The slap of fish breaking surface sounded almost as steadily as the beat of the cedar paddles. Gulls wheeled overhead on steady wings, turning their smooth heads slowly as they scanned the water for prey. When the canoe skirted the shore, cranes flapped heavily into flight. Sometimes mallard and coot skittered along the green surface, or a helldiver flipped under.

The party landed and bought salmon and potatoes and mats from some Indians who were smoking clams near the beach. They camped for the night—too low the first night and the tide drove them off, to spend the night on the water. Maynard lost a skillet cover and got his gun wet.

The next day a southwest wind came up and rain fell. The Indians raised a sail, and the dugout ran with the waves under a flat roof of clouds that stretched from the dark islands to the dark shore. In the rain Maynard coasted past the sandy spit where, within a year, Seattle would be founded, and in the rain reached the Stilquamish. The record of his exploration for coal is lost. He is believed to have found some traces and, on his return to the upper Sound, to have sold the pages of his journal describing the location to another explorer.

Maynard settled in a small community on Budd Inlet, three miles north of Tumwater. The place, now called Olympia, was then known officially as Smithter, though most people called it Smithfield, both names honoring Levi Smith, a Presbyterian divinity student who settled there in 1848 but lost his life when he suffered an epileptic attack in a canoe. While Maynard was living in Smithter, Congress awarded the town a customs house, and it became the first port of entry on the Sound.

The town prospered—but not Maynard, whose money ran out. There were not enough people on the upper Sound to support a doctor, so he borrowed an ax and between calls on the widow Broshears he cut wood. He kept cutting for half a year, and by the fall of 1851 he had four hundred cords piled at tidewater. Maynard persuaded Leonard Felker, captain of the brig *Franklin Adams*, to haul him and his wood to San Francisco. There the wood brought him more than two thousand dollars. He used the money to buy a stock of trading goods from a wrecked ship.

Before returning north Maynard looked up his old friend John Weller, who was reconverting himself to politics after serving as a colonel during the Mexican War. Weller tried to talk Maynard into staying in California, but the doctor protested that life in the gold camps was too rowdy: in two days he had been called to treat four gunshot victims. He would return to Puget Sound, where life would be more orderly. Weller told Maynard of two other Ohioans, Henry Yesler and John Stroble, who shared Maynard's conviction that western Oregon had a future and who planned to start a sawmill somewhere in the Northwest. Weller said to Maynard, "Doctor, let me advise you. You have the timber up there that we want and must have. Give up your profession. Get machinery and start a sawmill. By selling us lumber you'll make a hundred dollars for every one that you may possibly make in doctoring, and you'll soon be rich."

He was right, of course, but Maynard did not have enough money to buy machinery and he was tired of cutting trees by hand. He sailed back on the *Franklin*

Adams with his stock of trading goods. Going down the
Sound, the vessel passed a cluster of cabins on a spit near
the mouth of Duwamish River, a settlement which,
Maynard was told, was derisively called New York-Alki,
meaning "New York-pretty soon."

Maynard rented a one-room building in Olympia and
opened his store. His business methods were unorthodox,
even for the frontier. Since he had purchased his goods at
half price, he sold them at half the price asked by other
merchants. If he was feeling particularly good—and alcohol often made him feel particularly good—he was in-
clined to give his customers presents; he offered unlimited
credit. Maynard was popular with the townsfolk but not
with other merchants, among them Mike Simmons, who
felt that Maynard was not only hellbent for bankruptcy
but was a bad influence on customers. His business rivals
suggested that Maynard would probably be happier selling
his goods somewhere else.

One day an Indian named Sealth (pronounced See-alth
and sometimes See-attle), the tyee, or chief, of the tribe
living at the mouth of the Duwamish River (which was
also known as the Duwamps and the Tuwamish and, to
everyone's confusion, as the White), paddled up to Olympia on a shopping trip. Sealth was a big, ugly man with
steel-gray hair hanging to his shoulders; he wore a breech-
clout and a faded blue blanket. His arrival caused some
stir in the little community, for the whites considered him
one of the most important tyees in Oregon Territory; they
certainly were more impressed by Sealth than the Indians
were. The tribes along the Sound were of the Salish family; the Nisquallies, the Duwamish, the Muckleshoots, the
Puyallups, the Suquamish, the Snohomish, and other
groups varied in number from less than a hundred to
more than a thousand, but they all seem to have had the
same notion about the role of a chief: a chief had little
authority. He was merely a rich man with some elo-
quence, a man whose opinions carried more weight than
those of his fellow tribesmen. Since wealth was hereditary,
the chieftaincy often stayed in one family, but it did not
necessarily go to the eldest son; the tribe might agree on a

younger son, on an uncle on anyone who was rich, or at least generous and wise, or at least persuasive. A tribe might agree to have more than one chief; nearly all had one leader for peace and another who took over during war.

Sealth appears to have been an exception to this rule; he was a peacetime tyee, but there was a story current in his lifetime that he had distinguished himself as a strategist in some distant campaign and that his military genius had established his people's hegemony over the lands at the mouth of the Duwamish, on the western shore of Lake Washington, and on the eastern side of Bainbridge Island. Sealth was, as the settlers put it, "an old Indian," meaning he refused to wear "boston"—that is, American—clothing, and he would speak neither English nor the trade jargon called Chinook; he talked in Duwamish, and anyone who wished to speak with him either learned Duwamish or found an interpreter. Nevertheless Sealth was considered to be friendly toward the whites and was on good terms with the storekeepers in Olympia. It may have been Mike Simmons who suggested to Sealth that he speak to Maynard about moving his store up to the little settlement of New York-Alki. Maynard agreed. He held a hurried sale, loaded his remaining goods aboard a scow, and, accompanied by Sealth and a squad of Duwamish paddlers, started north. The forty-mile trip took four days and three nights. Maynard and his companions landed on the sandspit of New York-Alki late on the afternoon of March 31, 1852.

3.

New York-Alki was a community of seven men, five women, and twelve children, living in four houses, two made of logs and two of cedar puncheons, set close together on the narrow plain between water and forest. The settlement was five months old and, Maynard soon learned, most of the settlers were ready to give up. They had come to the Sound country to found a town, not to

farm, and though Alki point was beautiful, offering a wide
view up and down the Sound and on clear days a pan-
orama of the Olympics to the west, it was no place to load
ships. The only commodity the settlers had for export was
timber, much in demand in San Francisco, but at Alki the
trees stood well back from the shore and the beach was
shallow and exposed to the wind.

Eighteen years earlier Dr. William Tolmie, the factor at
the Hudson's Bay post up-Sound at Nisqually, had examined the Alki plain as a possible site for a trading post and
had scratched in his journal his reasons for deciding
against it:

It is about a mile in length and from one hundred to one
hundred and fifty yards in extent, raised about thirty feet above
sea level, towards which it presented a steep, clayey bank.
Surface flat and dotted with small pines, but soil composed
almost entirely of sand. . . . At its northern extremity the
coast is indented with a bay five or six miles wide, and
perhaps three long, into which a river flows. . . . The south
side of bay and river is inhabited by the Tuamish Indians,
of whom we saw several parties along the coast, miserably
poor and destitute of fire arms. . . . A fort well garrisoned
would answer well as a trading post on the prairie where we
stood. It would have an advantage of a fine prospect down
the Sound and of proximity to the Indians, but these would
not compensate for an unproductive soil and the inconveni-
ence of going at least one-half mile for a supply of water.

A number of Americans scouted the site after Dr.
Tolmie's visit. In 1841 young Lieutenant Wilkes and his
naval party drew a beautiful and accurate chart of the
harbor, which Wilkes named Elliott Bay in honor of the
chaplain of his exploring expedition. He made no reference to the place as a possible site for commercial activities.

In 1850 a skinny youngster from Iowa, nineteen-year-
old John Holgate, paddled around Elliott Bay in an Indian canoe and went a few miles up the Duwamish River,
which flows into the bay. He liked the valley so much that

he chose a site to homestead, but he neglected to file papers for his claim, and while he was back east in Iowa to round up his relatives, someone else moved onto his land. (Holgate had made an amusing mistake earlier that same year: he brought with him across the plains a seedling fir so that he would not be lonesome for evergreens while on the West Coast.) Though as a farm boy Holgate selected bottom land for his own homestead, he was the first to predict the possibilities of the harbor.

Colonel Isaac Ebey, who later was beheaded by Indians in revenge for the murder—by someone else—of one of their tyees, paddled down-Sound from Olympia a few weeks after Holgate. Like the Iowan, he was greatly impressed by the valley of the Duwamish. In a letter to Mike Simmons, Ebey reported: "The river meanders along through rich bottom land, not heavily timbered, with here and there a beautiful plain of unrivaled fertility, peeping out through a fringe of vine maple, alder or ash, or boldly presenting a view of their native richness and undying verdure." It is probable that Maynard read Ebey's description of the valley southeast of New York-Alki; perhaps he even read it aloud to Simmons, for Simmons, like many other Northwest pioneers, could read little other than his name.

The Duwamish pours from a glacier high on the northwestern slope of Mount Rainier and, after flowing twenty miles as a mountain stream, slows down and meanders, rich and brown and placid, northward between the foothills of the Cascade Range and the highlands that form the eastern shore of Puget Sound. The valley is rich and easy to farm, though threatened (and replenished) by spring floods. In 1851 a man named Luther Collins gave up trying to farm the glacial silt of the Nisqually valley at the head of the Sound, and staked out a claim on the lower Duwamish in what is now Georgetown. Three friends[1] followed him within the month.

Collins brought his wife and daughter to the Duwamish

[1] Joseph Maple, his son Samuel Maple, and Henry Van Asselt, a Hollander, who took a claim that includes the present site of Boeing Airfield.

in a scow, then went back to Nisqually to pick up his cattle. After an unsuccessful attempt to move them by scow, he hired an Indian and drove his livestock north along the beach. When Collins herded the beasts around the southern head of Elliott Bay he found three young Americans—Lee Terry, John Low, and David Denny— building a log cabin. They told Collins that they had picked this as the site of a town, which they would call New York after Terry's birthplace. They had come to the Sound to scout homesteads for a party recently arrived, overland, from the Midwest and were dissatisfied with the crowded conditions in the Willamette valley. The others were waiting south of the Columbia River. Collins tried to talk them into settling on the Duwamish, but they wouldn't hear of it.

Five weeks later, on a rainy day in mid-November, the rest of the party—A. A. Denny, John N. Low, C. D. Boren, W. N. Bell, and their families—arrived on the brig *Exact*, Captain Folger, after a rough passage from Portland. Three of the four women cried when the brig's boat put them ashore on the salt-smelling beach. Portland had been rude and the ship awful, but this was worse: the only habitation was a log cabin, still roofless, and the only neighbors a host of bowlegged Indians, the men wearing only buckskin breechclouts, the women skirts of shredded cedar bark, the children naked. The sky was low and gray, the air sharp with salt and iodine; but soon the women were too busy to weep.

While Collins and his friends were breaking ground for their farms on the Duwamish, the New York settlers were building four houses. In December the brig *Leonesa*, Captain Daniel Howard, hove to off the point. The skipper asked if the town had any timber for sale; he wanted to pick up a cargo of pilings for San Francisco. They had none cut but they had the makings; the men promised by the time the *Leonesa* got back from Olympia they'd have a load ready. They did too, and the town's line of development was fixed. It would cut lumber for export, and that meant it needed a deeper harbor.

Early one morning in February Arthur Denny, Bell,

and Boren set out in an Indian canoe to find a better anchorage. They paddled north across Elliott Bay and began to take soundings at what was later called Smith's Cove. They worked back around the shore toward Alki. Bell and Boren paddled while Denny heaved the lead, using a bunch of horseshoes tied to a length of clothesline. To their delight they found they had to stay close to shore to reach bottom at all. Deep water stretched for miles along the eastern shore.

Elliott Bay was deep, but the banks were steep. The narrow beach rose to a shallow shelf and the shelf folded into a raw clay cliff. The sides of the cliff were set and steep, and at the top stood a tangled jungle of fir. As the canoe coasted south the bank became gentler. Denny noticed the mottled trunks of alder among the evergreens and, after climbing the bank to investigate, "found a gently sloping hillside over which a fire had passed, deadening the trees. Some of these, particularly the alders, had fallen over, leaving an opening." Denny later built his house in the clearing. South of the clearing the bluff diminished from thrity or forty feet down to fifteen, to five; then it disappeared, and they came upon a little winding tidal stream, with muddy banks and salt grass on the margin, running through a tiny meadow. They landed and walked over to a circular knoll thirty or forty feet high, with steep sides. From the top of the knoll they could look over the meadow: the only sign of habitation was an Indian house, long deserted and partly overgrown with wild roses, standing near the present corner of First Avenue South and Yesler Way. To the south the land sloped down to marshy tideflats and the mudbars off the mouth of the Duwamish. When the explorers returned to their canoe and lowered the horseshoes again, they found that the deep water ended off the marshlands. Their city, then, would stretch along the deep water. Boren staked out a tentative claim on the low land nearest the Duwamish, Arthur Denny took the middle strip, and Bell the land to the north. David Denny, who came over later to look around, decided on a narrow strip reaching from the bay to Tenas Chuck, a small lake he found about a mile from salt water.

This was the situation when Maynard arrived at New York-Alki. Four of the men were ready to move to their new claims, leaving the Terrys and Low in possession of the spit. Both groups wanted Maynard to stay with them, though it is probable that Low and Terry, having started a small store of their own at New York-Alki, were not thrilled by the prospect of their only neighbor's being a competing merchant. They didn't need to worry. Maynard thought the new town on Elliott Bay more promising than the old. But there was one trouble: he wanted some deep-water frontage, and as near as possible to the Indian villages on the Duwamish; he had work for the Indians to do and goods for them to buy. It was not hard to arrange. The others wanted Maynard to stay among them "for the benefit a good man brings," and they moved their claims north by an eighth of a mile. Maynard measured out his claim so that it included about three hundred yards of the most southerly deep-water frontage; for the rest he took marsh and hill.

4.

So they planned a town. They planned it with the conviction that it would grow to be a great city, though they were not more confident of success than were the men who had already built Steilacoom and Olympia and the others who would found Mukilteo and Whatcom (now Bellingham) and Townshend and Port Gamble and Port Ludlow and a score of other settlements around the Sound. For a time their settlement was nameless, but when a clerk in Olympia tentatively called it Duwamps, the pioneers hastily got together to pick a less repulsive name. At Maynard's suggestion they called their town Seattle, a name they adapted from that of Maynard's Indian friend Sealth. There is no trustworthy account of how the old chief took the honor. He may well have been horrified: the Indians had a superstitious dread of having their names mentioned after death.

For Maynard the first years of the new town may well have been the best years of his life. He was older than the others, richer in experience, better educated, and now he had more money. He was the town's first capitalist. He hired some Indians to help him build a place down by the Sag, as they called the low land by the water, and within a few days he was selling goods in his new store, the Seattle Exchange, a building eighteen feet long and twenty-six feet wide, with log sides, a shake roof, and over the front part a low attic that Maynard used as living quarters. The store sold, according to an advertisement Maynard wrote for the paper in Olympia, "a general assortment of dry goods, groceries, hardware, etc., suitable for the wants of immigrants just arriving."

Maynard was as interested in supplying the wants of immigrants to California as he was in supplying those of western Oregon. San Francisco, a thousand miles away by sea, was the only population center on the coast large enough to make much of a market for products of the fisheries and the forests. From the time two years earlier when the ship G. W. Kendall nosed into the Sound in misguided search for icebergs (the ice to be used in drinks on the Barbary Coast) and had to settle for a load of piling, timber was the paycrop on Puget Sound. Maynard had some to harvest; there was a stand of fir directly east of his store, so near that the needles fell on his shake roof. He hired Indians to fall and trim and buck the trees. They cut the trees with axes and soon learned to cut a high stump; they cut notches in the trees high above the under-brush (and away from the worst flow of sap), set boards in the notches, and then, balanced precariously, they hacked away at the great boles. Some of the lumber was split into shakes, some squared, some cut into cordwood. While this was going on Maynard set other Indians to catching sal-mon and making rude barrels, roughly hooped. When Maynard's old friend Captain Felker brought the Franklin Adams to the tiny dock at the edge of Maynard's property that October, the doctor-merchant had ready for shipment

1000 barrels of brined salmon, 30 cords of wood, 12,000 feet of squared timbers, 8000 feet of piling, and 10,000 shingles. The salmon spoiled, and the loss ate up much of Maynard's profit on the lumber.

Nothing dimmed Maynard's enthusiasm for long. The extravagant optimism and exuberant friendliness that had brought about his financial disaster in Ohio made him an ideal pioneer type. Anything that was good for Seattle was good for Maynard, especially since he was one of the largest landholders. Maynard decided that the thing to do was to force up the price of land by making Seattle boom, and the way to do this was to get more population. So, when visitors from Olympia came to town in Indian dugouts or on the square-rigged two-masters, he would push his octagonal glasses high on his forehead, pull his dark coat over his white shirt, leave his log store, and stroll down to the spit to greet them. At once he would go into his real-estate-agent's routine about the future of Seattle.

On the day when the settlement's most important visitor arrived, Maynard was down in the Sag, helping the other men roll a big log to water. The stranger, a solid-looking man in his forties, came in a dugout; he walked among them unexpectedly, a big-nosed, trim-bearded god of good fortune. His name, he said, was Yesler, Henry Yesler, of Massillon, Ohio, and he was looking for a place to build a steam mill.

This was the Yesler whom Maynard's friend, Colonel John Weller, had said intended to start a sawmill "somewhere in Oregon." Now here he was, hunting a site. He had inspected New York-Alki across the bay and found it promising. Of course, this side of the bay looked good too, but the best land on this side was taken. The ideal place for a mill would be right on the spit, where Maynard had set the Indians to salting salmon. The spit had level ground with deep water alongside, but this was Maynard's property and Boren's, and they had already done some clearing. Of course they wouldn't want to give up cleared land; that was understandable. Well, it was a pleasure to have met them and he wished the town well. Yesler strode

back toward his dugout to return to Alki for another look.
Maynard and Boren went into a quick conference.

A mill meant jobs for the citizens. It meant regular calls
by the lumber ships, and that in turn meant the population would grow. A mill meant the land would be cleared
rapidly. Property values would rise. No other town on the
Sound had a steam mill; there was a water-driven rig at
Tumwater built by Mike Simmons, but it cut boards half
an inch thicker at one end than at the other. The town
that got Yesler's steam mill would have a toehold on the
future. There was only one thing to do, and Maynard and
Boren did it. They told Yesler he could have the strip of
waterfront where the Maynard and Boren claims joined.

Yesler agreed and Seattle got the mill. Again the stakes
were lifted and the claim sites marked off anew. Maynard
made the biggest sacrifice, giving up the best section of his
waterfront. Yesler took an umbrella-shaped claim, with
the narrow handle of land reaching up between Boren's
and Maynard's holdings, then spreading over the timberland on top of what is now Capitol Hill.

While Yesler was in California arranging for the shipment of his machinery, the townsfolk built a big open
shed of planks, to house the boiler and the saw, and a
cookhouse of logs for the millhands. The paper in Olympia remarked. "We have heretofore neglected to notice the
fact that there is a new steam mill in process of erection
by Mr. H. L. Yesler at Seattle, mouth of the Duwamish
River, and which, we are told, will be ready to go into
operation early in November 'and no mistake.' Huzza for
Seattle! It would be folly to suppose that the mill will not
prove as good as a gold mine to Mr. Yesler, besides
tending greatly to improve the fine town site of Seattle and
the fertile country around it, by attracting thither the
farmer, the laborer, and the capitalist. On with improvement!"

That was Maynard's idea too. As he cleared land he
sold it cheap, expecting to make his profit off the later sale
of his remaining property. He gave one of the best lots in
town to Captain Felker for twenty dollars and a promise
that Felker would build a big house on it. He donated two

acres to the Methodist missionaries, asking only that they clear it as soon as possible. He was always looking for people who would be useful to the community. Sea captains for prestige and as traveling salesmen; missionaries for tone; blacksmiths for skill. He wanted a blacksmith very much (he blamed the failure of his barreled salmon enterprise on faulty coopering), and when none answered an advertisement he put in the Olympia *Columbian* he set up a blacksmith shop of his own. He was not a good hand with an anvil. One day a visitor from the White River valley stood by the open door of Maynard's smithy, watching him work; the stranger kept shaking his head. "What's the matter?" Maynard asked at last. "You don't know much about this kind of work, do you?" "Could you do better?" Maynard asked sharply. "It's my trade," the man said. Maynard sold him the shed and equipment, title clear, for ten dollars.

Maynard preached the gospel of Seattle's certain greatness not only to his neighbors but in every community where he could find listeners, and especially in Olympia, the biggest town north of the Columbia River. He was continually going up the Sound by canoe to visit the widow Broshears at Olympia. Years later, in their reminiscences, several pioneers recalled their astonishment at seeing, as they camped on some wilderness beach under the shadow of the dark firs, a dugout manned by Indian paddlers and carrying a large, dapper man in a dark suit with white linen and black tie, sometimes talking the Jargon with his paddlers, sometimes peering through octagonal glasses at a leather-bound book. Maynard became quite an authority on dugout travel; he usually advised travelers to take along a large supply of hardtack, because if the wind shifted they might be pinned down on some beach for days before their Salish paddlers would risk setting out again.

Travel overland was even more difficult and costly. One of the men who reached Seattle a few months after Maynard estimated that it cost him two hundred and fifty dollars to bring his family from Salem, Oregon. They went by wagon from Salem to Portland, then on to the Tualatin Plain, where they boarded a boat and crossed the Columbia to St. Helens. They loaded the wagon on a scow and went down the Columbia to the Cowlitz, where they took the wagon apart and packed the pieces in canoes for the upstream paddle to Cowlitz Landing; one of the men drove the horses overland. At the landing the wagon was put back together for the drive through the forest to Olympia. From that point the women took the boat north; the men drove the wagon to Steilacoom, where they again disassembled it for transport in dugouts the final thirty miles to Seattle. The horses were left to graze at Steilacoom. When one of the men returned for them, he got lost and wandered for two days in the Puyallup and Duwamish valleys until he reached Seattle half-starved.

The residents of Oregon Territory who lived north of the Columbia felt that they were getting a bad deal in the Territorial Legislature, partly because the problems of the heavily populated Willamette area dominated the meetings and partly because communications were so poor that sometimes a session of the legislature was over before a northern delegate knew he had been elected. The northerners wanted to become a separate territory, to be called Columbia. In October 1852 Maynard made the long, slow trip south on business that was both official and personal. He was a Seattle delegate to the Monticello Convention, a semiformal congress of northern citizens who sought to divorce their part of the territory from that south of the river, and he was also bound for Oregon City to persuade the Territorial Legislature to pass an act that would give him a divorce from his wife Lydia.

Maynard was an effective lobbyist, smooth in speech and dress, quick to tip a bottle or remember a face, and a known supporter of the Democratic majority. The legislature passed his divorce, though one Whig senator objected on the not unreasonable ground that Mrs. Maynard did not even know she was being divorced. A few days later, when the legislature reorganized the counties north of the Columbia, it chose Maynard's store-residence as a county seat.[2] Maynard was appointed justice of the peace and notary public.

On his return trip, Maynard stopped in Olympia long enough to tell Mrs. Broshears of his divorce, ask her to marry him, and obtain her consent. He hurried on to Seattle to straighten up his house, but within a few days, during the coldest week of the coldest winter the settlers had suffered on the Sound, he paddled back to Olympia. Though Mike Simmons had threatened to shoot Maynard if he persisted in his courtship and had once imprisoned her at home to keep her from seeing the doctor, Catherine Broshears was waiting for him. They were married at a farm outside of Olympia and on the same day sailed for Seattle to honeymoon in the new county seat.

Maynard's first official duty was a marriage. Eight days after his own wedding he read Seattle's first wedding ceremony, uniting in wedlock twenty-one-year-old David Denny and his sister-in-law's sister, Louisa Boren. He was the first to kiss the bride, first to give them a wedding present—a book. He also wrote out the first marriage license in his big, bold hand and filed it in his safe.

When he was fulfilling his other functions as justice of the peace, Maynard held court in Yesler's cookhouse, an outsized log cabin, twenty-five feet square, with an enormous fireplace, which made it the most comfortable as well as the most spacious building in town. At the conclusion of the first trial Justice Maynard decided that the mate of the brig *Franklin Adams* had, as charged, appropriated the moneys and goods of the vessel for private purposes. Since there was no jail and a shortage of manpower, he let the culprit off with instructions to keep his books in better order.

Maynard's own papers were in some confusion. When he had first come to Seattle he took a married man's claim of 640 acres, 320 for himself, 320 for his wife Lydia.

[2] At the same time it honored another deserving Democrat, William Rufus King, the newly elected vice-president of the United States, who died shortly after taking office, by naming the county King County. Pierce County, the next one south, was named for President-elect Franklin Pierce.

Now, having divorced Lydia, he sought to change his claim so that her share would go to Catherine. He felt he was justified in doing so because Lydia had never lived on the property. He sent a sworn statement to the land commissioner about the change, saying that he had been "intermarried with Lydia A. Maynard until December 24, 1852," and was "legally married to his second wife Catherine B. on January 15, 1853." The commissioner, not being aware of the peculiarities of Maynard's marital affairs, assumed that this meant Lydia had died; he filled out the forms accordingly. There was another complication. Between the time Maynard filed in Lydia's name and the time he applied again for Catherine, the donation laws had been changed. Catherine did not qualify under the new provisions, a fact that nobody noticed at the time.

There was also confusion in the platting of the township. When Seattle became a legal entity in 1853, it was necessary to file a formal plat. Maynard surveyed his property and Arthur Denny went over the Denny and Boren holdings. Each planned to have streets paralleling the bay. But since the meeting place of the two plats—Mill Street, down which ox-teams skidded logs to Yesler's Mill—was also the point where the water front curved, the streets did not meet. Denny talked to Maynard about it, hoping to work out an agreement, but personality as well as geography worked against a compromise. Denny was a Whig and a teetotaler; Maynard was a Democrat and a bit of a drunk. The doctor had been hitting the bottle when he conferred with Denny and insisted that since his streets not only paralleled the bay but ran due north and south, they should be continued across the Denny-Boren holdings. Denny, while admitting that it would be neat to have the town four-square with the compass, felt that it would be more convenient to have the streets in his section parallel the water too. "Maynard had taken enough to make him feel that he was not only monarch of all he surveyed but what Boren and I had surveyed as well," Denny remarked dryly. No agreement was reached. The next morning, the day of filing, Denny turned in his plat first; some hours later Maynard, nursing a hangover, appeared at the cookhouse and gave his version of the plat to Yesler. Neither man would back down, so instead of the streets curving together across Mill Street (now Yesler Way), they hit it uncompromisingly, as far apart as the proprietors. They remain far apart to this day.

The town grew, Maynard's section faster than Denny's, probably because the doctor was so free and easy with his acres.[3] In 1854 when Justice Maynard strolled down Commercial Street from Yesler's cookhouse to his store, he passed on his right a big two-story frame building and a store; to his left was a combined residence and shoeshop and the blacksmith shop that he had all but given to Lewis Wyckoff. Most of the buildings were of boards, for Yesler's Mill made sawed lumber available so soon that nobody who could afford boards would build a log cabin. The showplace of Seattle was the house that Captain Felker built, two stories high with a wide porch and three chimneys and hardwood floors and good white paint and a white picket fence.

But though there were big buildings, everybody was broke. The town was built on speculation; even the missionaries were writing home hinting that they could make a financial killing if only they had cash. What capital there was in Seattle was tied up in land and timber; even the rich were land poor.

Things were so bad, cash-wise, that it is hard to guess how the community came to realize that one of its members, Edward Moore, was a pauper. Perhaps the determining factor was, in the words of Maynard's report, that Moore was "a stranger, and insane besides."

In a pioneer community like Seattle nobody knew what to do with an insane pauper. Finally Maynard offered to look after him if the county would pay his board bills. Maynard should have known better: King County had so little money that it was unable even to supply him with an official seal for his notary work. He kept the poor fellow for several months but, realizing that he would never get

[3] A year after the plats were filed there were only four buildings north of Mill Street.

paid for it, at last turned him over to Dr. M. P. Burns of Steilacoom, who gave him a receipt for "an insane and crippled man, a stranger without acquaintance or friends." Burns agreed to look after Moore until the Territorial Legislature took action on the subject of relief; he presented a bill for $621 to the legislature for "custody and care of a non-resident lunatic pauper"; but the legislators, establishing a tradition, couldn't agree as to the need and didn't vote a cent. Dr. Burns loaded his patient into a canoe, paddled him back to Seattle, and left him. Maynard didn't want him again; nobody did. The county commissioners decided that "Edward Moore, the pauper, now in Seattle, be sold at public auction to the lowest bidder for his maintenance to be paid out of the county treasury, said bid to be left discretionary with the Commissioners to accept or reject, on Saturday, the 7th day of June, at 2 o'clock in the town of Seattle." Moore disappears from the official records with that. Apparently there were no bidders; at least no bid was accepted, and the insane man was left to wander the streets. At last the townsfolk took decisive action. They caught Moore, amputated his toes, which had been frozen, cleaned him thoroughly, put new clothes on him, and paid his passage on a ship bound for Massachusetts.

Seattle found it somewhat easier to solve the problem of what to do with its first white-skinned murderers: it let them go. When in July 1853 an Indian known as Massachie Jim—*massachie* means bad in the Jargon—beat his wife until she died, some of his neighbors on the White River, who had long deplored his habits and admired his property, decided that this was as good a time as any to bring law and order to King County. They hanged him.

The other Indians didn't show much concern about Bad Jim's demise; his reputation with them was not good either. But when a white man disappeared on a trip to Lake Union a few weeks later, there were rumors that he had been killed in revenge for the hanging of Bad Jim. Relations between the natives and the whites grew strained. Nine months after Bad Jim's death there was a Mrs. Catherine Blaine, the wife of the local Methodist missionary, wrote of it in a letter to the folks back in the Midwest:

One day last week a man started from Alki to go down the Sound in a canoe with three Indians. The Indians returned with his canoe, clothing, watch, money, etc. and were quite badly wounded so that one of them died. Suspicions were raised that all was not right, and last Saturday three white men, and three Indians of another tribe, went to make inquiries.

The Indians who were suspected of murder had left Alki and were found among their own tribe. The whites demanded them and they were given up without hesitation. They put them in a canoe, but it was aground which caused some delay in getting away, during which time the Indians from the land rushed upon the men with drawn knives, and one man fired upon them. This commenced hostilities and the whites killed from five to ten (they do not know the exact number) of the Indians. During the fracas one of the Indians they had arrested managed to escape. The other behaved so badly they shot him. The whites were all wounded, one of them mortally. He died last night. Mr. B. preached his funeral sermon this afternoon. Another was wounded in the thigh, the bullet going through it. The other received a bullet in his cheek, which flattened against his teeth and he spit it out. One of the Indians they took with them was wounded so they think he cannot live. Their return to this place yesterday excited the people very much.

A company immediately volunteered to go this morning and attack them, but upon more mature thought they decided to refer the case to the governor for his action upon it. The citizens convened last night, drew up a set of resolutions informing him of affairs and requesting him to take immediate action. They sent it off in a sloop to Olympia, but unless the winds should be very fair, we cannot hope for aid from him before Saturday. . . .

The governor's decision was that a rule of law and order should be established. It was necessary to show the Indians that no one, white or red, could violate the law without being subject to trial. Sixteen months after Bad

Jim was lynched, the first District Court was held in King County with Maynard as court clerk.

First the grand jury studied the information the government had obtained about the hanging of Bad Jim. One of the men who helped to hang him was William Haebner; he was also a member of the grand jury. Haebner sat with the others while they returned indictments against Luther Collins and David Maurer, but he was excused while the jury considered his own case. He was indicted too.

Then came the trial. Maurer, a simple-minded German with a fine feeling for the truth, was the first to be brought before the bar. He looked bewildered when the charge was read. It was a statement that the government considered him guilty of having committed murder in the first degree by depriving one Massachic Jim, a resident of King County, of his life. Maurer was asked how he pleaded. He told Chief Justice Edward Lander that he didn't understand what all the words meant. The judge explained that Maurer was accused of helping to string up Bad Jim and was supposed to say whether he had done so or whether he hadn't. Maurer looked relieved. He was happy to have it cleared up. Sure, he'd helped the boys with that.

It was the wrong answer. The court quickly appointed an attorney for him; the attorney changed his plea to not guilty. From that point the trial was routine. Maurer, of course, was acquitted. So was Haebner. The prosecuting attorney gave up and asked that charges against Luther Collins, the solidest citizen of the accused trio, be dismissed. If the Indians were favorably impressed by this display of the rule of law they did not say so.

There were two ways to look at the Indians. The usual view of the pioneer whites was summed up by the Reverend David Blaine, who quickly decided the Indians weren't worth his trouble. His wife shared his opinions and mentioned them in another letter to her parents, who wrote back chiding her for intolerance and saying that she would have to love the Indians if she was to help them. The Reverend Mr. Blaine decided to set them straight. He wrote his mother-in-law:

You tell Kate that she must love the coarse, filthy, debased natives in order to do them good. We can imagine in some degree your feelings on this subject, and you will need the help of imagination to appreciate our situation and relation to these pitiable objects of neglect and degradation.

Once we could have hoped to do them good, but alas, they are most undoubtedly beyond our reach. . . . Those who cannot talk the jargon or Chinook are beyond our reach because we cannot converse with them except through an interpreter. They have already learned enough of religion through the Catholics to make the sign of the cross and say *ikt papa ikt sockala Tiee*, one pope and one God.

They are taught that there is a lower region and an upper one and that the good and bad will be separated in the future state, but moral feelings seem to be quite blunted or blotted out, and they lie, gamble, steal, get drunk and all the other bad things almost as a matter of duty because it is so deeply innate and so fully acquired by habit.

Those who can speak the Chinook are apparently more intelligent because from their intercourse with the whites they have acquired some cunning and artifice, but they are even lower in immorality than their less informed elders who speak not the jargon. They have also associated with the worst of white men and their example and influence have been most pernicious. Seeing the whites paying no regard to their religious obligations nor even to moral principle they could scarcely do otherwise.

The principle which actuates almost all here is, "Get all you can and keep all you get," no matter how you get it. This is fairly illustrated by a case that occurred a day or two since. An Indian wore a very nice pair of pants when he came to call upon us, and when Kate, who was in the house alone, asked him if he got them by working in the sawmill, he replied, "*Wake, nika iscum momook tolo*," meaning, "No, I got them by gambling." When she said, "*Momook tolo tias mussachee*"—"Gambling is very bad," he replied, "*Wake mussachee, wake mussachee, iscum hiyou dolla.*" "No bad, no wicked, gets plenty dollars." This is the principle. Nothing is wicked which gets plenty of dollars. . . .[4]

---

[4] In a letter home a few months later Dr. Blaine said, "If I had

Maynard took a different view from the man of God. He could understand how anyone with a multitude of problems might be led to lift the bottle too often. And instinctively he liked people; he liked everyone who was not a Whig, and he even liked some Whigs. The Indians had helped him; he helped them. He learned their language, doctored their illnesses, drank their liquor, paddled their canoes. He was especially close to Sealth. "My heart is very good toward Dr. Maynard," Sealth told the Indian agent; and Maynard's heart was good toward Sealth and most of the Salish along the Sound. He knew how it was with them, and he was sorry.

5.

They lived in a living world: the fish they ate, the animals they skinned, the very hills they climbed, were cousin and brother to the Salish of Puget Sound.

They lived with their world on terms of genial equality. It had much to give and they took as their portion whatever was necessary, wanting little more. The women dug clams on the muddy beaches and smoked them for the winter; the children gathered wild blackberries and the dusty, tart Oregon grape, black raspberries and the fragile, grainy salmonberry. The men caught the Chinook salmon in nets, traps or weirs, on hook and line, or, during the spring run when the salmon clogged the shallow streams, by clubbing them. The women dug the starchy bulbs of the blue-flowered camass plants, the men hunted deer and elk with bows made of yew or dogwood. They lived in cool houses of woven grass mats during the summer, and in winter in lodges of split cedar. They dressed in buckskin or dogwool blankets if they were wealthy; in cloth

the value of that mill here, or even half of it, I could buy the whole town plat of Seattle that remains unsold, as the times are depressed and money scarce just now, and this in ten years would increase in value ten-fold. . . . One of our town proprietors, Dr. Maynard, a good friend to us, has given us some two acres more or less, a short distance from the town plat, laying on the shore of the bay, for a garden and orchard. The land is very rich and in a few years will be included in the town and needed for building lots.

woven from the inner bark of the cedar if they were poor. When they worked near the water, as they often did, they went naked. They rode the swift, short rivers and the ever-changing waters of the Sound in beautifully designed dugouts, painstakingly burned and carved from cedar.

They had a life of daily change within a fixed pattern, a life of constant challenge, but of challenges that were familiar and could be mastered. The mysteries of life they explained in their spoken literature, in the tales told around the work fire, the stories that made all the world alive and kin to the Salish tribesmen; in their legends they explained how man discovered the use of fire and lost it and recovered it, why snakes were poisonous east of the Cascades but not around Puget Sound, and how the Salish wiped out their enemies in every battle.

It was only in their legends that the Salish tribes killed all their enemies. They never really became involved in wars of extermination, nor did they occupy the lands of defeated tribes. They raided and retreated. They fought to avenge affronts to tribal honor but seldom for personal gain. It was simpler and safer to hunt or dig or snare or chop than to fight; so much easier, in fact, that when the warlike Kwakiutl—the Smoke of the World people, who lived a harsher life on Vancouver Island—came raiding down the Sound, the Salish usually found it expedient to take to the bushes instead of standing to do battle. The more northerly tribes on the Sound tended to be a bit belligerent, and each tribe had its list of tribes it tended to like or to distrust. But the occasional wars were actually raids. The object was to sneak up on the enemy's village, burn it, capture a few prisoners to serve as slaves, and get away. A war was not for killing.

Then the white men came. They brought with them wonderful things: tools that would cut the great trees, blankets larger and brighter than those of the richest chief, liquor more stimulating than *kinnikinnik*, a local drug the Salish sometimes smoked, and guns and beads and medicines. The Indians were pleased to have in their midst these people of perpetual supply.

But the white men brought other things. They brought new diseases. They brought a religion that said many things the Salish had always done were wicked and should be done no more, though the reasons were not clear. They brought the idea of private property. The Indians had owned some things individually, but not land, which belonged to the people and was used by the people. When the whites took acres and miles of land and shut the Indians off from it, the Indians could not understand; but they were slow to anger, and there was much land. By the time they realized the danger it was too late. The very pattern of their life had unraveled, and the whites were on the Sound in strength. In such a situation there were two things an Indian leader could do. He could fight or he could temporize.

6.

After 1854 it was obvious that there was going to be serious trouble between the Indians and the whites on Puget Sound. With the benefit of hindsight we can see now that the Indians' cause was hopeless. The Salish never had a chance; in a sense they did not even have a choice. They were certain to be pushed into reservations. To some Indians, however, it seemed there was an alternative: they could fight.

The whites too were bound by conditions they could not control. They were compelled to adopt a policy that led straight to war. Until the Indians ceded their land by treaty, no settler would have legal title to his property. It was therefore decided by the men who had the power to make decisions—white men, of course—that the Indian policy in the Northwest, as elsewhere, would be a reservation policy. It was for the Indians' own good, they believed. The Indians would be put on reservations, then the reservations would be gradually reduced in size; by this means the whites would not only get legal title to the remaining land but the Indians would be forced to give up their hunting and fishing economy (which required much land) in favor of farming, a peaceable pursuit. It may have been that this policy was in the long run the best policy for the Indians, but the decision to follow it was not theirs, and it never has been easy to persuade men that they ought to give up a career of hunting and fishing for the greater security that comes with tilling land. The man whose duty it was to persuade the Indians to remove to the reservations was General Isaac Stevens, a diminutive, able, alert, vain West Pointer who had distinguished himself in the Mexican War.

Washington was separated from Oregon on March 2, 1853, when President Millard Fillmore signed the bill creating the new territory. A few days later Franklin Pierce was inaugurated as President; one of his first acts was to name Stevens, who had supported him in his presidential campaign, governor of Washington Territory. Stevens reached Olympia in November after a five-month trip from St. Paul, and on November 28 he proclaimed Olympia the territorial capital. He chose Mike Simmons, a deserving Democrat if ever there was one, as Special Indian Agent; Simmons in turn suggested his Democratic brother-in-law, Doc Maynard, as agent for the Seattle area.

Of all the tasks Maynard undertook on behalf of the community, this was to be the most successfully executed—and the most disastrous to himself. While the other citizens labored on a stockade and blockhouse, Maynard moved among the Salish tribesmen, listening to complaints, passing out medicine, delivering babies. Indians came for miles to be doctored by him. Maynard could set a bone, lance an infection, or deliver a baby; for more complicated complaints he relied upon the patient's belief in the curative powers of colored water and pink or blue pills, and upon his own belief in the beneficent effects of staying in bed in a warm, sunny room. With the Indians this type of treatment was especially effective, for in following his advice they stayed away from the sweat lodge, a Turkish-bath treatment the Salish considered a remedy for everything from impure thoughts to smallpox. Maynard's therapeutics had their limitations but were an

improvement over the medicine man's, which tended to
kill rather than cure; the doctor's reputation as a healer
rose steadily among the tribesmen, and the good will he
acquired as physician helped him as diplomat. When Governor
Stevens wanted to talk to the Indians, Maynard had
no trouble arranging for the meetings.

The first of the great conferences on the central Sound
took place in front of Maynard's store in Seattle. Stevens
and his party came from Olympia on a paddlewheeler.
The Indians came by canoe from across the bay and from
up the Duwamish, the Snohomish, the Puyallup, and the
Skagit. Maynard, dapper in his inevitable dark suit, his
curly hair neatly brushed, introduced the little governor,
who wore riding breeches and a red flannel shirt. Stevens
was an able orator of the high-flown school. He told the
Indians what the Great White Father had decided was
good for them. He spoke of the money the government
would pay them for their lands, of the schools that would
be started, of the workshops that would be furnished. He
spoke well and with dignity. Sealth, wrapped in an old
blanket, his hand resting at first on Stevens' head and
then, after the little general edged away, on his shoulder,
replied that the Indians had no choice but to accept.

Some months later Maynard arranged for a treaty conference
at Point Elliott, a few miles north of Seattle.
Representatives of four thousand Indians living along
the northern shores of Puget Sound, listed in the treaty as
"the Snohomish, Skokomish, Duwamish, Muckleshoots,
Queelewamish, Seawamish, Snoqualmie, Sakequells,
Scadgets, Squinamish, Keekallis, Scoquachams, Swim-
mish, Nooksacks, and Lummy," agreed to sell their title to
two million acres and move to reservations in return for
$150,000 payable over twenty years in usable goods. His-
torians still argue about this treaty and others that Governor Stevens negotiated in his swing around the territory.
The Indians had to rely on translators to tell them what
was in the treaty. The translation was made not in the
language of the individual tribes but in the Jargon, a
bastard tongue composed of about three hundred words of
Indian, English, and French derivation and better suited

to barter than precise diplomacy. The possibility for misunderstanding was enormous even if the translator was scrupulously accurate. Among those Indians who understood the terms there was not complete satisfaction. Unhappiest of the tyees was Chief Nelson of the Muckleshoots; his tribe considered their neighbors, the Duwamish, to be something less than human, but both tribes were assigned to the same reservation.

An immediate showdown was prevented by the fact that the Indians were not required to move until confirmation of the treaty was received from the national capital. In the meantime Stevens crossed the Cascades, where he had even more trouble making treaties with the Plateau Indians. He was handicapped by the fact that on the dry side of the mountains he had no one with Maynard's peculiarly persuasive status to front for him. Even worse, though, was the discovery of gold in eastern Washington Territory. The rush of prospectors to the brown hills and dry creekbeds was, to the Indians whose land was involved, an invasion. They began to pick off strays from the army of goldseekers, and soon the trouble spread back across the mountains.

In the fall of 1854 a man named A. L. Potter, who was homesteading Potter's Prairie on the White River, circulated a story that the Muckleshoots had crept up to his cabin intent on a massacre and that only the happy fact that he had taken to sleeping in a near-by tree had saved his life. The rest of the families in the valley, on hearing of Potter's trouble, fled to Seattle, where they stayed for a couple of weeks, booming business and helping to build up the defense of the town.

Charles Mason, a pudgy young lawyer who was acting as governor while Stevens was away, talked to the settlers, then under armed guard went up the Duwamish until it became the White and talked with the Indians, who assured him they were good Indians. Mason looked at the farmhouses—which were unburned—and went back to Seattle to spread the word that all was calm. The settlers ought to return to their homes, he said. There were crops to be harvested.

The settlers returned. The following week a number of them were massacred, partly as the result of a second error by Mason. After telling the settlers to leave the protection of the Seattle stockade, he began to have doubts and issued a call for the formation of two companies of volunteers. He then dispatched a group of these irregulars to arrest Leshi, a strong-minded Nisqually chief who had refused to retire to a reservation. The posse surprised Leshi in the subversive activity of sowing winter wheat in the Nisqually valley, but he was a superb horseman and escaped capture. The irregulars pursued him toward the White River. On the third day of the chase they ran into an ambush and four of the posse were shot dead.

That was on a Saturday. The following day, a cool, brilliant Sunday morning, some Muckleshoots, aided by members of the Klickitat tribe, to which Leshi was closely related, attacked the cabins of settlers living along the White River between the present towns of Kent and Auburn. Three children, spared by the Indians on the order of Chief Nelson, who had admired their mother though he had found it necessary to shoot her, made their way downstream to Seattle with news of the attack.

This was war. The town mobilized. Riders left Seattle to warn all settlers to return to the stockade. Dispatches were sent to Olympia and Portland and Washington, D. C., asking for more military support. All through the next day wagons loaded with household goods creaked over the narrow roads leading to town. Children drove the sheep and hogs and geese; men herded cattle. The valleys nearby were deserted by nightfall. But Seattle was never so crowded, never more active.

Maynard was as busy as everyone else. He and Catherine took charge of the three children orphaned by the Indian raid, a boy of seven, a girl of four, another boy of two. He wrote a blistering memorandum to the War Department, saying that it was time for the military—and for governors of all categories—to get over the idea that a handful of whites could outfight a host of Indians. "The number, valor and prowess of the Indians have been greatly underrated," he said. And he moved among the neighboring tribes, assuring them that the whites still loved them and would protect them against the Klickitats and Nisquallies and Muckleshoots.

That was certainly not true. The whites were far from sure they could protect themselves, let alone any friendly Indians. Nor were most of the settlers sure they wanted to protect any Indians. How could you be sure an Indian was friendly? How could you even be sure about a fellow like Maynard? He spent an awful lot of time with the Indians, didn't he? What was he up to? The man was an Indian lover.

Two weeks after the killings in the valley Mike Simmons sent Maynard word from Olympia that he was to round up all the friendly tribesmen in his area and move them across the Sound. Indians did not want to go. It was the wrong time of year to be leaving their winter houses. Maynard promised them that the government would supply lumber to build new houses at Port Madison and Suquamish.[5] They protested that November was no time to be moving household goods by canoe: Maynard said he'd hire a schooner. They said their food supplies were short: Maynard wearily assured them he'd see they didn't starve. So, reluctantly, they agreed to go.

In mid-November more than a thousand Indians camped just outside the raw-planked stockade that protected Seattle. Inside the walls Maynard worked desperately to keep his promises. The government had not appropriated a penny to meet the expense of moving the Indians. Mike Simmons at Olympia sorrowfully answered Maynard's plea for funds with the admission that it would be months before any money was available. But the danger in breaking promises to the friendly tribesmen was obvious, so Maynard used his own money. He bought a load of lumber for the houses, he rented a schooner, he used food supplies from his own store.

On a gray day late in November the Indians embarked

[5] Suquamish was the site of one of the most remarkable structures ever raised by the American Indian—the Oleman House, a community lodge nine hundred feet long divided into forty apartments.

in their long, black dugouts, Maynard went aboard the schooner, and the flotilla moved across the leaden waters toward a destination hidden in mist. The citizens of Seattle were happy to see them go.

During the next two months Maynard shuttled back and forth across the Sound, rounding up most of the friendly Indians who had not moved with the main party, bringing rumors that had been relayed to him by his charges, picking up news of the war.

The war was not going well for either side. Whenever a party of soldiers caught up with a band of hostiles, the Indians turned on them and drubbed them. But Salish warfare with its emphasis on the quick punitive raid against an unsuspecting enemy had developed no tactics for attacking prepared positions or for exploiting a siege. Though the warrior bands roamed the forests and swamps and unguarded valleys, the whites remained safe behind their stockades throughout both Washington and Oregon Territory.

The pattern of life of both Indians and whites was disrupted. The tribesmen could not follow their usual trade routes, could not visit many of the camass fields or clam beaches, could not venture safely on the Sound to fish. The Indians grew hungry, their ammunition ran low, and as winter deepened they felt the pinch of cold. As for the whites, they might be safe but they were going broke. The farmers could not work their fields or save their cabins from the torch. The merchants for a time benefited by having their customers close by, but their customers soon ran out of money; the merchants had to extend credit and risk not being paid, or refuse credit and risk losing customers who were also friends. In either case they would go broke. Mills shut down for want of logs. Real-estate prices dropped to literally nothing. The winter rains turned the streets to filthy mud and kept families inside the crowded clapboard houses and log cabins. Rumors spread. The army was sending help from California; the army was withdrawing what troops it had on Puget Sound and sending them to Oregon. Two thousand Plateau Indians were coming over the pass to join the hostiles; the

Muckleshoots had retreated over the pass to eastern Washington. Governor Stevens was trying to arrange an armistice; the Indians wanted to surrender but Stevens was determined to defeat them in the field. You heard everything and believed what your temperament directed.

Among the friendly Indians at Suquamish rumors also flourished. Chief Sealth picked up one that he felt should not be ignored: a hostile warrior intended to sneak into the reservation when Maynard was there and assassinate him. This rumor had the sanction of being true to the Indian concept of war, which centered on killing the enemy leader, the symbol of the opposition. Maynard, as Indian agent for the Seattle area, was a natural target. Chief Sealth persuaded the doctor to take off his dark suit and wrap himself in a blanket. Maynard even put aside his octagonal glasses to make it more difficult for an assassin to spot him, but after a day he put them back on with the comment that he'd rather be killed than stumble to death.

The rumors were worrisome, but worse for Maynard and the friendly Indians was knowing that something important was happening and not knowing the details. On January 25 the Active steamed past the reservation, headed north. A canoe went out and brought word that Governor Stevens was aboard. He was optimistic. Seattle was in no more danger from the Indians than New York was. The warship Decatur with a complement of Marines was there, and a troop of volunteers had just come in from the blockhouse on the Duwamish. The latter had come to be discharged, their three months' enlistments having expired. None of them was willing to sign up again, but they were in town and probably would fight if the Indians attacked—only the Indians wouldn't attack. They'd all gone back into the hills. There weren't any hostiles within miles. He was sure of it.

When Maynard awoke the next morning, January 26, the sky was overcast but there was no rain. Clouds stretched low over the gray water. As he walked along the damp, steel-gray beach, his eyes fixed on the point where Seattle would be visible on a clear day, Maynard heard the rumble of distant thunder. Strange: thunder is rare on

Puget Sound and never comes on a gray day. But again the boom rolled across the water, and Maynard recognized it as the sound of artillery. Seattle was having visitors. The visitors were welcome enough to be given a salute, or unwelcome enough to be fired upon. Reinforcements or Indians?

The howitzer sounded intermittently. Straining to hear, Maynard thought he could make out the crackle of small arms. Some of the Indians who joined him on the beach thought so too. Seattle was under attack.

For Maynard the day of January 26 was perhaps the longest in his life. He could not cross the Sound to see what was happening; Suquamish was his post. Indians volunteered to go, but he could not send them; his job was to keep the Indians on the west shore. He could only wait. All day the rumble of the howitzer rolled across the water, and at night there was the distant glow of burning buildings.

The next morning the news that reached Maynard was not bad. Shortly after Governor Stevens had sailed from the town, a party of hostiles crossed Lake Washington in canoes and slipped into the forest east of Seattle. Friendly Indians, who had been permitted to remain in Seattle, warned the whites of their presence and sentries patrolled the town. Nothing happened. In the morning, acting on a tip relayed from an Indian to Henry Yesler to the commander of the *Decatur*, the Marines lobbed a howitzer shell into the woods above the town. The Indians fired back.

Settlers rushed from their cabins to the protection of the blockhouse. The volunteers formed ranks. The Marines opened up with small arms, and the howitzer. As a battle, though, it wasn't much. The Indians made no attempt to storm the stockade, and none of the whites—not the settlers, not the discharged volunteers (some of whom declined to shoulder arms at all), not even the Marines— saw any sense in charging across the open fields to get at the enemy in the forest. The battle raged, in a manner of speaking, throughout the day: the Indians maneuvering behind the cover of the dark forest, firing down into the

village, the settlers replying frugally with small arms, the
Marines alternating volleys of gunfire with shells from the
howitzer. Both sides paused for dinner (the Indians dining
off the settlers' livestock, the Marines going aboard the
Decatur for mess, the settlers eating whatever their wives
brought them), but they all came back for a few twilight
shots. Before calling it a night the Indians set fire to two
houses outside the stockade.

In the morning the Marines were prepared for some
more long-range fighting, but the Indians had disappeared. They never returned, armed. It had been a safe
fight for the cautious Marines and the invisible Indians,
but a fourteen-year-old boy and a young volunteer who
neglected to stay under cover were shot dead; no one who
remained inside the stockade was wounded. As for the
Indians, no one knew—or knows. When Maynard
learned of the battle he was told that two thousand Indians had joined in the attack, that more than a hundred
were killed, another hundred wounded; but not so much
as a single body was found, nor even a sign of blood. It is
possible that the Indians left the battle as undamaged as
the Marines.

The settlers suffered greatly as a result of the war.
Many who lived outside the town lost their houses. After
the attack they did not want to return to the valleys: the
war might be over, but did the Indians know it? Some
were still at large, among them Leshi. He once offered to
surrender and to cut off his right hand to prove he would
not take up arms again, an offer that was not accepted.
Finally Leshi was betrayed by his nephew, who received a
reward of thirty blankets for turning him over to authorities at Fort Steilacoom. He was tried for the murder of an
officer who had been ambushed during the war. (One of
the two attorneys for the defense was H. R. Crosby, Bing
Crosby's grandfather.) The first trial ended in a hung jury,
10-2, for conviction. A second trial before a new judge in
another district resulted in Leshi's conviction. He was
sentenced to death. A strong minority of pioneers, including Maynard, felt that Leshi was being made a scapegoat,
that Governor Stevens was blaming the Indian for harm

that had really been caused by unfair treaties. When the day came for Leshi's execution some of his partisans arranged to have the sheriff and marshal who were to hang him arrested on a trumped-up charge. The execution was delayed, new appeals were made to the Territorial Supreme Court and the Territorial Legislature, but in vain; after another half-year Leshi was led to the gallows. The man appointed to hang him said later, "He was as cool as could be—just like he was going to dinner.... He did not seem to be the least bit excited at all, and no trembling on him at all—nothing of the kind, and that is more than I could say for myself.... I felt I was hanging an innocent man."

Even with Leshi dead[6] and the other raiders off on the reservations to which they had been assigned, the homesteaders had their doubts. How could you ever be sure? They hated and feared the Indians, all Indians.

7.

For Maynard, when he returned from Suquamish, that was the greatest misfortune of all. It cut him off from the town he loved, since he was the known friend and associate of redskins. It was useless for him to point out that it was his duty to mingle with Indians, useless to say that his friendship with some of them had lessened the danger to the community. His friends understood; those who knew him less well he could not reach. He was an Indian lover.

He was a Democrat too, in the shifting climate of opinion. Nationally the Whigs had given way to the new Republican Party, and the other leaders of Seattle—Yesler, the Dennys, Dr. Smith—were of Republican kidney. Maynard, the friend of the Indian, was the foe of the Abolitionist. He was a states' rights man, a moderate, and,

---

[6] Years later, reaction set in and Leshi was considered a martyr. When Yelm Jim, a friend of Leshi, shot the nephew, he was not indicted. Today a lovely park in Seattle is named for Leshi.

in time, a defender of Secession. There were those, later, who called him Copperhead.

So, in the dark days following the Indian War, wĥen business was at a standstill and land was worth almost nothing, when half the families left town, Maynard found himself estranged from much of the remaining community. Catherine stood firmly by him; so did Chief Sealth and a few others. But this man who had been a mover and shaker, this booster who had been a one-man chamber of commerce, found himself put aside. And not only did Maynard receive scant gratitude for his work with the Indians, but he failed to get back most of the money he had supplied. His claims on the government were disapproved. He had not gone through channels.

As the Civil War approached and passions rose, Maynard, the friendliest of men, found Seattle unbearable. He longed to escape to the solitude of a farm. In 1857 he traded 260 acres of his land—the area directly south of Yesler Way, the section which became the headquarters for the northern gold rushes—to C. C. Terry, in return for a 319-acre farm on Alki Point. There, in a fine clapboard house with a wonderful view of the Sound, he and Catherine almost starved. Maynard was no farmer. He could not follow the quiet discipline of farm life and he would always knock off work to help a friend.

One day young Christopher Columbus Simmons, Big Mike's boy, who had drawn his historic given name because he was born on the banks of the Columbia during the overland trek, pulled his canoe up on the beach below Maynard's house. With him was a very young girl. They wanted to get married, Chris said, but their parents thought the girl too young. Maynard asked, "Well, how old is she?" "Thirteen," the boy admitted, but they loved each other very much.

Maynard, who had encountered Big Mike's objections when he courted Chris's aunt, thought that anyone in love ought to get married. He hit on a stratagem, childish but effective. He took two pieces of paper, wrote "18" on each of them, and had the girl put them in her shoes. Then he took them to the residence of the Reverend Daniel

Bagley. The Minister said the girl looked pretty young. Maynard allowed that she did but added, "Nevertheless, I'm positive that she's over eighteen, absolutely positive."

So, with Maynard as a witness, the ceremony was read at six in the morning. That afternoon the parents arrived. They upbraided poor Bagley for marrying a girl so young. He took them to Maynard and demanded an explanation. Maynard explained. They were not amused.

Sixty-three years later the patriarch Christopher Columbus Simmons recalled that after the ceremony Maynard had taken him aside and said, "Look here, young fellow, this is a pretty serious affair." And Chris had replied, "All right, I'm willing to take my medicine." And, Simmons added, "I'm still taking it and enjoying it. We have at present in our family sixty, including ourselves, children, grandchildren, and great-grandchildren."

Maynard had many other visitors at Alki. The house was on the main canoe route along the Sound. The Indians made their friend's house a camping spot, coming and going. They nearly ate him out of house and farm.

Official duties took Maynard from the plow quite often. Though the Republicans were gaining power, the Democrats still controlled the Territorial Administration; Maynard was again appointed justice of the peace for the Seattle precinct and court commissioner for the county. After he and Catherine had been gone for a week on court business, they returned to find their house burned to the ground. It was almost a blessing. The Maynards moved back to Seattle and opened a hospital.

As usual Maynard couldn't concentrate. The hospital took up only two rooms in the small, two-story frame building he lived in. Catherine, who had no formal training at all, was put in charge of the lying-in ward. Another room was set aside as drugstore and notions counter. Tradition says that Maynard's hospital did not thrive because the doctor insisted on treating Indians as well a whites. One of his patients was Sealth. The aged chief spent much of his time with his people on the reservation across the Sound, but when he came to Seattle he called on Maynard for treatment; one school of local historians believes that the doctor joined his friend in taking some high-proof medicine; others insist that Sealth would never touch alcohol. The chief died suddenly, of a heart attack, on June 7, 1866.

We will never know, for sure, the stature of Chief Sealth. He may have been, as the pioneers said, a great man and a great statesman; he may have been, as some Indians of the generation that followed his have argued, a shrewd and conniving subchief who turned the power of the white men to his own advantage, a Quisling who guessed right about the outcome of a struggle for power. The truth probably lies somewhere between these two estimates, but either way he was a good friend of Doc Maynard's, and that friendship was important for the future of Seattle.

Two years after opening his hospital Maynard hung out his shingle as a lawyer. He had been admitted to the bar by an act of the legislature in 1856 but had never practiced. As a physician Maynard had at least the recommendation of his own good health; as a lawyer his personal affairs should have been as helpful as a quarantine sign: they were in a mess. Most of Maynard's legal troubles grew out of his switch of wives and his casual conviction that since Lydia had never lived on the land he had registered in her name he could transfer it to Catherine. When Lydia learned—probably from some busy patriot who did not care for "Copperhead" Maynard—that she had not only been divorced but had been divested of a considerable portion of downtown Seattle, she started west. One day Maynard heard she was to arrive on the afternoon steamer from Olympia. He stopped at his favorite barbershop and said, "Fix me up in your best style."

"What's up, Doctor? What are you going to do?"

"I'm going to give the people here a sight they never had before and may never have again. I am going to show them a man walking up the street with a wife on each arm."

When the steamer arrived, Maynard and the second Mrs. Maynard met the first Mrs. Maynard and together they went to the Maynard house, where the three lived in apparent harmony until Lydia had completed arrangements for her legal business.

The business turned out badly for all concerned. The litigation wore on and on. Lydia's claim for the land was not allowed because she had never lived on it; Maynard had a brief moment of happiness, believing that Catherine would surely be awarded the disputed title, but the court ruled that Catherine had not settled on the land in time to claim it. Her half of the Maynard property would have to be returned to the government.

That raised new problems and started more suits. Did the dividing line between the property of husband and wife run north and south or east and west, and which side belonged to which partner? Hundreds were vitally interested in the decision because Maynard had disposed of most of his land; whichever way the ruling went, a considerable portion of Seattle's property owners were going to find themselves without a valid title to their land. But to Maynard it no longer made much difference. The few lots he still held title to were so scattered that no matter how the line was drawn he would lose a number of them. He resigned himself to their loss. In the final decision, which he did not live to learn, the court ruled the property line ran at right angles from the shore and that Maynard had owned the northern portion; the southern part reverted to the government. The decision that mattered to Maynard was the one that deprived Catherine of her claim.

Liquor became for Maynard less a stimulant than a consolation. He drank more than ever, but as he became an alcoholic he regained much of his old popularity. He was an institution, and there was probably pity in his popularity. "Old Doc Maynard is a better doctor drunk than the rest of them are sober," the people said. But still he did not prosper as a physician: he hated to send bills.

If there was a change in Maynard's attitude once he realized the inevitability of his failure, it was in his relations with public officials. Whenever he had held office, Maynard had tried to use his position to help people, but it seemed to him that other officials operated on a different principle. They had short-changed him for his services, they had deprived him of his land grant, they would not even repay the money he spent in line of duty as Indian agent.

One day when Maynard went to the post office to pick up his mail before catching the steamer to Olympia, he found the door locked. The postmaster was sorting mail. Maynard shouted that his boat was leaving and he wanted his letters, right now. The postmaster said he'd have to wait, just like everyone else. To Maynard it seemed he had been waiting most of his life for the government to give him what was rightfully his. He kicked down the door and snatched the letters from the startled postmaster.

But he could not stay angry. When he came back from Olympia he brought with him new hinges for the door and put them on himself.

He changed very little. One of his last acts was to deed to St. John's Lodge of the Masons, the first Seattle lodge, of which he was a charter member, one of the few pieces of property to which he still held clear title. The Masons were raising funds for a new cemetery and Maynard thought the project worthwhile. He was on the committee that selected the site of the graveyard.

A few months later, in 1873 he died. His funeral was the largest Seattle had known. His body lay in state at Yesler's Pavilion, a big new frame building at Front and Cherry. The whole town came to say good-by. One of his fellow citizens, speaking from the floor, said "Without him, Seattle will not be the same. Without him, Seattle would not have been the same. Indeed, without him, Seattle might not be."

It was a fitting tribute, though delayed, and even in death Maynard had to wait. His was to be the first body buried in the new cemetery, but the ground had not been dedicated. When the funeral procession left the Pavilion it moved along the narrow dirt streets, past the big, unpainted clapboard houses on the hill, to the old cemetery. There the coffin was stored in the toolhouse. When the Masonic ground was finally consecrated, Maynard resumed his final journey. Seattle had at last caught up with one of his visions.

Mercer's Maidens

The troubles of Doc Maynard, an exceptional man, stemmed from his possession of a plurality of women; the troubles of other Seattle males were quite the opposite in origin.

The bulk of the white population on Puget Sound was young and unmarried and masculine. Only one adult out of ten was a woman, and rare indeed was the girl over fifteen not spoken for. At least three-fourths of the men in town had to be chaste or sinful, and even the latter course raised the question of whom to be sinful with. With a population of less than two hundred in 1860, the community was too small for adultery to be inconspicuous. That left the lusty with the choice of marrying Indian girls, a solution frowned on although practiced, or of taking Indian mistresses. The Indian girls were not unwilling, either way. The Salish culture had a different sexual ethic from the white; men who wanted relations with Indian maidens had little difficulty persuading the girls, or their parents. But there were other problems. The whites had brought venereal disease, and it was ravaging the tribes. Nor did the Indian habits of sanitation lend enchantment; some tribes piled excrement around the house walls to add warmth in winter; even the more fastidious girls reeked of smoked fish and clams and washed their hair with urine. Although there is little reason to think that the bearded and unwashed Anglo-Saxons were much less noxious than the girls, the men *believed* that they smelled better. In spite of smells there was considerable intercourse between

55

the settlers and the tribeswomen, but much of it was desperate and impromptu.

The plight of the Puget Sound male was indeed sad. The *Herald*, up-Sound at Steilacoom, came out with periodic editorials bemoaning the impossibility of adequate sexual activity. Where demand was so sustained and so obvious, somebody was certain to try to hustle up an adequate supply. That somebody was a Barbary Coast gentleman named John Pennell.

How Pennell came to desert San Francisco for Seattle is uncertain. Probably some seaman from one of the lumber ships told him of the yearnings of Puget Sound males; and with the supply in Pennell's line almost exceeding demand along the Barbary Coast, he may have decided to prospect the virgin territory to the north. In the summer of 1861 Pennell debarked from a lumber schooner on the sandspit beside Yesler's Mill. A single glance at the pedestrians on the dusty reach of Front Street, who were as predominantly male as the crew of a ship, must have confirmed the reports he had heard in San Francisco. An examination of Seattle's economic base could only have made business prospects seem bright. Here was a town of bachelors, a town with no commercial entertainment, a town with an established payroll. Here was a town just waiting for the likes of John Pennell.

Within a month of his arrival there stood on the shore of the bay, not far south of the point where the logging road reached the mill, a pleasure palace of rough-sawed boards, the pioneer of a long line of establishments which were to give this part of town a distinctive character. The lot on which this bawdyhouse was built was "made land," a fill created on the tideflats by pouring in the sawdust from Yesler's Mill. It was not desirable land, for the flats stank when the tide was out; but Pennell could not be too particular, and the site had the advantage of being only a few minutes' walk from the mill and in plain view of the ships entering the harbor.

The Illahee, as Pennell named his house, was in the great tradition of the Old West. The oblong building of unpainted boards housed a large dance floor, which was flanked by a long bar. Along one side of the floor was a hall leading to a number of small rooms. Pennell imported three musicians (a fiddler, a drummer, and an accordion player) from San Francisco; the rest of his help was native. He traded Hudson's Bay blankets to local chiefs for a supply of Indian girls. These recruits were vigorously scoured, their long hair was combed and cut, they were doused with perfume and decked out in calico.

A girl would dance with anyone without charge, but her partner was expected to buy a drink for himself and his companion after each dance. (The bartender usually substituted cold tea for whisky in the girl's glass, though the charge was for whisky.) When a man's tired of purely social intercourse, he could always buy a couple more drinks and lead his partner down the hall to one of the little rooms.

There was no attempt to conceal what was going on at the water's edge. One historian has argued that it was the establishment of Pennell's place that led straight to Seattle's present-day dominance of the Northwest, the scholar's thesis being that word swiftly spread throughout the timberland about the type of entertainment offered at the foot of the skid road in Seattle. The town had, in that historian's words, "the best mouse trap in the woods; hobnails and calks were deepening all the paths to its door."

While this economic argument gives more importance to sex than even Freud would be likely to admit, there can be little doubt that Pennell drew his clientele from all over the Sound country, and that the men who came to town primarily to enjoy the girls also spent money on more legitimate trade. Some respectable members of the little community accepted Pennell's establishment as a necessary evil; others deplored it but failed to convince Sheriff Wyckoff that he should close the place as a nuisance.

Somehow the name Illahee—which meant "homeland" or "earth" in Chinook—didn't catch on. It may have been among the straitlaced that the establishment first came to be known as the Mad House, but the nickname stuck and was later applied to other houses whose stock-in-trade was of Indian origin. Those who did not call the brothel the Mad House sometimes referred to it as the Sawdust Pile or Down on the Sawdust. The inhabitants were known as Sawdust Women.

During a depression period in San Francisco at the end of the Civil War, Pennell rounded up a handful of out-of-work Barbary Coast girls and shipped them north. They were the first white women north of the Columbia to ply the oldest profession. Though it is doubtful that prostitutes unable to prosper in San Francisco were unduly attractive, their presence in the Illahee, according to a chronicler of the period, "had a powerful imaginative effect on the whole male population of the Puget Sound country, and old-timers still relate fabulous legends from those happy days." The legends were the standard ones of the red-light district. There was the tale of the ladylike whore who murdered the men she learned were carrying large amounts of money. There was the legend of the girl who fell in love and demurely denied her swain the favors she still sold, albeit unwillingly, to everyone else. And, of course, there was the story of the girl who married a client and moved into one of the white clapboard houses on the hill.

That some Seattle families grew out of love affairs in the Illahee is not inconceivable. Women were few and a man could not be choosy, especially a man who patronized the establishment. There were, however, many who considered such marriages undesirable, and among them was a righteous and energetic youngster named Asa Mercer, fresh from the civilized Midwest.

Young Mercer was the brother of Judge Tom Mercer, a solid citizen who had arrived in 1852 with a team of horses and had prospered as Seattle's first teamster. Asa worked as a carpenter on the new Territorial University building, which was going up on the hill northeast of the skid road, and when the building was finished he moved inside as president and faculty of the institution. One day during a conversation on the territory's Topic A—the shortage of maidens worthy to become the wives of pio-

neers—Judge Tom remarked that in the interests of posterity the territorial government should appropriate public
funds to bring west a party of acceptable young ladics.
The idea had an understandable appeal to the twenty-two-
year-old university president who was unmarried and moral; he took it up with the governor. William Pickering,
Washington's fourth governor,[1] was a husky, spade-beard-
ed man in his mid-sixties; he agreed as to the need but
sadly called Mercer's attention to the lack of public
money. Asa decided to carry off his venture as a private
enterprise.

He talked to a number of Seattle's frustrated young
men and, after pocketing an unspecified amount of contributions, caught a ship for Boston. The daughters of that
sedate community were not to be talked into venturing
west, but in Lowell the young proselyter found more
attentive listeners. Lowell was a textile town, racked with
depression since the Civil War had cut off Southern cotton
from its looms, and there Mercer found eleven virgins
willing to forsake the land of the cod. They sailed from
New York, crossed the Panama Isthmus, rested briefly in
San Francisco (where some enterprising Californians tried
to talk the maidens into easing that region's shortage of
pure females) and went by schooner to the Sound. They
debarked at Yesler's wharf about midnight, May 16,
1864, and were welcomed by a delegation headed by Doc
Maynard.

[1] Isaac Stevens resigned the governorship in 1857 after having
been elected territorial delegate to Congress; he later re-entered the
Army and was killed at Bull Run. Fayette McMullen, a Virginian,
succeeded Stevens and used his time in the territory mainly to get
a legislative divorce and to court, sucessfully, an Olympia girl. The
third governor, Richard Gholson, served less than a year, resigning
after Lincoln's election because he was "unwilling, even for a day,
to hold office under a Republican." Lincoln named William H.
Wallace as Gholson's successor, but Wallace instead ran for the
better-paying position of territorial delegate and was elected. (Later
Lincoln appointed him governor of Idaho and again he ran for
Congress instead of serving.) In Wallace's place, Lincoln named
Pickering, an Oxford graduate who had been chairman of the
Illinois delegation to the Republican convention in 1860.

With the exception of one girl who took sick and died unwed, all the girls soon found husbands. The details of the courtships are unknown, and it is uncertain whether the maidens married the men who had financed Mercer's trip. As for Asa, his grateful contemporaries elected him—unanimously—to the upper house of the Territorial Legislature. The young legislator thought less of laws than lasses. He wanted to import young women not by the short dozen by by the hundred. Soon he was circulating through the territory, talking confidentially to lonesome bachelors. His proposition was simple. For three hundred dollars paid in advance, he would bring a suitable wife. There were several takers, how many only Mercer knew, but enough so that he started east in high spirits and with great confidence. He talked of bringing back enough girls to provide mates for every single man west of the Cascades.

Everything went wrong. Lincoln was shot, and Asa, who had known him slightly, lost a potential ally. Mercer didn't know President Johnson, but General Grant, who knew from personal experience how lonely a man could get among the rain forests, promised to lend Mercer a transport, but the Quartermaster General quickly pointed out that such use of federal property was illegal. Then, out of nowhere, appeared an angel, a wartime speculator named Ben Holladay, who offered to buy the surplus transport and carry Mercer's five hundred charges around the Horn to Seattle "for a minimum price." Mercer quickly signed a contract. The trouble was he didn't have five hundred passengers; he didn't have half that many; he didn't even have a hundred. For this Mercer blamed the New York Herald and its cross-eyed editor, James Gordon Bennett. The recruiting drive had been going well, Asa wrote his backers, until it attracted the attention of the Herald, which ran an "exposé" of the project. The exposé implied that most of the girls were destined for waterfront dives on Puget Sound and if anyone did gain a legal mate, she must resign herself to the fact that he would probably be ugly, ill-mannered, illiterate, and probably diseased.[2] Massachusetts authorities investigated too, though hardly thoroughly. Since no politician is likely to admit that young women would do better to leave his state, the report implied that Mercer's girls might be headed for a fate worse than Mormonism.

Besides getting a bad press, Mercer was up against the fact that it was easier for his prospects to say they'd make the voyage than it was for them to walk up the gangplank, leaving behind them all that was familiar. When the day came to sail, January 6, 1866, fewer than a hundred nubile passengers appeared. Mercer sold passages reserved for girls to men and married women, but he was far short of filling his five hundred reservations. Holladay demanded payment in full. He didn't get it, but he got every cent Mercer had. Once at sea, Asa figured his financial worries were over. Three months later the ship docked at San Francisco. The captain ordered everyone ashore. This, he said, was as far as he was going.

Mercer argued and lost. When they put him ashore, he rushed to the telegraph office and wired Governor Pickering: "Send two thousand dollars quick to get party to Seattle." Pickering wired back his best wishes, collect. In desperation Mercer appealed to the skippers of the lumber schooners that plied between Seattle and San Francisco; these gentlemen, pleased at the prospect of feminine companionship on what was usually a dull voyage, took them fare-free. A few of the girls decided to stay in California, and who can blame them? Mercer himself must have been tempted to stay. He had spent every cent that had been given to him; he had brought back fewer girls than he had promised, and those not on schedule. He must have known the home folks weren't going to elect him to the legislature for this performance.

On Mercer's return to Seattle rumors spread, wild and ugly. On May 23 the *Puget Sound Daily* carried a front-page story saying that "Honorable A. S. Mercer will address the citizens of Seattle and vicinity, at Yesler's Hall,

[2] A Seattle woman who has been doing research on the Mercer expedition for three years tells me that she has been unable to find the *Herald* editorials quoted by Mercer.

this evening, for the purpose of refuting the numerous stories that have been circulated in regard to himself, in connection with his immigration enterprise." The editor urged, "Turn out, everybody, and hear the other side of the question."

The report of the meeting is irritatingly incomplete. "Rev. Daniel Bagley was called to the chair, who briefly stated the object of the meeting, which was to hear an address by Mr. A. S. Mercer in regard to his experience while in the East conducting the famous immigration enterprise. Mr. Mercer than addressed the audience, to which address marked attention was paid, the speaker being frequently applauded. The audience was composed, in part, of the fair immigrants who had so recently arrived, and it is a fact, that has no little weight in the vindication of Mr. Mercer's reputation against the assaults that have been made upon it, that those immigrants place the utmost confidence in him. At the close the chairman made a few very appropriate remarks, after which the meeting adjourned, apparently with the best of good will towards Mr. Mercer and all concerned."

The night after Mercer's speech a "Marvellous Magical entertainment" was held at Yesler's. No matter how impressive the legerdemain—and the paper also gave it a rave notice—it could hardly have been as remarkable as Mercer's feat of pacifying with words the angry men who, after waiting almost a year for delivery of the women they had ordered, found themselves without brides and minus three hundred dollars.

Mercer himself married one of his imports, Annie Stephens, a few weeks later. They soon removed to the Rocky Mountain area, where Asa lived out his days as a rancher, as far from ships as he could get.

John Pennell faded from the Seattle scene at almost the same time as Asa. He left for parts unknown. But the type of institution that he had founded on the sawdust fill south of Yesler Way did not vanish with him. Other entrepreneurs built bigger and better houses. The honkytonk was there to stay.

The Skid Road had been born.

II

Mary Kenworthy and
the Railroads, 1873-1893

1.

For some towns, as for some people, maturity comes gradually. For others it comes abruptly with the death of a father or the death of a dream. Seattle came of age in 1873, four years after it was incorporated, four months and a day after Doc Maynard died. Maturity was implicit in an eight-word telegram sent on July 14 to Arthur A. Denny from Kalama on the Columbia by two commissioners for the Northern Pacific Railway. The message read: *We have located the terminus on Commencement Bay.*

Commencement Bay was twenty miles away. For Seattle this was disaster.

The pioneers of Puget Sound had cut their trees and built their cabins and forced the wilderness back from a dozen beach-heads. They had fought the Indians and the fleas, they had endured the damp and the mud and one another, they had gone without salt and flour, they had left friends and relatives and comforts two thousand miles behind—all this they had done to earn and to hold the claims that were in effect tickets in the great railroad lottery.

Whatever town got the terminus would get rich; its landholders would see the value of their lots rise, and its businessmen would have customers by the hundreds instead of by the dozen. Every Puget Sounder knew by rote the reasons why this town should become the tidewater terminus. The eighteen hundred inhabitants of Olympia were sure the railroad builders would not bypass the territorial capital, the largest town (Seattle disputed this claim) and the oldest town on the Sound. The three hundred people at Steilacoom bespoke the advantages of their Army post and their lovely houses; they pointed out that Steilacoom was twenty miles nearer the ocean than Olympia. True, the eight hundred residents of Port Townsend agreed, but look at us, we're right up here where the Sound and the Strait of Juan de Fuca meet. Yes, said the handful of millworkers up the Sound at Whatcom, but you're stuck out there on the Olympic Peninsula; who's going to build a railroad clear around the Sound to reach Port Townsend when we're here? And while the debate went on and on among those who were not in position to make the decision, the people of Seattle were smug in their conviction that geography was on their side.

Seattle, in spite of its late start, was challenging Olympia for the lead in population. In 1872 the town formally claimed 2000 residents and 575 buildings. Although 50 of the buildings were barns and stables, there were 57 two-story structures and 151 of one-and-a-half stories. With a tannery, a brick works, a shipyard, a blacksmith shop, and two sawmills inside the town, and a number of coal mines nearby, Seattle was the leading industrial community in the territory.

Behind the town lay Snoqualmie Pass, where the Cascades dipped to three thousand feet, and it was logical that a railroad should cross the mountains here and bring to the Sound, for shipment by water, the grain harvest of the rolling hills of eastern Washington. (The alternate route was along the Columbia, which meant money for Portland.) Seattle, lying at the mouth of the Snoqualmie funnel, expected to handle that grain. And since the town dominated the narrow shelf of flatland between the water and the mountains, it expected to make money off all north-south rail and road traffic. The site was the natural focal point of Puget Sound commerce.

This logic of economic geography, plus the payroll of

Yesler's Mill, had brought about two thousand people to Seattle. But the very fact that so many people bet on Seattle as the railroad terminus hurt Seattle's chances. Why should an empire builder raise the value of other people's property when he could pick an unpopulated site for his terminus and make for himself the profit off the rise in land prices?

2.

In 1833, only two years after the first locomotive in America chugged down a short stretch of track, the editor of the *Emigrant*, an obscure weekly in Michigan, suggested that rails be laid from coast to coast. He was smiled at by the few who read his visionary proposal; twenty years later, in 1853, Congress authorized the exploration of four possible transcontinental routes.

The most northerly route was assigned to General Isaac Stevens. He was the first to complete his survey and, like the men assigned to each of the other routes, he felt that the terrain he had explored must be the best. He assured the people of Puget Sound in 1854 that they would get a railroad "within five years," and in his official reports he pointed out that his route was the shortest, perhaps the easiest, and that the Puget Sound ports were hundreds of miles nearer to the Orient than San Francisco. As territorial governor and as delegate to Congress he thumped the drums for a northern railroad, but California had the population, the glamour of gold, and more effective lobbyists. No one in the East saw much point in running a railroad two thousand miles at an estimated cost of a hundred million dollars for the benefit of a dozen or so Indian villages. No one saw much point in it, that is, until 1864, when crusty old Thaddeus Stevens pushed through Congress a bill offering a grant of lands to aid in building a railroad and telegraph line from Lake Superior to Puget Sound by the northern route.

The Northern Pacific Railroad Company was organized immediately. Under terms of the law it was supposed to start laying track within two years. In that time the company was able to raise about two hundred thousand dollars, and to spend about two hundred thousand dollars, but it laid no track. The board was then reorganized to admit some experienced railroad men, who knew enough to look to Congress for help. They asked for more time before starting to build (granted) and for a cash subsidy (refused). Next they turned to financial circles for help. In December 1869 the men of the Northern Pacific found a backer in the handsome form of Jay Cooke, a Philadelphia banker who specialized in floating bonds.

Cooke was a perfect flower of the Gilded Age. He lived in a fifty-two-room mansion outside Philadelphia; he could summon the President of the United States to dinner to talk over business matters. He owned a half-dozen senators and as many governors. When he became interested in the Northern Pacific he consulted the Chief Justice of the Supreme Court, himself a financier, about its prospects, and that worthy assured him, "I should like to be in the Board of Directors, as to which I suppose there will be no difficulty, and am half tempted to offer myself as a candidate for the presidency of the board; ... my antecedents and reputation would justify a good salary."

It was not surprising that after Cooke had undertaken to finance the Northern Pacific, Congress enlarged the land grant until it covered sixty miles on each side of the right of way—more than seventy thousand square miles in all, a grant half again as large as all of New York State.

Land, not transport, was probably uppermost in Cooke's mind. He saw the possibility of turning the West into a personal fief. In his agreement with the Northern Pacific, Cooke inserted a farsighted clause: "A company shall be organized for the purpose of purchasing lands, improvement of town sites, or other purposes, and the same shall be divided in the same proportion; that is, the original interests shall have one half, and Jay Cooke shall have one half."

Cooke began operating as Northern Pacific financier in December 1869, and only two months later crews were smoothing the hard prairie ground west of Duluth. In

May, after the Northern Pacific had made a deal with the
Oregon Steam Navigation Company, under which the latter agreed to let the transcontinental line use its tracks
along the Columbia, work started in the West. The company picked Kalama, an undeveloped site on the north
shore of the Columbia, as the base for its western operations, and it started laying a narrow gauge line north to
Puget Sound.

But where on Puget Sound? No one knew. The sus-
pense mounted steadily and over a long period. The company was required by Congress (which at Cooke's request
had obediently amended the charter) to build only twenty-
five miles the first year and forty miles a year after that
until it reached tidewater. The NP directors were in no
hurry to reveal their plans. As the line inched north, the
company negotiated with rival towns, seeing which would
offer the most. By 1871 it was popularly believed that
only three places were still in the running: Olympia, Seattle, and Mukilteo, the last a tiny settlement just south of
present-day Everett.

In 1872 the NP crews were working across the plain
southeast of Olympia. It became apparent they were going
to bypass the capital; the best Olympia could hope for was
a spur, and the railroad said the town would have to build
that itself. Seattle was still in a happy glow over its rival's
discomfort when the wire came locating the terminus on
Commencement Bay.

No news could have been worse. This meant not only
that Seattle would be deprived of the terminus, but that
the hamlet of Tacoma, with two hundred residents, a
settlement barely two years old, would swiftly grow to
challenge Seattle's industrial leadership. The new town,
only twenty miles away by water, would undoubtedly
dedicate itself to the economic destruction of its nearest
rival. The two thousand residents of Seattle, with no effective allies, were pitted against a community sponsored by
a transcontinental railroad which was backed by the nation's leading banker, who had the personal support of
the President of the United States and the Chief Justice of

the Supreme Court, as well as the votes of a substantial number of senators and representatives.

A number of Seattle pioneers caught the next paddle-wheeler south to Commencement Bay. Their decision to desert was understandable. What is hard to understand is the stubbornness, which amounted to vision, of those who remained on Elliott Bay. Soon after the NP message ticked off the wire the pioneers of Seattle assembled on the sawdust by Yesler's Mill and assured each other that all was not lost. They would raise enough money to build a line across the mountains and meet the transcontinental tracks in the Walla Walla country. There was no sense, they told one another, in traffic being detoured down the Columbia and then north. A straight line is the shortest distance between two points. Yes, sir. All they had to do was raise the money and build the cutoff, and grain and goods and wealth would flow to Seattle.

There was one trouble: no one would invest in Seattle's road. Few would invest in Mr. Cooke's railroad either. The messiest scandal in American political history, the Crédit Mobilier affair, had just broken, and it concerned the financing of the Union Pacific. The public had learned that "every step in that mighty enterprise had been taken in fraud." A private holding company, made up of individuals who risked almost nothing, had milked between thirty and fifty million dollars in profits from the semi-public funds used to finance the first railroad to reach the Pacific. The graft had been made possible by the blindness of public officials, and the public learned that its officials had profited from their blindness. Among those "taken care of" by the financiers were both of the Republicans who served as vice-president under Grant, the Democratic floor leader in the House, and a gaudy array of senators and representatives. The pride the public had felt in the gleaming tracks that stretched from sea to sea turned to disgust. They refused to buy more railroad bonds. No advertising pamphlets that Jay Cooke's publicity men could revise, no editorials that his paid editors could write, no sermons that the ministers he subsidized could preach, convinced the people they should finance the Northern Pacific.

In September the bronze doors of Jay Cooke's central bank closed, and the great man, a symbol of his age, stood weeping behind them. The panic of '73 was on. Work on the Northern Pacific shuddered to a halt, but not before the line from Kalama to Tacoma was completed.

Seattle could snicker at the dedication ceremonies at Tacoma. It rained all day the day the line was completed. There was no money to buy a golden spike, and the workers, who hadn't been paid and weren't going to be, climaxed the festivities by blockading the track with logs and threatening to remove a few bridges and hold them as security. It was a farce all right, but there was no laughing away the railroad. The steel bands stretched from the Columbia to the Sound; Tacoma had the terminus, and the local railroad officials took pleasure in bedeviling Seattle. They arranged the train-boat schedule so that anyone coming up the Sound from Seattle en route to Portland had to wait for twenty hours in Tacoma, and it was the same going back.

As the months wore on and nobody stepped forward to finance construction of the Snoqualmie cutoff, Seattle citizens grew worried. They held another mass meeting and talked one another into desperate optimism; they agreed to lay the line over the mountains with their own hands. On May Day 1874 the people assembled on the east bank of the Duwamish and bespoke their determination; as they grew more and more long winded in praising what the citizenry was about to do, single-minded old Henry Yesler got more and more impatient. When his turn came to speak he picked up a shovel and said eloquently, "Let's quit fooling and get to work."

That, of course, was harder. When the sweat had dried and the blisters had broken and the muscles had grown stiff and the first enthusiasm had been rubbed off, the people of Seattle realized that though, as the speakers had said, their destiny was now in their own hands, their hands were not calloused enough, or skilled enough, or numerous enough, nor were their backs strong enough, to push the road through; it would take them a century to get the tracks across the mountains. Work dwindled. Eventually a Scottish engineer named James Colman took over the aborted project and reshaped it into a line to the coal fields behind the town of Renton. As such it served Seattle well and made Colman a millionaire, but it did not solve the problem of direct connections with the East.

Many in Seattle had come to have a deep hatred for high finance. The realization of the degree to which their destinies could be controlled by the decisions—even the whims—of a Philadelphia banker and a few of his economic henchmen had shocked them deeply. Hostility to Eastern capital became a persistent strain in the community consciousness. Yet it was high finance at its dizziest pinnacle that gave Seattle a breathing spell after the Northern Pacific picked Tacoma as its terminus.

The collapse of Jay Cooke and his railroad bonds had been brought about, at least in part, by a rival banking house, Drexel, Morgan and Company. This outfit had been formed in 1871 when Anthony Drexel, the second biggest banker in Philadelphia, had combined forces with the rising young financier J. P. Morgan; they had dedicated themselves to capturing some of the public and semi-public business on which Cooke had almost a monopoly. Drexel controlled the Philadelphia *Ledger*, which carried on a sustained crusade against the Northern Pacific.

With Cooke's failure, work halted on the transcontinental line, which had been laid as far as Bismarck, North Dakota, and Seattle was given a chance to reorganize for its war with Tacoma. When a decade later, the Northern Pacific was completed, it was high finance that placed, momentarily, a friend of Seattle in the office of the president of the line.

Henry Villard was a Bavarian who had come to this country at the age of eighteen. He taught school, edited a German-language weekly in Wisconsin, covered the Lincoln-Douglas debates for the *New Yorker Staats-Zeitung*, married the daughter of William Lloyd Garrison, and, during the Civil War, distinguished himself as a war corre-

spondent for Horace Greeley's *Tribune* by scoring a beat
on the Union disaster at Fredericksburg. As a reporter
Villard became the intimate of the great, and after the
war he found an interesting job in Boston as secretary of
the American Social Science Association, work which permitted him "to study public and corporate financing, including railways and banks." He studied himself into a
nervous breakdown and went back to his native Black
Forest to recuperate. In Germany as in America, he min-
gled with bankers; many of them had been taken in by the
promotion pamphlets of the railroad builders in America
and held bonds now worth a cent on the dollar. Villard
agreed to serve as the agent of the foreign bondholders of
the Oregon and California Railroad, an incomplete coastal
line which had fallen into the hands of Ben Holladay—the
financier who had so outmaneuvered young Mercer on the
steamship deal—and see what he could salvage.

In pursuing his studies of corporate financing in the Far
West on behalf of his new clients, Villard examined the
structure of the Oregon Steam Navigation Company,
which controlled traffic along the Columbia. What he
learned interested him. He made a few practiced financial
gestures and took control of the OSNC. Then he talked to
the directors of the Northern Pacific, who had a few crews
out making motions at construction beyond Bismarck.
Villard suggested a deal in which OSNC would become
the western section of the Northern Pacific, but the directors weren't co-operative.

Villard went to New York, talked to his friends among
the financiers, told them he needed a lot of money but not
what he needed it for. Such was Villard's reputation as a
financial wizard that his admirers advanced him eight
million dollars on no other security than his name and
with no intimation of what it would be invested in. With
these funds Villard bought control of the Northern Pacific. He hired enough men to push the line through to the
Columbia, where it joined the rails of the OSNC, and he
drove the golden spike himself.

To Seattle's joy, Villard indicated that he saw no reason
to ruin the town on Elliott Bay. He bought the little rail

line to the Renton coal fields and started work on a spur leading north from Tacoma to Seattle. He came to Seattle to receive a hero's welcome; and then he went broke.

A financier rather than a railroad man, Villard had moved too fast, had spent too much, had not thought of a profitable investment so much as he dreamed of a world empire of trade. He over-reached himself. When he fell, in Janurary 1884, men with their eyes on the account books instead of the horizon took control of the line Villard had completed. Again these were men who preferred that Seattle should not prosper. They canceled the service along the spur north from Tacoma, and the city was cut off from direct trade with most of the continent. With the end of construction work on the railroad, the Northwest again slid into a business depression.

Many people in Seattle resented the instability of the frontier economy, none more so than Mrs. J. T. Kenworthy.

3.

Mary Kenworthy was a tall, slender brunette who had crossed the plains in a covered wagon with her tailor husband. She was thrity-five years old at the time she left her native Illinois, a handsome, high-spirited woman who found life on the frontier fascinating.

The Kenworthys built a big frame house at Fifth and Union, just across from the university campus. Housekeeping kept her busy, but not so busy that she failed to attend the lectures that constituted Seattle's chief cultural activity. In August 1871 she heard handsome Mrs. Laura De Force Gordon lecture in Yesler's Hall on "Our Next Great Political Problem—Woman Suffrage." She was deeply impressed, and later the same year she was among those who crowded into the Methodist Brown Church to cheer Susan B. Anthony, the national leader of the suffrage movement, and Abigail Scott Duniway of Portland, the Northwest's first female literary figure.

Mary Kenworthy joined the Woman Suffrage Association, the radical wing of the movement. Through the seventies she attended nearly all the suffrage meetings, but she was elected to no offices and attracted little attention. That was to come later. Perhaps she was held back during those years by her husband, a dark, shy little man who worked hard at the tailor's trade and made a good suit and a good living. Mr. Kenworthy seems to have had little interest in politics or in abstract economics, and his wife may have deferred to him. He died in 1880, and after a brief period of formal mourning Mary Kenworthy emerged as a character in her own right.

The widow Kenworthy had watched Seattle grow from a village with stumps in the streets to a town with planks for pavement and board sidewalks and twenty buildings of brick. When she had arrived everybody in town, the whole thousand of them, had known Doc Maynard, but a decade later less than a third of the townsfolk could remember him. The population was 3533 in 1880, and Mary Kenworthy was to see it rise an average of 3500 a year for the next decade. The railroad brought the new population, but the increase was not an unmixed blessing. Mary Kenworthy had read the newspaper reports of the progress of the tracks across the plains and mountains, tracks that were laid by the cheap labor that Villard had imported, mostly Irish and Chinese. She had watched the fights among the financiers for the profits from the line, watched her fellow townsfolk bask in the sun of Villard's smile and shiver under the calculated neglect of Villard's successors. She saw her town grow in size and saw the property of those who had come early (including herself) rise in value. She saw the deserving and the undeserving make fortunes through blind luck, and she saw others just as deserving or undeserving go broke. She dreamed the old dream of a society in which this could not happen.

Mary Kenworthy wanted to reform the world, and she listened to anyone who was sure he knew a way. She took up with spiritualists and union leaders, with vegetarians and socialists, with prohibitionists and single-taxers, with anyone who stood for change.

The big frame house hard by the university campus

came to be a center of agitation against "the interests." She entertained the leaders of the Knights of Labor and of the agrarians. She spoke at union meetings on behalf of the Knights' One-Big-Union idea. She spoke for the free silver people and the Populists and the unaffiliated People's Party that arose to oppose businessmen's government in the city. Years later a man who had watched her activities in this period said, "Mary wasn't brilliant. She was a good woman who let her emotions guide her politics. She just couldn't help being for anybody who was agin something." She bought her bread from a baker who quoted Karl Marx.

Mrs. Kenworthy and the rest of the women of Washington got the vote in 1883. The Territorial Legislature amended the code by omitting the word "male" in the section dealing with suffrage. The measure was supported by the Good Templars, a lodge then active in the political-reform movement; they lobbied for woman suffrage because they felt women would, as they put it, "vote moral." The bill passed the House easily and squeaked through the Senate by one vote. For the next four years, until the law was overturned by the Territorial Supreme Court, the women had full political rights as voters, jurors, and office-holders. Their delight in citizenship is reflected in the memoirs of a Bellingham woman, who wrote, "I took my turn on petit and grand jury, served on election boards, walked in perfect harmony to the polls by the side of my staunch Democratic husband, and voted the Republican ticket—not feeling any more out of my sphere than when assisting my husband to develop the resources of our country."

The enfranchisement of the women did not make the municipal election of 1884 any less bitter, although no women stood for office. The candidates used charges of corruption, incompetence, and favoritism. "One word about the police court," an Out candidate declared. "I say, and I challenge contradiction, that there never was such a rotten nest anywhere on the face of God's footstool as the police court of the city of Seattle."

The campaign was fought against the background of the depression that gripped the town after the collapse of the Villard boom. Though Seattle was still growing rapidly, jobs were scarce and money was tight. (Nationally the Democrats, behind Grover Cleveland, were about to win the presidency for the first time since the Civil War.) The women got their baptism of political fire in a noisy campaign in which the Business Man's Ticket was battling to hold the city hall against the assaults of the People's Ticket.

The Business Man's man for mayor was John Leary, a Canadian-born lawyer turned promoter. He had been one of the leaders of the abortive Seattle and Walla Walla railroad project, had recently purchased control of the company that furnished the town with water. The Business Man's candidate promised economies in the city administration and the creation of an economic climate attractive to outside capital.

The People's people were for Reform. They wanted to do away with vice and corruption, which they feared were widespread among their fellow citizens. Their oratory was directed toward two groups—labor and women. To labor they promised protection against exploitation and "fair treatment in police court"; to the women they promised civic righteousness.

The town was ripe for a little righteousness. The Skid Road was rapidly acquiring a reputation for toughness rivaled only by the Barbary Coast. A considerable portion of the newcomers to Seattle were men who had been working on the railroad construction gangs, tough men, alone, and with little sense of civic responsibility. Some of them settled down and became good citizens; some found rooms in the dives that had sprung up along the Skid Road. As the population grew more congested on the flatland south of Mill Street, more and more establishments opened to cater to their tastes.

There had been periodic efforts to clean up the Lava Bed, as the district was called during this period. Grand juries refused to indict the operators of bawdyhouses and Sheriff Wyckoff—the man who had succeeded Maynard as

blacksmith—was always looking the other way, but once
in the early seventies the Illahee had been closed and
Seattle briefly without the services of a brothel. This state
of affairs had been achieved by a stratagem on the part of
the county commissioners. Having come into possession of
a valuable farm, which had been owned by a man who
died without heirs, the commissioners traded the farm to
the new owner of the Illahee and in return received the
whorehouse. Since the farm was much the more valuable
property at that time, the trade was something of a bribe
given the proprietor by public officials to induce him to
abandon his traffic in women. The commissioners and the
whoremonger were pleased with their deal but the courts
weren't. A judge decided that the county had no right to
make such a trade and the deal was called off: but while in
possession of the Illahee the commissioners had thoughtfully had the house torn down. Other establishments, bigger if not better, soon took its place.

The denizens of the Lava Bed were not only immoral
but sometimes criminal. The area naturally came to harbor a considerable number of burglars and bandits and
strong-arm men as well as tarts and pimps and gamblers.
Crimes of violence increased even faster than the population.

On the night of January 17, 1882, George Reynolds, a
middle-aged businessman, was walking home after dark.
Two armed robbers stepped from behind a tree and told
him to put up his hands. He reached for his back pocket.
They shot him and ran away. Reynolds died two hours
later. Someone started ringing the firebell. When the men
of the town had assembled they were told about the
attack. They formed a "vigilance committee" and began a
citywide hunt for the killers. One of the searchers saw a
man's foot protruding from a pile of hay on a wharf. The
haystack was surrounded, the foot seized; two men were
found hiding in the hay. Some of the citizenry were eager
to hang the two men from the wharf without further
formality. Sheriff Wyckoff drew his revolver and persuaded the posse that it would be better to wait until it was

proved that the two men had done something more criminal than sleep in a haystack on the night of a murder.

The prisoners were taken to jail. The posse took the
men's shoes and compared them with impressions found
in soft mud near the scene of the murder. The shoes
matched the impressions nearly enough to convince most
of Seattle that the prisoners were guilty.

The next morning the men were brought before Justice
of the Peace Samuel Coombs. The preliminary hearing
was held in Yesler's Pavilion, and the place was packed
with angry citizens, some of them armed. Among those
present, but unarmed, was the ailing Roger Sherman
Greene, chief justice of the Territorial Supreme Court,
who had climbed out of bed to make sure the two men
got a fair hearing. The prisoners offered no defense other
than to deny guilt. Justice Coombs turned them over to
the deputy sheriffs, ordering that they be held without bail
until they could be tried. From the back of the hall came
a shout, "Let's get 'em," and the crowd surged forward.
As the deputies drew their revolvers a door behind them
opened and a group of men rushed them from the rear
and disarmed them. Somebody threw a sheet over Judge
Greene's head. Others seized the prisoners, hustled them
outside, and dragged them down the alley to Front and
James. The mob placed a pair of railings between the
forks of two maple trees, tossed ropes over the railings,
slipped nooses over the men's heads, and strung them up.
Just as the prisoners were hauled clear of the ground,
Judge Greene pushed his way through the mob and ran to
the struggling men. He pulled out a pocketknife and
slashed at the ropes. The crowd dragged him from the
scene. The prisoners died.

A lust for "law and order"—or for blood—seized the
citizenry. At one o'clock in the afternoon someone rang
the firebell three times. Five hundred men assembled in
front of the city hall, chopped down the door to the jail,
overpowered the guards, and took from his cell a man
accused of having killed a policeman three months earlier.
They lynched him too.

Soon after the lynchings Sheriff Wyckoff dropped dead.

His friends said he was brokenhearted over the failure of his men to protect their prisoners. Wyckoff was widely mourned, but few grieved for the victims of the mob. The coroner's jury, made up of prominent citizens, investigated the death of the man who had killed the policeman and reported that, though it could not guess who had killed him, "substantial and speedy justice has been subserved." The grand jury refused to indict anyone for the triple killings.

Only Judge Greene continued to protest. "Those hangmen were in revolt against Magna Charta," he said. "The lynchers were co-criminal with the lynched. Many of the actors were professed Christians. Unwittingly they were illustrating the doctrine of original sin and total depravity.

"That lynching set a bad example to other communities and to posterity.... The pernicious example of Seattle's citizens still remains, and will continue to remain, a widely approved but fallacious precedent, to invite, and sophistically to justify or excuse, here and elsewhere, future similar disorder."

His prediction came true. Two years after the lynching the memory of the bodies swinging from the scantlings between the great maples had ceased to deter criminals. Conditions were worse than ever in the Lava Bed. Much of the appeal of the People's Ticket in 1884 lay in the promise of its spokesmen that they would tighten up on saloons in general and Lava Bed establishments in particular. They claimed the city administration was in alliance with the "rum vendors and pink-cuff[1] hoodlums."

Mary Kenworthy introduced the speaker at the People's mass meeting one warm July afternoon and she led the applause as he described John Leary, the water-company president, as "the candidate of alcohol and aqua pura."

"Who are the prime movers in the Business Man's movement?" the Populist orator demanded. "Why, it's S.

[1] "Pink cuffs" refers to the pink shirts often worn by West Coast gamblers.

Baxter, a wholesale liquor dealer, who sells to those Lava Bed dealers by the jug, and W. A. Jennings.

"I visited the Business Man's convention. And among the businessmen I saw a banker, one of the first bankers who went into that business in the town. Fourteen years ago I saw him carrying on his banking business on a public sidewalk in Seattle on the Fourth of July. I refer to Barney Crossen, a member of the protective association, and proprietor of a faro bank.

"I thought at first it was all whisky, but I found it was all water. Bailey Gatzert turned out for the meeting for the first time since Beriah Brown was nominated for mayor [1878]. Mr. Leary and Mr. Gatzert are the principal stockowners of the Spring Hill Water Company. I want the city to buy plenty of water and I want it bought from the Spring Hill Water Company, but I don't want John Leary, as mayor, to sign a contract with John Leary, as president of the Spring Hill Water Company, for such supply."

Then the speaker introduced a new element into the campaign. He pointed out that "notwithstanding the fact that Mayor Struve, one of the best lawyers in the territory," had been serving as mayor, the city had just made the mistake of constructing the Jackson Street grade across government land. After the grade was made the city learned it could not tax, or confiscate, the government land to raise money to redeem the script it had issued to pay for the construction.

There was eighty-seven thousand dollars' worth of Jackson grade script outstanding. A large part of it was held by the Puget Sound Bank, of which the McNaught brothers, James and Joseph, were stockholders. Joe was running the city council; his brother James had issued a statement saying that the taxpayers at large must redeem the script instead of the people whose property benefited by the improvement. "Many good lawyers differ with him," the orator remarked dryly. Then he said, "Wa Chong, the contractor, holds ten thousand dollars' worth of Jackson Street script, and an attempt is being made to saddle this amount off onto you and me and other tax-payers."

Thus was the Chinese question introduced, somewhat obliquely, into Seattle politics.

John Leary was elected in spite of the watery mud splashed on him by the Populists.

A steady stream of newcomers poured into Seattle during the next year, many of them men let off by the construction crews, others drawn west by easy transportation and the advertising pamphlets circulated by the railroads. They found few jobs. They joined the ranks of the unemployed and listened to the oratory of Populists like Mary Kenworthy, who was belaboring the Business Man's backers with such salty epithets as "our dog-salmon aristocracy." In 1885 the threat of the People's ticket was so great that the Business Man's group felt it necessary to call back into the political arena the town's most loved tycoon, blunt, four-square old Henry Yesler, who eleven years earlier had spent a quiet and profitable year as mayor. Yesler was elected again, but there was nothing quiet about his second term. Hell broke loose over the Chinese question.

4.

The Chinese had been popular once. They had been imported in large numbers by the railroad builders when cheap labor was needed. When the Chinese arrived the Western people had looked on them as genii who would bring from the East on their narrow backs the much desired tracks. The Chinese, one and all, were called "John," and the stories of John's prowess as a construction worker almost reached the status of folk legend. John could work twelve hours on a handful of rice; impassive John could handle blasting jobs that other men were too nervous to carry out; brave John would work all day at the end of a hundred-foot rope, chiseling notches for trestle supports; inscrutable John had the best poker-face in a poker-loving nation. Good old John.

And then the final sections of track were laid, the golden spikes were driven, and the construction workers poured into the western cities, into Tacoma and Portland, San Francisco and Seattle. The streets teemed with restless men, men with money to burn; restless men, soon broke, the Chinese among them. The fact that the Chinese were accustomed to receiving less than the white men no longer seemed laughable to the white workers; with the construction boom over and business slow, there was competition for every job—and fear of economic competition always increases prejudice. The hard-working, industrious Chinese who were willing to take any job, to accept any wage, became symbols of discontent to the unemployed. "Go Home, John," the slogans said, "Go, John."

Some of the anti-Chinese argued that since businessmen were protected against the competition of cheap Chinese goods by a tariff, laboring men ought to be protected against cheap Oriental competition by a ban on immigration. When Congress, after a long wrangle, did curtail the entry of Asiatics, the leaders of the anti-Chinese movement were not satisfied; they wanted the Chinese already here to be expelled, and their arguments were the arguments of hate. In a single story the *Seattle Call*, which claimed to speak for labor, spoke of "the two-bit conscience of the scurvy opium fiend ... the treacherous almond-eyed sons of Confucius ... chattering, round-mouthed lepers ... those yellow rascals who have infested our Western country, the rat-eating Chinamen."

So spoke the voice of labor. And the "better element," as they called themselves, agreed that the Chinese were undesirable. "We are in substantial agreement that the Chinese must go," their spokesmen said repeatedly. The quarrel was about the way in which the Chinese should be expelled: radicals advocated direct action—load the Chinese onto ships or boxcars and ship them away; the conservatives sought suasion—"talk the Chinese into going home." In Seattle only the Methodist Episcopal Ministers' Association had the temerity to go on record as believing the entire anti-Chinese movement was "cruel, brutal, un-American, and un-Christian."

The violence started in small communities, where raids were easy to organize. At Rock Springs in Wyoming Territory unemployed miners led an attack on the Chinese who had supplanted them in the pits. The mob drove the Chinese out of town, killing nine men and two women, and then burning their shacks. Word of the attack—"the successful action," it was called in anti-Chinese papers—spread swiftly through the West. Four days after the disorder in Wyoming a group of Indians and five whites resorted to violence at the Wold Brothers' hop ranch in the Squak valley about twenty miles east of Seattle. They raided the camp of thirty-five Chinese hop-pickers, attacking at night, shooting indiscriminately into the tents of the sleeping Chinese. They killed three, drove the rest into the brush, and burned the camp. Later the same week the Chinese working in the mines at Coal Creek and Black Diamond were terrorized.

Realizing that they were completely unprotected in the mining towns and on the ranches, the Chinese moved to the cities, where there were police forces and the rule of law. The police sided with the mob, and the Chinese found themselves outside the law.

Laboring men in the cities saw that a large pool of cheap Chinese labor would permanently depress wages. They demanded that "The Chinese Must Go," and they meant "Right Now." When lawyers and ministers and public officials temporized, citing American treaties with the Chinese government, quoting the Bill of Rights, pointing out the injustice of arbitrary action, the workers questioned the motives of the speakers. They believed that those who spoke for a rule of law spoke really in behalf of the rule of the railroad and the land companies, in behalf of the Interests.

There had arrived in the Northwest a short while earlier a man named Dan Cronin, an organizer for the Knights of Labor. He came north from Eureka, California, where he had organized the Sinophobes of that community. A good organizer and a superb propagandist, Cronin shrewdly organized labor's part of the anti-Chinese movement on the basis of distrust of the motives of the moderates. By overstating the radical case he offended the moderates and caused them to hesitate; then he cited the hesitation as proof to the radicals that their allies were insincere. All this tended to increase the militancy of the radicals, not only with regard to the Chinese but on other matters. It widened the gap between labor and capital, and that was what Cronin wanted.

While conducting a membership drive for the Knights, Cronin also formed a secret organization dedicated to the expulsion of the Chinese, called the Committee of Nine. It was made up of interlocking cells of nine members, and each member of each circle was expected to recruit a full new circle of nine. There was an elaborate ritual of oaths, a carefully calculated atmosphere of secrecy and dedication. While the purpose of the Committee of Nine was the expulsion of the Chinese, Cronin was known to have more extensive aims. He admitted his belief in a society organized for production for use; he talked of a division of wealth. In his speeches on behalf of the Knights he held to the line that the Chinese were only pawns in a game played for the benefit of capitalists. In Tacoma, where Cronin was most active, property owners hired detectives to infiltrate the circles of nine; Cronin had his men spying on the detectives. Fears that the anti-Chinese agitation would overflow into revolution became so acute that leading figures in the community took to wearing sidearms. Even Tacoma's Presbyterian minister made his pastoral rounds with the butts of two army revolvers bulging ominously beneath his Prince Albert.

Cronin heightened the tension by arranging for a Congress of Sinophobes from most of western Washington in Yesler Hall on September 28, 1885. Delegations came from eight communities and seven labor unions.[2] The Anti-Chinese Congress elected as its president the German-born mayor of Tacoma, R. Jacob Weisbach; the

---

[2] Colby, Black Diamond, Newcastle, Seattle, Squak, Sumner, Tacoma, and Whatcom were the towns represented. The unions sending delegations were the Seattle Turn Verein, Seattle Typographical Union, Seattle Labor League, International Workmen's Association, and the Knights of Labor of Renton, Seattle, and Tacoma.

other officers all came from Seattle. Meetings were held morning, noon, and night. Cronin, working behind the scenes, pushed through a set of resolutions that claimed most of the Chinese had entered the territory illegally and demanded that they all get out by the first of November. The Congress declared ominously that "we hold ourselves not responsible for any acts of violence which may arise from the non-compliance with these resolutions." After voting "aye" to this ultimatum, the delegates listened to a fiery speech in which Mary Kenworthy accused "the dog-salmon aristocracy" of being insensitive to the plight of labor.

The Congress instructed each delegation to hold a meeting as soon as possible to elect another delegation, which would tell the Chinese that they must leave. Seattle's representatives booked Yesler Hall for October 3. The Better Element was alarmed at the anti-capitalist tone of the Congress, and the elevation of Tacoma's mayor, "a foreigner who can hardly speak English," to the titular leadership of the anti-Chinese movement offended those Seattle citizens who felt no Tacoman could possibly be better than a Seattleite at anything, even at hating. On the day the radicals met at Yesler Hall the moderates (including Yesler himself) gathered at Frye's Opera House.

The Anti-Chinese party selected a Committee of Fifteen to arrange for the expulsion of the Chinese. They wanted Sheriff John H. McGraw, who had succeeded the late Sheriff Wyckoff, to head their delegation, but McGraw was at the Opera House, deputizing the moderates and organizing them into a semi-military Home Guard.

The two factions thought the worst of each other. The Opera House party looked on the Congress as a gang of toughs who were using the Chinese issue as a means of fomenting revolution. The Congress agreed with Mary Kenworthy when she called the Opera House party "the representatives of iron-clad monopolies" and "the lackeys of those thieves who stole our timber and coal lands."

Many Chinese left, but hundreds stayed on, some because they had investments too valuable to dispose of quickly, others because they were too poor to buy passage anywhere. The November 1 deadline passed quietly, but on November 3, in Tacoma, the Committee of Nine took action. Before dawn Cronin's men circulated through the community, giving word to the underground to be ready to strike. When the steam whistle at Lister's Foundry sounded at 9:30 a.m., hundreds of Tacomans poured into the streets. They marched through a steady rain to the Chinese shanties that dotted the business district and stretched along the waterfront, told the occupants to pack up, escorted them under armed guard to the railroad tracks, flagged a train, and while the conductor shouted joyously, "Put 'em aboard! I'll haul 'em," herded the Chinese into boxcars. After waiting a day in the rain at a siding the displaced Chinese were taken to Portland. The whole affair was carried off without violence, indeed, with a horrible friendliness that enabled the vigilantes to chat with their victims as they forced them into boxcars. Among the whites were men who could say that some of their best friends were Chinese.

When news of the mob action in Tacoma was received in Seattle the town braced itself for violence, but there were men on each side ready to compromise. On the afternoon of the Tacoma expulsion three leaders of the Knights of Labor, four leaders of the business community, and five important Chinese met to talk over the situation. The Knights spoke of their determination to protect their standard of living; then Mayor Yesler, ex-Mayor John Leary, and his partner Bailey Gatzert told the Chinese it was unfortunate but that their countrymen could not be protected and had better leave. The Chinese agreed but asked for time. The Knights acceded.

A mass meeting for November 5 was scheduled by the Knights, and as a gesture of good will speakers from the Opera House party were invited. Since the Chinese had agreed to leave, the meeting was something of a victory celebration for the anti-Chinese. More than seven hundred people, most of them laborers, crowded through the Marion Street entrance of the big red-brick Opera House, moved down the green velvet carpets, and found seats under the great gas-flame chandelier.

Feeling was so good that one of the Sinophobe leaders, George Venable Smith, a lawyer then completing plans for a utopian colony to be founded at Port Angeles, made a surprise nomination for chairman of the meeting: Mayor Yesler. The mayor was chosen by acclamation. The speeches were redolent of good will. The problem was solving itself, the Chinese would soon be gone. If all this harmony distressed militants like Dan Cronin and Mary Kenworthy, they needn't have worried.

Judge Thomas Burke was perhaps the best lawyer in Washington Territory. Though he was exceptionally prosperous he was well liked by labor, for he was as Irish as a clay pipe, and many of the newcomers to Seattle were recent immigrants from Ireland. They liked Burke's stumpy figure and his homely beer-mug of a face. They liked the way he nicked the wealthy for substantial fees and refused to charge the poor for his services. But they didn't like the surprising fact that he opposed the Knights on the Chinese question and helped organize the Opera House meeting. Many who had considered him an ally now called him an apostate.

When Burke was introduced at the meeting there were scattered boos and hisses. Others in the crowd hushed the demonstrators—perhaps they thought Burke would recant. He paused, stared at the men and women sitting tense and hostile in the brown plush seats, and began to speak.

He started softly, saying nothing more controversial than that "false stories have been put into circulation inciting hostility against the Chinese." But as his rich voice boomed on his words took on anger. "We are all agreed that the time has come when a new treaty should be made with China restricting Chinese immigration to this country. But by the lawless action of irresponsible persons from outside, the people of this city are called upon to decide whether this shall be brought about in a lawful and orderly manner or by defiantly trampling on the laws, treaties, and Constitution of our country."

There was little doubt how Burke would decide this rhetorical question, and there was no doubt, as the boos increased, that the crowd disagreed.

"Would you, men of Seattle, even if you had the power, overthrow the law of the land and set up brute force and violence in its stead? ...

"For the first time in the history of this territory an attempt is made to divide the community into two classes —laborers on one side and all other workers on the other. This attempt is as wicked as it is un-American.... The man who would now seek to divide us on Old World lines is an enemy to all."

And then he spoke as an Irishman to the Irishmen in the crowd. "... I cannot conceive how it is possible that any man of Irish birth could be so base, could be guilty of such black ingratitude, as to raise his hand in violence against the laws, the Constitution, or the treaties of this country.... If the Irishman is true to his own nature, he will love justice and his sympathies will go out in overflowing measures to the weak, the lowly, the despised and oppressed. He will not deprive any of God's creatures, not even the defenseless Chinaman, of the protection of that law which found the Irishman a serf and made him a free man. ... Those who come from other lands to live here must obey the laws and respect and honor the institutions of our country or go back to where they come from."

Boos drowned Burke's words. George Venable Smith jumped from his seat and shouted at the crowd, "I hope the workingmen will be patient and listen to what Judge Burke has to say." Hot with anger, Burke brushed Smith aside. "Excuse me, Mr. Smith," he snapped, "I can assure you that I need no one to intercede for me with a Seattle audience.... I recognize the insidious and unworthy appeal to workingmen. But to them I say that if there is anything certain in human history it is that of all men the workingman has the most vital interest in upholding the authority of the law. 'Where law ends tyranny begins,' and where tyranny reigns the workingman is a slave.

"By conducting ourselves as true Americans pursuing lawful measures for the redress of any grievance, real or imaginary, this little trouble that in the mirage of passion now looms so large will soon vanish like a bad dream and we shall all wonder what we were so wrought up about. I thank you for this patient hearing. I knew you would listen to me whether you agreed with me or not, even though I say things ever so distasteful to you."

Burke's speech may well have been the greatest ever made in the Puget Sound area, more powerful even than the legendary oration by Chief Sealth, but it did not save the Chinese. Indeed, it may have made violence inevitable. Nothing is so painful as truth told by a former friend, nothing so infuriating as an unanswerable argument.

Next day the territorial governor asked the U. S. Secretary of War to send troops to Seattle to preserve order; three hundred and fifty men and officers started north from the Vancouver, W. T., barracks. Mayor Yesler issued a proclamation asking everyone to uphold the law and warning that "prompt arrest and punishment awaited all riotous violators of the law." Sheriff McGraw passed out rifles to the Home Guard. The revenue cutter *Wolcott* moved into the harbor and showed her guns.

The anti-Chinese were furious at what they felt was a doublecross engineered by the Opera House party. They were angried still when a grand jury, with J. C. Colman, the railroad engineer, as foreman, indicted seventeen Seattle men, among them George Venable Smith, for conspiring to deprive the Chinese of their rights. Smith told a mass meeting that his indictment was "an attack upon free speech, upon the rights of labor, upon every man who earns his living not by speculation and plunder but by the sweat of his brow." Mary Kenworthy explained to the same gathering that they were engaged in class war, that labor and capital were "marching toward irrepressible conflict." But the Sinophobes avoided violence while the troops were in town.

The soldiers were hardly an unmixed blessing to the Chinese. While the officers were being entertained at the homes of the Better Element, some of the troopers entertained themselves by beating up the Orientals they had been sent to protect; others roamed the Chinese district, shaking down the inhabitants for a personal protection tax.

The soldiers were withdrawn in the middle of November. An uneasy truce lasted for ten more weeks; both sides settled down to wait for the verdict in the conspiracy trials and to see if the legislature, which convened in December, would pass measures to force the Chinese out of the territory.

In January 1886, a law forbidding Chinese to own real property was passed, but three other laws designed to exclude Orientals from obtaining public or private employment were blocked in the Senate after passing the House. The man who led the fight against them was Orange Jacobs, a former mayor of Seattle, who argued that they were unconstitutional. The same week that the legislature adjourned, the case of the anti-Chinese conspirators reached the jury. It took the jurymen only ten minutes to find all fifteen not guilty. The stage was set for the showdown.

The Sinophobes called a mass meeting for Saturday, February 6. They assembled in the new Bijou, the most luxurious of the saloon-theater combinations located along the Skid Road. The proprietor of the establishment, who had been trying unsuccessfully "to induce auditors of the gentler sex to visit my theater," must have blinked as the crowd assembled; more than a hundred women were among the eight hundred persons who crowded into the auditorium. Mary Kenworthy made another impassioned address. She was cheered when she interpreted the legislature's action as meaning that the "dog-salmon aristocrats" would pass laws to protect rich men against the competition of Chinese merchants but would never pass legislation to protect the worker. She was cheered again when she said the time for delay had passed, the time for action was at hand. She did not say that no jury would convict a white man for violating the legal rights of a Chinese: she did not have to. The fifteen "conspirators" were all on the stage.

When Mrs. Kenworthy left the platform a new Committee of Fifteen was appointed. The meeting passed resolutions instructing the committee to check and see if the Chinese were violating city regulations concerning the number of persons per cubic foot of air in residences. (They undoubtedly were: the regulations had been drawn with the Chinese in mind.) They were also to plan a boycott on all employers who hired Chinese, including Mayor Yesler. The committee was instructed to report back at a mass meeting the following week.

After the crowd had filed out under the Roman arches, the real work of the Sinophobe leaders began. The rally, with its public plans for future action, had been camouflage. The anti-Chinese intended to solve the problem permanently the next day.

5.

The Better Element and the Chinese were taken by surprise when the Sinophobes struck on Sunday morning, February 7, 1886. The troops had gone back to Vancouver, the cutter *Wolcott* was cruising the upper Sound, the Home Guard had returned its guns. The anti-Chinese had timed their move perfectly.

Shortly after seven o'clock the mob moved into the Chinese district. The Sinophobes were organized in groups of five: "order committees," they called themselves. The leader of a committee would pound on the door of a Chinese house and say they had come to see if the city health regulations were being obeyed. Once inside, the leader would inform the Chinese that the building was condemned as a hazard to health and warn them that if they wished to avoid serious trouble they would get out of town at once. The steamer *Queen of the Pacific* was at the ocean dock, about to sail for San Francisco. Did they want to leave with her? The Chinese had no choice. With their doors open and hundreds of determined workingmen milling in the street outside, they could only say yes. Once the Chinese had agreed to go, the chairman would tell the people waiting outside "to help out the heathens." The mob would rush in, carry out all the household goods and pile them in wagons, and hustle the Chinese off to the ocean dock.

So unexpected was the Sinophobe assault that nearly two hours passed before the town was aware of what was going on. Judge Thomas Burke was at breakfast when a panting Chinese rushed in to tell him that his people were being driven out of town. Burke at once informed W. H. White, the United States Attorney in Seattle.

White hurried to the waterfront, where policemen were standing by while the mob led the Chinese to the dock. He ordered the policemen to break up the mob, but the officers said they could do nothing more than see that no physical harm came to the Chinese. White cursed the police as cowards. He ordered the crowd to disperse, and when they jeered at him he cursed them too. He was still railing at the mob when Mayor Yesler and Sheriff McGraw arrived. The three men hurried off to Engine House Number One to sound the alarm. One of the agitators, tried to stop White from ringing the firebell, but Sheriff McGraw grabbed him. At 10:30 a.m. the bell clanged the call to arms for the Home Guard.[3]

Meanwhile Territorial Governor Squire, who happened to be staying in Seattle, was informed of the outbreak. He issued a proclamation warning lawbreakers they would be punished and urging all citizens, except those deputized to enforce the law, to stay home. The proclamation was hastily printed. It was read from the pulpits of most of the town's churches that morning. To United States Deputy Marshal Henry fell the awkward task of reading the proclamation to the mob. Protected by thirty armed deputies,

[3] The anti-Chinese faction later expressed indignation at "this willful violation of the ordinance prohibiting the ringing of firebells except for fire or drill."

Henry made his way to Commercial and Main, and from the steps of a building he read the proclamation. He was booed and hissed. Members of the mob, still shouting threats, followed him back to the courthouse.

Governor Squire heard the shouts. It sounded like a revolution to him. He wired General Gibbon to send troops at once from Port Townsend. The general wired back, "There is no one in America who can order the interference of troops except the President of the United States." So, after considerable indecision, the governor wired President Cleveland.

In the meantime the mob had herded nearly all of Seattle's three hundred and fifty Chinese to the Ocean Dock at the foot of Main Street, where they huddled on the planks under the black hull of the steamer. An enormous crowd of workingmen—many of them from Tacoma and Renton—milled around the shore end of the dock, waiting to see the Chinese board the Queen of the Pacific. The Chinese said they were anxious to go. But there was a hitch. Captain Jack Alexander of the Queen wanted seven dollars a head to take the refugees to San Francisco. Only nine of the Chinese had money to pay their fare. A committee passed the hat through the crowd and raised six hundred dollars toward paying the fares, and eighty-six more Chinese went up the gangplank. But times were hard and the rest of the money could not be raised.

Mary Kenworthy and a dozen men solved the financial problem. They signed a personal note jointly guaranteeing fifteen hundred dollars to pay the rest of the passage money. Captain Jack was willing to accept the note. But before the Chinese could be put aboard, a man pushed through the crowd and handed Alexander a piece of paper. It was a write of habeas corpus. A Chinese merchant had appeared before Judge Greene and protested that his countrymen were being unlawfully detained aboard the ship. Alexander was ordered to appear in court with his passengers at 8 a.m. the next day.

That seemed to end the possibility of deporting the Chinese that day. The town settled into a state of siege. The Chinese were confined in a warehouse on the dock. A guard was placed around them and a committee formed to bring them food. During the afternoon one Sinophobe thought of a new appraoch. The writ was only for the Chinese who had boarded the *Queen*. Why not deport the rest by rail? A committee was sent to the Northern Pacific office and the superintendent agreed, for a dollar a passenger, to haul the remaining Chinese to—of all places—Tacoma.

Word of these negotiations reached Sheriff McGraw. He warned the railroad superintendent that if he transported any Chinese against their will he could be prosecuted for kidnaping. The superintendent immediately dispatched all his rolling stock to Tacoma, empty.

Then the sheriff ordered the Home Guard to take control of the dock. The nervous guardsmen, their new rifles feeling huge as cannons in their cold hands, marched to the dock. They met no resistance. The crowd, tired after more than twelve hours of standing around, had dispersed. A dozen sentries were watching the Chinese. The Home Guard locked the sentries in the warehouse with the prisoners.

Early the next morning the Chinese were marched to the courthouse at Third and Yesler for their hour in court. Judge Greene told them that those who decided to stay would be protected. The Chinese, however, had come along streets lined with angry workingmen, and all but sixteen wanted to go. They were taken back to the dock and they started to board the *Queen*. But the *Queen* could carry only a hundred and ninety-six passengers, and Captain Alexander was now anxious to keep his operations strictly legal. He refused to take on any more.

At noon the *Queen* stood out to sea, leaving about a hundred and eighty-five Chinese on the dock. The next steamer, the *George W. Elder*, was not due for six days. George Venable Smith suggested that the Chinese stay at the dock, if not until the *Elder* arrived, at least until the crowd dispersed. The Home Guard overruled him. It was decided to take the Chinese back to their homes. The major of the guards asked Smith if he thought the crowd would make trouble. Smith said that since his advice was not being followed anyway, he wouldn't try to guess.

Shortly after noon the Home Guard started to escort the Chinese back to their shanties in the Lava Bed. The waiting crowd, who had seen the Queen leave, now saw the Chinese returning to their homes. They did not know of the agreement that the Chinese would take the next boat, or else did not believe it would be kept. They wanted the Chinese to stay at the dock. As the Home Guard moved forward, the workingmen milled around them. At the corner of Commercial and Mill the crowd was so thick the Home Guard could not push through. The situation was tense—and someone panicked.

A big, bearded logger pushed up against the front rank of the Home Guards, asking where they thought they were going with all those Chinamen. Somebody shouted, "Arrest that man!" One of the guardsman pushed the logger and said, "Come with me." The logger grabbed at the guard's rifle. Another guardsman clubbed him; then the shooting started. Five men fell wounded, one fatally— the big logger.[4]

---

[4] He died thirty hours later, but not before dictating his own account of the riot. "My name is Charles G. Stewart. I will be 34 years old in May. I have no home. I work in the woods when I can get work. Been in Seattle two months and a half. I think I will die from the effects of my wound if I get much worse. I don't expect to recover if the pain continues but will die inside 24 hours. Dr. Smith says my chances of recovery are very slim and I believe him.

"I was standing on the New England corner having come from the wharf when I saw the Chinamen coming. We came to the New England corner to stop them and to see where they were going. When they came up, we stopped them till the officers come, to see what they were going to do with them. We stepped in and said: Hold on, gentlemen. What are you going to do with these Chinamen?

"A man named Dave Webster, a tall, sandy complexioned man, said, You come along with us. I told him, No Sir, I have done nothing to go with you for; nor we don't intend to, not a man of us; but we want to move the Chinamen out of Seattle, and do it decently and quietly if we can.

"He pulled and jerked me and another fellow caught me. I think the other fellow's name is Carr; he is tall with black beard and a lawyer, a young man. So this Webster raised his gun and struck me

When the shooting started two other groups of militia were on guard. The Seattle Rifles were on the wharf and Company D was at the courthouse. The Rifles heard the shots and rushed on the double to the scene. They joined the Guards in a hollow box around the Chinese, who had sensibly fallen to the ground behind their baggage.

Judge Roger Greene and Judge Ike Hall were walking down Yesler Way when they heard the shots. They turned and sprinted to the courthouse to inform the troops there. Greene, though older, was the better runner. He reached the courthouse first and told Private James Hamilton Lewis[5] to tell Captain Hanes to hurry Company D to the scene of action. Lewis did.

The crowd cheered when Company D came running down the street. Its members were drawn largely from the working class and Captain Haines was popular with the common people. They half expected Company D to do battle with the Home Guard, or at least to arrest Judge Burke, for a rumor that he had given the order to fire was spreading through the crowd. Company D fell in with the Rifles and the Home Guard.

Captain Haines mounted a box and informed the crowd that the Chinese would leave on the next boat. Hecklers shouted, "Burke! Burke! Give us Burke!" He told the crowd they ought to go home. "Burke! Burke! We want

---

across the head and at the same time something hit me on the arm and I fell. It happened to be a bullet. I found that out after I came up here. I squatted down with my feet under me from the effects of the blow on my head and wound in my arm. Some man at that moment shot me in the body when I was down; who it was I do not know but I think it was that lawyer [Carr]. I do not know his name. All I know is what I was told, but I think it was Carr from the place where he stood when they picked me up. That's all I have to say. I did not see anybody shoot me. I heard Carr say if I did not come he would shoot. Did not see him. . . .

"I don't know whether I will be able to make another statement or not. I have no hope myself of recovery. Dr. Smith tells me I cannot recover and as he has doctored me before I have confidence in him."

[5] Lewis had a distinguished political career in Seattle and later was elected senator from Illinois. As senator he attempted to have Mrs. Maynard awarded a government pension, and he once proposed that the Army be abolished and replaced by Home-Guard units.

Burke!" He said that if those who had fired into the crowd had acted illegally, they could be prosecuted, and that statement probably saved further disorder. The mob broke up. The militia escorted the Chinese to their homes.

The idea of bringing the law down on Judge Burke fascinated the Sinophobe leaders, who hunted up a justice of the peace and had him swear out warrants for Burke, the Reverend L. A. Banks, E. M. Carr, Frank Hanford (whom they had confused with his brother, Cornelius), and David Webster. The warrants charged shooting with intent to kill. They were given to Constable H. G. Thornton.

The constable found the five men at the courthouse. When he tried to arrest them, Judge Greene—who feared that Burke would be lynched and perhaps the other four as well—told him that all five were members of his court and could not be arrested. Thornton went off to ask for advice, and before he came back, Greene talked Governor Squire into proclaiming martial law. Under marital law, civil warrants could not be served.

Judge Greene read the proclamation to the crowd assembled outside the courthouse, and the crowd dispersed. By 3 p.m. the trouble was over.

Legal purists had some doubts about a governor's authority to declare martial law, but there was no doubt at all about President Cleveland's, who made it official the next day. On Wednesday eight companies of the 14th Infantry arrived in town. For some time after that things were very quiet indeed. The Monday after the shooting most of the remaining Chinese left aboard the *Elder*. Martial law was lifted on February 22, though the troops remained. Things returned almost to normal, but a few details remained to be taken care of.

Burke and the four other men who had been accused by the Sinophobes of shooting with intent to kill were at last arrested. At their preliminary hearing the judge agreed with their argument that the case against them was political rather than factual; he released all five on bail. They were never brought to trial.

The case against Burke rested on the fact that he had

been carrying a double-barreled shotgun when the trouble
started, and a shotgun blast had ripped into the wall of
one of the buildings on Main Street. Burke declared—and
proved to the satisfaction of his friends—that his shotgun
had not been fired. He certainly had not shot the logger,
who was hit twice by rifle fire.

Though he was legally cleared, thousands in Seattle
continued to blame him for the trouble. He was often
threatened and insulted. "So many people know the
answers before they know the questions," he wrote bitterly
to a friend.

Who did kill the big logger was never determined. Two
men believed that they were responsible, Private R. B.
Partridge and Captain J. A. Hatfield of the Home Guards.
Each told Sheriff McGraw that he had fired the fatal shot.
Partridge was so upset about it that he died a month later.
He was probably not responsible. Hatfield's story was that
he had shot at Stewart from a distance of seven feet, so
close a range that he could hardly be mistaken about
hitting him. McGraw had told each man to keep his
secret. To announce his responsibility would have made it
almost impossible for either man to remain in town. Hatfield's story was not made public for twenty years, not
until he was dead ten years and his son of age.

George Venable Smith, who had emerged as the strongest man among the anti-Chinese, left Seattle for Port
Angeles, where he was a midwife at the birth and a
pallbearer at the death of the Puget Sound Co-operative
Colony, an experiment in socialism.

Some of the agitators dropped from sight, among them
Dan Cronin. Six of the Sinophobes were, months later,
brought to trial on charges of conspiracy. The defense did
not even bother to sum up its case and the jury promptly
acquitted all six.

Eventually Congress, "out of humane consideration and
without reference to the question of liability," appropriated $276,619.15 as full indemnity for the losses and
injuries sustained by Chinese subjects at the hands of
American citizens in the agitation on the West Coast. The
money was paid to the Chinese government.

6.

Mrs. Kenworthy and Judge Greene had few political convictions in common. They both believed, however, that the anti-Chinese agitation was part of a planned drive toward a socialist state.

Mary Kenworthy had no doubt about it. She believed what she had told the mass meetings, that the conflict between labor and capital was irrepressible, and she had enlisted for the duration of that dubious battle.

When the annual municipal election campaign began in June 1886 she was as active as ever. The election was certainly an extension of the fight over the Chinese. The Business Man's ticket this time was called the Loyal League. At its head was Arthur A. Denny, the pioneer who had measured the harbor with a horeshoe on a clothesline. Against him was William Shoudy, a political unknown. For chief of police the People's Party was running William Murphy, who had been forced by Mayor Yesler to resign as chief because he had not protected the Chinese. Murphy's opponent, a Colonel Scott, told the voters, "I believe there is but one issue in this campaign: law and order on the one side, and anarchy, disloyalty, and trouble on the other, as we had on the seventh of February."

Murphy was elected; so was Shoudy, though he beat Denny by a bare 44 votes out of 2400. For the first time the People's ticket was triumphant in Seattle. In the November elections the Populists made a clean sweep of county offices. A friend of Mary Kenworthy's said that Mary wept for joy when she heard the result of the election. Her dream soon faded. The candidates who had roared like socialist lions from the platform, who had frightened even Judge Greene into believing they might attempt a redistribution of property, were lambs in office. Responsibility sobered them, and returning prosperity eased the pressure that had forced them into office. The People's officials did little to change things, and if Mary

Kenworthy wept again it was not for joy. Then, in January 1887, the Territorial Supreme Court declared that the enfranchisement of Washington's women had been unconstitutional (Judge Greene dissenting). Mary and her sisters had lost the vote: the People's people lost the next election.

In 1889 Washington became the forty-second state, and the Republicans elected Elisha P. Ferry its first governor. With that, Mary Kenworthy withdrew from active participation in politics. She made an occasional speech, but the razor edge of her tongue was dulled. She remained a radical, but the fight was no longer in her. "I've lived too long," she told a friend when ex-Sheriff McGraw was elected Governor of Washington State in 1892. There is no record of what she thought when she learned that a new railroad was coming over the mountains and that again Seattle hoped to become the western Terminus of a transcontinental line.

The Great Northern was the creation of Jim Hill, probably the soundest of all the men who dreamed of steel tracks. Hill knew engineering and finance and marketing and mining; he laid out a line that was a hundred miles shorter than the Northern Pacific, had fewer degrees total grade, and had its steepest climbs concentrated so that it was easier to double-team engines. The Great Northern cost more to build than the NP but was cheaper to operate; one of the things Hill had in mind was hauling Pacific Coast lumber to the Midwest, and to do that he had to keep rates low—otherwise Douglas fir could not compete with Southern pine. As a businessman Hill certainly considered the financial possibilities of the evergreen forests through which his railroad ran, but his excitement was undoubtedly stimulated by the man who lived next door to him on Summit Avenue in St. Paul—Frederick Weyerhaeuser, the man most lumbermen consider the greatest lumberman of them all. Weyerhaeuser was not only Hill's neighbor but his associate, and he became a director of the Great Northern. Even before it reached the Pacific, the new line was deeply involved in the politics of lumber.

When Hill pushed his tracks through the Red River valley in 1891 he claimed the land that Congress had offered thrity-four years earlier to the first railroad to cross the valley. The courts upheld his claim, but the people who had settled on the land in the third of a century since the original offer protested stenuously. Congress heard them. When Hill suggested a solution Congress happily accepted it: the Great Northern was given the right to choose equal amounts of government land elsewhere. Hill picked timbered lands (they turned out to have minerals too), and so it was that Hill and Weyerhaeuser came west not only as operators of a railroad but as the biggest property owners in the area.

While the Great Northern was accumulating stumpage, Hill was pursuing the old policy of keeping everyone guessing about the terminus. Judge Burke constituted himself a one-man committee to see to Seattle's interests; the Irishman talked so persuasively that Hill agreed to make Seattle his terminus—and hired Burke as attorney, to represent him in his negotiations with Seattle property owners and city officials. Burke got the land for Hill, though a crusty city engineer named R. H. Thomson, and called "That Man Thomson," blocked Burke's efforts to get the city council to give the Great Northern most of the waterfront.

The first of Hill's trains rolled into Seattle in July 1893. The city scheduled a major celebration, but again a panic gripped the nation's economy; the businessmen from the east who had been invited were too busy—or too broke—to come west, and the celebration was called off except for some routine Fourth of July oratory. Seattle didn't much miss the party: it consoled itself with the terminus. There was another consolation: the Northern Pacific had gone broke again, and this time Jim Hill helped pick up the pieces. With a friend of Seattle in charge of both the rail lines the city could expect a brighter future; no longer would the Northern Pacific oppose Seattle's progress.

The panic of '93 concentrated the power of the railroads in Hill's hands. It also led to a resurgence of the Populists. Mary Kenworthy saw her old enemy Governor McGraw defeated for re-election in 1896; in his place the people of Washington put John R. Rogers, a radical from Maine who had made his political reputation by pushing through the state legislature the Barefoot Schoolboy Law, said to be the first state law guaranteeing every child a common-school education—a terribly socialistic doctrine for the time.

Two years later the Orientals came back to Seattle in grand style. Jim Hill had learned that a Japanese steamship line had decided to start regular service to the West Coast and that the Japanese had about made up their minds to use San Diego as port of entry. He sent an agent to Tokyo to sing the praises of Seattle and the Great Northern; the agent sang sweetly, and on August 31, 1896, the *Miiki Maru* of the Nippon Yuson Kaisha Line steamed into Elliott Bay. When the liner was sighted the churchbells and firebells clanged, the bands began to play, and tens of thousands of Seattleites flocked to the water front to cheer as she was made fast to the dock, the first steamer to cross the Pacific on a regularly scheduled voyage with cargo and passengers. The dream of Seattle as the gateway to the Orient was coming true.

With the arrival of the *Miiki Maru*, Seattle's attitude toward the Oriental came full cycle. Again the Asiatics were looked on, not as a menace, but as the solemn symbols of the wealth of the Far East. There was little objection among the townsfolk when some Japanese, and later Chinese, settled in Seattle; after the Spanish-American War there was an influx of Filipinos.

Mary Kenworthy, who thought she had lived too long when she saw women lose the franchise, lived long enough to vote again in a Seattle election in 1911. She died a few months before the event which, in all Seattle's history, would probably have aroused the most enthusiasm in her, the General Strike of 1919.

Many people still living remember the widow Kenworthy as she appeared in their youth, a tall woman with gray hair and a black dress; women who are old now but were girls when they came to know her recall that she was "nice but sort of queer." A reformer who knew her when she was still active politically remarked of her recently, "She was a fiery one, Mary Kenworthy, a fiery one. Said what she thought, with something added. You knew where she stood, all right, no doubt of that. She'd tell Old Nick to his face, she would. But you know—I don't want to do an injustice to the dead, mind you—but you know, I wouldn't be surprised, not at all surprised, if she was a bit of a free thinker."

Fire

No rain fell during the first week of June in 1889. Day followed day in soft brightness. The wind held from the north, and the thermometer dropped to the fifties at night, rose to the seventies during the day. It was the best of all possible seasons. The salmon were striking out in the bay, and in the valleys the vegetables matured early. Farmers hauled wagonloads of lettuce and peas and rhubarb along the plank streets to the markets, and the children came back from berrying with baskets of red raspberries and black raspberries and salmonberries. The firs were fringed with new green and ferns covered the dead grass of winter.

The city was growing like a young alder. The railroads were hauling people west and Seattle was getting its share of the influx. The population had been 3533 in 1880; now it was almost ten times as much.

Among those impressed by the town's possibilities was a young man named F. M. Gordon, newly arrived from Maine. At 2:30 p.m. on Thursday, June 6, having made up his mind that Seattle was a place with a predictable future, young Gordon paid twenty-five hundred dollars—his entire capital—for a fourth interest in a tailor shop on Front Street.

At about the time that Gordon received his receipt, Madame Feitsworth-Ewens, who specialized in reading the future by means of colored clamshells, was giving a customer some advice in the near-by Pontius Building; in the office next to hers, Dr. Sturgens, a dentist recently from Boston, was peering into the mouth of a logger. On the ground floor, of the building J. P. Madigan was show-

ing some boots to a housewife. In the basement James
McGough, who ran a paint store and woodwork shop, was
finishing a cabinet. His assistant was heating glue over a
gasoline stove. Around 2:40 p.m. the glue boiled over.
Some of it, falling on the stove, caught fire; flaming gobs
of glue splashed on the floor, which was littered with
wood shavings and soaked with turpentine. The flames
spread over the boards. McGough tried to douse them
with water from the fire bucket; the water mixed with the
turpentine and burst into flame. McGough and his assistant fled.

Even before the cabinetmakers rushed from the building someone on the street saw the smoke and called the
fire department. The flames burst through the wooden
ceiling, driving Madigan and the housewife from the shoe-
store, Dr. Sturgens and the patient from the dentist's
office, Madame Feitsworth-Ewens and her client from the
farsighted clamshells.

A hose cart pulled from the station at Second and
Columbia by men and boys reached the scene first. Close
behind the cart came the town's first steam fire engine.
The hose company tied up to the hydrant at Madison; the
steam engine took the next hydrant south, two blocks
away.

The burning glue and leather threw off so much smoke
that the firemen had trouble finding the heart of the flame.
They shot water hopefully onto the outer walls of the
two-story wood building and onto the roof until someone
pried off the clapboards at street level: the basement was a
furnace. The firemen poured water into the basement but
it was too late: tthe fire was out of control. Flames ate
through the thin walls into the Denny Block, a ramshackle
two-story building that stretched along the west side of
Front to Marion Street. The first shop the fire reached in
the Denny Block was the Dietz and Mayer Liquor Store.
Whisky barrels in the basement exploded and showered
the walls with flaming alcohol. When the Crystal Palace
Saloon and the Opera House Saloon caught fire a moment
later more high-proof fuel was added to the flames.
Twenty minutes after the glue pot tipped over, the entire

block from Madison to Marion was aflame. Young Mr.
Gordon had only his receipt to show for the money he had
invested.

There was still a chance to save the investments of
other businessmen. Firemen struggled to keep the flames
from spreading. The wind was from north-northeast. The
buildings in most danger were the Commercial Mill, a
shed-like structure across the alley toward the bay from
the Denny Block; the Colman Building, on the west side
of Front Street, across Marion from the fire; and a three-
story brick building, the Frye Opera House, on the northeast corner of Front and Marion.

One fire company was pumping water from the bay to
the mill. Mill hands were spraying its sides with small
hoses and slapping wet blankets and gunny sacks on the
long shake roof. Steam Engine Number Two was on a
wharf behind the Colman Building, but the tide was out
and the hoses would stretch only to the side of the building away from the fire. Steam Engine Number One,
hooked up to the hydrant on Columbia, was trying to save
the Opera House. As more and more hoses were brought
into play, pressure fell. The water mains were too small.
The streams dwindled until little more than a trickle came
from the brass nozzles.

Several times wooden sills on the Opera House flared,
but each time the firemen doused them with a thin, well-
aimed stream. Shortly after three oclock a burning
brand, carried high by the great updraft of hot air from
the Denny Block, fell on the Opera House roof. The
streams from the hoses could not reach it and the roof
torched. Inside the building stagehands worked desper-
atley to haul scenery to safety. A rescue party climbed to
the Masonic Hall on the third floor and came out with the
more important effects, but the building was lost.

Almost at the same moment the north side of the
Colman Building burst into flame and the roof of the
Commercial Mill caught fire in several places. The wind
rose.

Square-jawed Robert Moran, the businessman mayor of
the town, took command from James Murphy, the acting

fire chief, who was distraught. (The regular chief was in San Francisco attending a convention on fire fighting methods.) The mayor ordered the Colman block blown up, to form a fire gap. A heavy charge of dynamite was placed under the Palace Restaurant. The crowd cheered when Moran gave the signal and the building fell in under the blast. But the fire swept across the wreckage. It spread to wharfs from the Commercial Mill. It climbed east up the hill toward Second Avenue from the Opera House. So great was the heat that the fire pushed backward against the wind across Madison Street into the Kenyon block, which housed in addition to stores the press of the *Seattle Times*.

By four o'clock the townsfolk knew that the business district was doomed. The pillar of purplish smoke rising above the town was plainly visible in Tacoma, twenty miles to the south. The roar of the flames could be heard for miles. The steamwhistles of the mills and on the ships moored along the waterfront shrieked steadily; churchbells tolled; the bells in the fire stations clanged. Frantic telegraph messages for more equipment went out to towns nearby—and to Tacoma, an hour away; to Portland, five hours away; to Victoria, half a day away by boat.

Businessmen and home owners began to empty their buildings of everything movable. Household goods were piled on street corners. Wagons loaded with goods rumbled over the plank streets. Those who couldn't hire wagons—most of the expressmen kept their charges down, although bids were reported to run as much as five hundred dollars for a single half-mile trip—carried what they could on their backs. Some struggled up the hill into the residential districts; others ran south before the flames; many headed onto the wharfs. When the wharfs began to burn, the ships hastily took aboard what they could and moved out to deep water.

Still the fire roared on. It jumped Columbia Street and swept south. It crossed Second Street and closed in on Trinity Church on Third. No one tried very hard to save the church. "It was a wooden structure and had on its front end a tall belltower," one volunteer fireman said later. "It was so ugly the fire would have been a failure if that tower had been left standing."

The courthouse, with its property records upstairs and prisoners in the jail downstairs, stood across the street from the Trinity. A murder trial was in progress in Judge C. H. Hanford's court. The judge hoped to avoid adjourning court and separating the jury, which was supposed to remain isolated until the end of the trial. He kept the court in session while firebells clanged in the streets below and smoke poured in the windows. But justice was not being served. The witness on the stand, a businessman, could not keep his mind on the questions he was being asked. The merchants on the jury peered anxiously through the smoke toward their stores. The crowd thinned until only the officials were present. With the flames mounting the Trinity belltower only a hundred feet away, Judge Hanford closed the court and told the bailiff to let the jurors go their separate ways until the following Monday. Before they could get out of the room he drafted some of them to try to save the courthouse.

Outside a hose company was trying without much success to get water above the first floor of the three-story wooden building. Clerks were hastily bundling records into baskets and sacks and carrying them up the hill. The jailers shackled their hundred and twenty prisoners and herded them toward the Armory. Few thought the courthouse could be saved—and beyond the courthouse stood the residential section.

"We got a ladder from somewhere," Judge Hanford recalled later, "but it was too short to reach the eaves of the building. It was long enough, however, so that if some of us held it perpendicular, an agile fellow could reach from the top end to the roof and pull himself up. The name of the agile young fellow who did that is Lawrence S. Booth.[1] He climbed up and stood on the roof. It was still smoking then. In a few seconds it would have been blazing. We used the halyards on the flagstaff to haul buckets of water up to him. He dashed the water on the roof where it was smoking. The courthouse was saved."

[1] Mr. Booth was still in business in Seattle in 1951.

A few other bucket brigades scored victories. To the north, the fire had backed four blocks against the wind, reaching as far as Front and University Streets. A few doors south of that intersection stood the solid, comfortable house of Jacob Levy, one of the town's most popular men. Sixty of his friends formed a bucket brigade and for two hours outfought the fire. At least fifty times, or so the firefighters agreed the next day, burning brands dropped from the purple sky on the dry cedar roof, but each time the brand was put out before it could spread. The house was saved.

In the business district another bucket brigade saved the Boston block. Yesler's fine residence steamed but did not burn under the cover of a hundred wet blankets. But the San Francisco Store, the finest commercial building in the city, thought to be fireproof because it was made of brick and equipped with iron shutters, burned after the intense heat exploded the shutters; a half-million dollars' worth of merchandise went up with the building. When the fire reached the Gordon Hardware Company, thirty tons of cartridges began to explode; the fusillade lasted half an hour. A few minutes later the flames ate into the Seattle Hardware Store, and another twenty tons of ammunition went off.

Other shots were fired in earnest. A patrolman, James Campbell, saw a man trying to get in the back door of the Puget Sound National Bank and ordered him to stop. The man shot at Campbell and Campbell fired back. Both missed. Another policeman shot at a man he saw carrying burning brands across an alley near Yesler Way. The man dashed into a house, which later burned; the newspapers speculated hopefully that the firebug died in his own trap, but no trace of a body was found in the ruins. Rumors spread that two plunderers had been hanged. Mayor Moran declared martial law, asked that the militia be called out, and swore in a Home Guard.

Thousands fled the city. Others came for miles to help fight the fire or just to watch. The last great battle was fought along Yesler Way. Moran ordered crews to tear down the shacks along both sides of the wide street. All the small buildings were smashed; a few of the larger ones were dynamited. The planks from the street were ripped up and carried away. But the rising wind of early evening carried the flames across the fire gap, and when the fire touched the wooden shacks of the Skid Road, there was no hope of stopping it. Whores and pimps and white-aproned barkeeps fled south before the flames.

Shortly before eight o'clock the blood-red sun dropped behind the mountains across the bay. As darkness settled, the glow of the burning city was reflected on the scattered clouds. The fire burned on until, around three in the morning, there was nothing more in the business district or the Skid Road or the waterfront to burn. The fire had swept through a hundred and twenty acres. Twenty-five city blocks, the heart of the town, were burned almost clean. Every wharf, every mill from Union to Jackson Streets, was gone.

The morning sun slanted down on a gutted city. Women slept, exhausted, on the street corners beside their household goods. Many had set up tents. Others had bedded down in lean-tos of boards ripped from partially burned buildings, and hundreds crawled into the fern thickets. There were refugees from the fire encamped on lawns, in the streets, along the shore of Lake Washington, up on the hill in Queen Anne Town. A mother nursed her child in the shelter of a tent made from two lace shawls. The men and women from the Skid Road hiked South to the race track, where Boeing Field now stands, and made camp on the infield. Sneak thieves roamed the ruins in search of loot. The militia marched the dead streets. Some toughs on the waterfront found a fifty-gallon barrel of whisky and enjoyed a riotous wake for the city. A saloon had rolled a hundred barrels of whisky into the bay, hoping to get them back later: they recovered two. T. W. McConnell, whose grocery on Cherry Street had been almost miraculously spared, stayed up all night serving coffee and crackers to the hungry. Boats with provisions came from Tacoma and Olympia and Steilacoom and Victoria. Captain Brown of the *Clara Brown* organized a sightseeing cruise to the ruins, then gave the fares to Seattle charities.

The first newspapers hit the streets in the early morning after the fire, tiny editions run off in job printing plants. They carried headlines that read:

A SEA OF FIRE

SEATTLE IN ASHES

TOMB-LIKE RUINS NEATH A GREAT RED CLOUD

The *Daily Press* lamented, "Oh, light-hearted, industrious Seattle, pushing rapidly to industrial and commercial greatness, with hearts full of cheer and hands so willing to work, to be reduced to ashes in a single afternoon, and to have the sun of prosperity darkened by a cloud of mocking smoke."

Many rumors of deaths were reported. One paper said flatly that seven people had died and guessed the total might reach into the hundreds. Another reported two theives shot. Several papers said a volunteer fireman had fallen two stories into the center of the flaming Boyd Building. But no paper had a confirmed story of anyone's being killed, either that first morning or later. A skull, a hand, and a bit of charred queue were found in the ruins of a Chinese establishment, but it was later decided that these came from the cadaver of an Oriental who had been kept in alcohol pending shipment back to the land of his ancestors.

The papers carried the mayor's proclamation of martial law, the warning that soldiers would shoot on sight anyone seen pilfering, a request that firearms be brought to the Armory for use by the Home Guard, and the announcement that saloons would remain closed during the emergency. The phrases repeated most often were "a pull all together" and "to rise like a phoenix."

The town did pull together too, though a few landlords boosted their rents ("Fifty dollars a room is too much," one paper editorialized) and some teamsters, perhaps regretting the money they had turned down during the excitement, doubled their charges, a practice all the news-

papers deplored. But for the most part Seattle was proud
of its own reaction to disaster. When someone at a public
meeting suggested that the $576 Seattle citizens had raised
before the fire to send to those made homeless by the
Johnstown Flood be used locally, the suggestion was
shouted down. The money had been given for Johnstown and it would go to Johnstown.

In Saturday's papers were the first announcements of
new locations for businesses. Merchants operated from
tents. When John Cort, a twenty-eight-year-old Irishman
from New York City who had come to Seattle in 1887,
reopened his Standard Theater under canvas, the routine
that brought down the house was one in which the straight
man asked, "How's business," and the comic replied, "Intense." [2] And business was intense. Five thousand men
had lost their jobs as a direct result of the fire. But there
was work for everyone rebuilding the town. A brick town.
No more fires.

Some of the newspapers suggested that the area south
of Yesler, the Skid Road, should again be the business
heart of the new Seattle. It had the advantage of being
fairly flat. "Never again need this section be used for
despicable purposes," declared the *Post-Intelligencer*. But
one by one owners announced plans to rebuild their
establishments on the sites they had previously occupied,
and brothelkeepers and gamblers felt the same way. When
the first of the new brick stores opened north of Yesler
Way four months after the fire, several brothels had been
back in business for weeks in wooden shacks on the Skid
Road. Some girls worked in tents, but even south of
Yesler most of the new buildings were of brick.

It takes many men to make a masonry town. Seattle
gained more than it lost by the fire. When the fire started
Seattle's population was estimated at 31,000. When census
takers counted the population in 1890, less than a year
after the fire they found that Seattle had 37,000 inhabitants.

[2] Half a century later a trio of veterans known as The Three GIs
used the same gag in advertising their war surplus stores, which
were also in tents. It was still good for laughs.

III

John Considine and the
Box-Houses, 1893-1910

1.

On the evening of the last Thursday in December 1897, a
large man wearing a brown derby, a gray raincape, and
white gloves, and leading a brindle bulldog on a silver
chain, strolled through the rain down Second Avenue
South, gravely declining the invitations of streetwalkers
and, on occasion, raising his cane in salute to a friend. He
paused for a moment at the corner of Second Avenue and
Washington to watch the men going down the steps into
the People's Theater. Even on a miserable midwinter
night the place was drawing well: young sports out on the
town, loggers in for the holidays, businessmen, and, most
of all, lonesome Easterners waiting for ships bound for
Alaska.

The big man watched thoughtfully, then went to the
head of the steps. He frowned at a black-and-gold sign
that read, "PEOPLE'S THEATER. Moses Goldsmith, Prop."
Nailed to the wall was a blackboard on which had been
written in crayon: "See Lady Osmena change clothes in
total darkness in a lion cage."

He went down the steps, paid fifty cents for a seat near
the stage, ordered a glass of "water, plain, unadorned
water," from an amazed waitress, and turned his attention
to the crowd. The place was full. The bar, which stretched
along one wall, was crowded; three bartenders were kept
busy. Nearly every table was occupied. Women with

painted cheeks and skirts nearly up to their knees roamed the room, smiling at the patrons; from time to time the girls went to the stage and sang a loud song or danced an awkward dance. From the curtained box seats in the low balcony came laughter and shouts and giggles and, most important, a steady ringing of bells as the box-hustlers summoned waiters with drinks.

The place was a gold mine, John Considine decided, a real gold mine. He'd have to get it back.

2.

It had taken a long time for anyone to make much money on culture, even popular culture, in Seattle.

In the early days the phrenologists and the minstrels, the genuine Atlantic seaboard celebrities and the temperance lecturers, the circuses ("The Startlingest Wonder of the Nineteenth Century") and the Swiss bellringers infrequently came and swiftly went, usually leaving the editor of Seattle's weekly the task of apologizing for indifferent attendance. The excuses ranged from unseasonable weather to bad roads, and sometimes the lack of quality, or sobriety, in the performers.

The town was twelve years old when Edith Mitchell, whom the *Washington Gazette* described as "an actress of noted ability and favorable celebrity," found herself stranded on the Sound while waiting passage to the Sandwich Islands, and staged the first professional performance in Seattle. The audience that assembled in the little hall above Charles Plummer's store to hear "personations of characters from Shakespeare and other great poets" was, the *Gazette* averred, "small but appreciative."

Not so the group that assembled later that same year, 1864, to hear a series of talks on physiology, phrenology, and medicines in Yesler's cookhouse. The *Gazette* explained that "those whose minds are too much occupied with old prejudices and established error are generally uneasy and disturbed by his teachings ... but such has been the way of old fogies in all ages." As a matter of fact, phrenologists seem to have been among the most frequent of the lecturers to appear during Seattle's salad years. They were invariably popular with the press, perhaps because they advertised. The following ad and editor's notice appeared in the *Territorial Dispatch* for July 24, 1871:

Dr. C. Pinkham. Lecture on Phrenology, Physiology, Physiogomy, Anthropology, Love, Courtship, Matrimony, the transfusion of desired qualities from parents to children, laws of health, diet, bathing, exercise, intellectual, moral, social improvements, ethical science, moral philosophy, universal reforms, etc. Illustrated with drawings, painting and lithographs and closing with the examination of two heads.
Admission for gentlemen $.25   for the course $.50
Admission for ladies $.10   for the course $.50
ED'S NOTE. There must be a mine of occult research contained in each lecture which to gents ought to be worth $.50 and to the ladies cheap for a short bit [ten cents].

Not all performances received automatic acclaim. When the Great Eastern and Royal European Circus suspended the free list and made the press pay its way into the tent, in 1869, the *Weekly Intelligencer*'s editor and critic reported, "The concluding piece was the sickliest attempt at amusement we have ever seen brought before an intelligence [sic] audience, but we understand it was eclipsed on Friday evening when the last performance was given."

Another time the *Intelligencer* found fault with a lecturer. "Dr. Dickerson, who it will be remembered lectured at Yesler's Hall one evening a few weeks ago, and on attempting a repetition the next evening failed to be so 'inspired,' has made two attempts to lecture in Olympia and weakened on each occasion. The 'spirits' under whose inspiration he holds forth would not vouchsafe their aid, and all attempts to rally them failed. Perhaps they were overproof." In 1875, commenting on a minstrel show, the *Intelligencer* noted sourly that it "was not very well attended. The fact is that some talent is a prerequisite for a good house here—unless it is a free entertainment."

Even when the critics approved the quality of a performance their praise sometimes rang dully. Of a circus the *Daily Pacific Tribune* remarked, "The performances were all good, especially those of two or three of the horses." And the *Intelligencer*, writing about the Seattle brass band, said with a perceptible sigh that the musicians had "erected a comfortable bandhouse adjoining Wyckoff's Livery Stable. We learn it is the intention of the band to Hire a competent teacher shortly."

Culture probably contributed more, in a financial way, to solid Henry Yesler than it did to the men who mounted the rostrum and trod the boards. In 1865 Yesler, whose cookhouse had been the first place for social gatherings, approached the Fourth of July committee of the Masonic Lodge and suggested that they subsidize him in building a hall on his property, suitable for the annual patriotic orations and Independence Day ball. The Masons gave him $200, the amount they had spent the year before on a temporary structure, and with it Yesler purchased $150 worth of planed lumber from the Freeport mill (his own mill having no plainer) and $43.75 worth of shingles. At the corner of his orchard, which touched First Avenue and Cherry Street, he built a one-story 30x100-foot hall—ample for the monologists and bell-ringers and ventriloquists and minstrels who came to town in the sixties. For more than a decade it remained the center of Seattle's cultural activity. At the height of its popularity the hall brought Yesler, he told a reporter, the sum of sixty dollars a month in rentals.

The first professional play to creak the boards was *Uncle Tom's Cabin*, which came to town in 1871 and reappeared frequently thereafter—once as an operetta, once with an all-colored cast, and again with a double cast including two Little Evas who went to heaven simultaneously and two sets of bloodhounds. The most elaborate repertoire offered by any visting company in the early days was that of the Fanny Morgan Phelps Dramatic Company, which in 1875 introduced to Seattle six plays— *Rip Van Winkle*, *The Lady of Lyons*, *Rosedale*, *The Ticket of Leave Man*, *The Taming of the Shrew*, and *The*

Gilded Age—besides giving devotees two more chances to suffer with Uncle Tom.

The reception of these visitors, though not financially overwhelming, was warm enough to inspire the organization of a Northwest troupe, the John Jack Theatrical Company, whose performances may not have been dramatically adequate but which nonetheless had elements of interest.

When Jack's players made their Seattle bow in *East Lynne* they suffered a minor disaster, duly recorded by the *Puget Sound Dispatch*. "In the third act Little Willie refused to pass in his checks in the conventional stage manner. Being frightened and unaccustomed to the business, the child couldn't see the utility of shuffling off the coil thusly, notwithstanding the desperate efforts of his heartbroken mother, Madame Vane, to make him lay down and die. Being unable to succeed, Mr. Jack was reluctantly obliged to ring down the curtain."

The company struggled on. Jack took his troupers on the road. They left Walla Walla with the blessing of the local editor, who said, "We hope they will have better houses than they had here." The company lost money in Lewiston and came to more grief in Victoria, where two of the performers, whose immorality, according to the press, "was almost sufficient to send them to the penitentiary," got drunk and refused to play their parts.

In time the troupe, bolstered by new and more sober thespians, returned to Seattle with a play tailored to their peculiar talents: *Captain Jack, or A Life on the Border*. Of this effort the *Dispatch* declared, "It is of the dime-novel melodrama description, and consisted of four abductions, one attempted poisoning, two bowie-knife combats, one chloroforming, and twenty-four homicides, and from the beginning to the end there was a running fire of revolvers, till persons on the outside supposed Chinese New Year's had broken loose again. Verily it must be seen to be appreciated."

Jack went broke. But the town was growing; during the eighties there was a large enough potential audience to draw bigger names. Opera companies came, and violinists and sopranos and a man who had "trained a cat to perform the marvelous feat of picking up a soda-water bottle and carrying it off the stage." Also heavyweight champions, on whom the legislature looked with disfavor. Boxing was barred by law. Only members of private clubs might legally spar among themselves, a provision that led fighters from distant points to join private clubs immediately upon their arrival in Seattle. A more ingenious evasion of the law was the creation of a play in which a celebrated pugilist acted the part of the hero and in the final act clashed with a local heavy. John L. Sullivan, Jim Corbett, Bob Fitzsimmons, and Jim Jeffries, the championship dynasty of the nineties, all appeared in Seattle in plays suited to their abilities.

"SEE FITZ," commanded an ad in the *Argus* when Ruby Bob Fitzsimmons came to town in *The Honest Blacksmith.* "Spar three rounds, Make a horse-shoe, Punch the bag, Shoe a horse, Sing a funny song."

None of the heavy-handed actors, not even Gentleman Jim Corbett, threatened to replace professional thespians in parts not calling for a display of the old one-two, but it was seldom that anyone had the temerity to object to their performances. Eugene Elliott, an authority on early-day entertainment in Seattle, tells a story he fears is apocryphal about the great John L.'s acting.[1] At a critical moment in the second act the Boston Strong Boy strode onstage and announced, "I'll save you, mudder." From the gallery came a shout, "Save her? You can't even pronounce her." The champion stepped to the footlights. "Who said dat?" No answer. He pulled his coat back onto his broad shoulders, returned to the wings, and made a second entrance. "I'll save you, mudder," he bellowed. He paused and looked into the audience. Silence. With the smile of a champion he clasped his hands over his head, shook hands with the crowd, and amid a burst of applause returned to the chore at hand.

---

[1] This story is from Eugene Elliott's lively monograph, *A History of Variety-Vaudeville in Seattle* (Seattle: University of Washington Press, 1944), and is quoted with the permission of the author and publisher.

Actors of more orthodox merit played Seattle too. Henry Irving, Maurice Barrymore and his elder son Lionel, Sidney Drew and Mrs. John Drew, Harry Langdon, W. C. Fields, Eddie Foy, and Sarah Bernhardt all appeared during the nineties. Miss Bernhardt's visit was probably the most remarkable. Not only did she sell out the house (gallery seats, $1; first floor, $5) for a performance given entirely in French, but she went big-game hunting within the city limits and bagged a bear. The fifty-year-old actress told admirers that now she had reached The Last Outpost of Civilization she wanted to go hunting. They obligingly took her to the shore of Lake Washington, put her safely in a blind, and ushered into her sight an ancient bear that had been left behind by a circus. She killed the bear and carried his skin back to France, along with a story of how she had "encountered a fierce bear and in hand-to-hand conflict killed the beast of the forest."

Though Bernhardt could sell out the house, less famous actors had trouble making expenses. It was a good year in which at least one troupe did not fold in Seattle; company managers and theatre owners were continually eluding creditors by catching the night boat to Victoria. The city's consciously cultured minority complained a good deal that "the only thing that will draw in Seattle is a minstrel show." That was not correct. There was one other type of performance that could be counted on to make money.

In 1885, for example, the *Post-Intelligencer* warned its readers about the approach of twenty women who were coming west in a troupe known as the Adamless Eden Company. "There is said to be no merit in the play," the paper lamented, "and less in the players, the chief and only attraction being its purpose and the practice of its actors to pander to the depraved tastes of the spectators. It is an indecent exhibition of a lot of women who, for what they can make out of it, parade their half-naked forms on the stage.

"It is needless to say," the paper said needlessly, "that the show draws immensely. In Salt Lake City, the performance was attended by an audience composed of

doctors, lawyers, city and county officials, landlords, cattle-
men, railroad men, bankers, merchants, music professors,
brokers, deputy marshals, latter-day elders, gamblers and
prostitutes.

"It is safe to say that whenever this company appears,
it is sure to have a full house. But it is a question whether
or not public opinion will secure its suppression before it
reaches the North Pacific Coast; in that event what intense
disappointment would be felt in certain quarters."

The Adamless Eden Girls did not reach Seattle, but
whatever disappoitment the paper's readers felt, they
could dissipate by a visit to one of the box-houses in the
Skid Road, where similar types of entertainment were not
unknown.

The box-house was a saloon with a theater attached.
The entertainment was rowdy, and the box-houses were
restricted to an area where they competed with establishments offering even rougher entertainment. The box-
houses were usually located in basements; they frequently
had to close during the rainy season, when the floors were
covered with water from an inch to a yard deep. Others
were built on pilings over the Elliott Bay tideflats, an
arrangement that made easy the disposal of boisterous
guests; dropped through trap doors, some waded ashore,
others were found floating; mostly it depended on the tide.

Some box-houses were tougher than others. Probably
the most respectable was one run by a mysterious English-
man reputed (of course) to be of titled family. He aimed
at refinement, and all the women employed in his establishment wore evening gowns. He wanted the carriage
trade. Even the songs at his establishment had a certain
elegance, the lyrics seldom slipping below the double en-
tendre. In time the proprietor married his most elegant
entertainer, then disappeared.

More typical of the box-houses was the Theater-
Comique, which was located in a basement under a liquor
store and cigar stand on Washington Street. A reporter
worte a highly seasoned account of it for the *Coast
Magazine*:

A nervous opium-eating individual was hammering away at a piano. In the hall-like space before the stage were a hundred or more men and boys. Not a woman was to be seen in the row of seats—only men smoking and chewing tobacco and boys eating peanuts. Around the sides of the room and at the end opposite the stage were built out of thin pine boards small apartments with an opening towards the platform and a barn-like door leading into the narrow passageway along the wall. In each room was an electric torch button which communicated with a bar set up behind the stage. The boxes were unlighted save as a stray beam might enter at the window. In these boxes were women, one in some, more in others. . . .

Women with dresses [reaching] nearly to the point above their knees, with stained and sweaty tights, with bare arms and necks uncovered over halfway to their waists, with blondined hair and some with powdered wigs, with faces rouged and powdered, eyebrows with winkers smutted up and blackened, there stood the female contingency at the doors and in the boxes.

The man who became king of the box-houses was John Considine, a teetotaler, a devout Roman Catholic, and a good family man. He was born in Chicago in 1868 and educated in the parochial schools there. He attended, briefly, St. Mary's College at Xavier, Kansas, and the University of Kansas at Lawrence. Classrooms could not hold him when he was offered a job with a traveling stock company. He drifted to Seattle in 1889, when, like the town, he was young, tough, promising, and nearly broke.

It would have been easy for a young actor to starve to death in Seattle if he had no other talent than acting, but Considine was more of a showman than an actor. He was a good talker, a good mixer, and a hard man to forget. A big man—he stood just under six feet but was heavy-boned—he wore conservative suits and white gloves and gaudy ties. He never drank but he chewed gum constantly. He didn't gamble, though he dealt a sure hand for other men's games. He seldom swore but he had a cold, furious temper when crossed. So equipped, he rose fast.

Within two years he was manager of the People's Theater, a profitable basement establishment dedicated to wine, women, and faro.

Like other box-houses along the Skid Road, the People's made its profits not from admissions, which usually started at ten cents, but from the liquor sold to patrons as they watched the show, and from the card tables. The girls who took part in the variety acts were expected to spend their offstage time circulating among the customers, tolling them to the bar. For every drink they cozened a customer into taking the girls received a metal tag, which the management redeemed in cash. If the girls wished to peddle more personal wares, the management did not object. Few of the houses had cribs attached, but the box seats were deep and the waiters discreet; for the bashful, there were rooming houses nearby. Under such a system most of the box-houses employed entertainers whose talents were not of the type to appear to the best advantage on a stage.

Such a setup offended Considine's theatrical instincts. He reasoned that except for the stage shows one box-house was pretty much like another. Therefore the way to build a bigger clientele was to offer better acts. The way to get better acts was to hire women who were professional actresses. That would be expensive, but the bigger the crowd the larger the sale of liquor and the higher the take at the tables. Considine established a system of specialized labor. His actresses stuck to the stage, while his box-hustlers plied their trade without having to worry about cadenzas.

The People's prospered—temporarily. For a time Considine was clearing two thousand dollars a month, but the depression that struck the nation in 1893 was particularly severe in Seattle. The take dropped. Although business was dull, life in the Skid Road remained lively. "There is no law south of the Deadline," the Telegraph complained. "Anything goes."

The papers were full of stories of brawls in the box-houses. Patrons complained of being drugged. The son of a prominent citizen lost an eye in a brawl over a hustler. The employees at the Palace, unpaid for several months, seized the wine room and drank up their back salaries in forty-eight hilarious hours. Considine himself broke into print for the first time in Seattle by his impromptu role as referee in a knife fight between two of his leading ladies. The trouble started when Lillian Masterson, a Spokane divorcee who Considine was grooming to be the top attraction in the variety end of his establishment, met Kitty Goodwin, the aging celebrity whose public she was stealing, at the bar. The two ladies entered into a discussion of each other's virtues, a chat that ended with Mrs. Masterson attacking Miss Goodwin with a beer glass. No damage was done.

About two-thirty the same morning the girls met again, and, according to the Telegraph, "but few words were exchanged when Kitty violently slapped Mrs. Masterson's painted cheeks. Some high kicking followed, only to have Miss Goodwin embed her fingers in Miss Lillian's bushy locks and with a jerk throw her upon the floor. At this juncture Mr. Considine and Billy King separated the women.

"Miss Goodwin ten minutes later seized an opportunity and renewed the fight. She again caught Mrs. Masterson in the hair of the head. Again Mr. Considine appeared a peacemaker. While he was trying to break Kitty's hold, Mrs. Masterson brought a small penknife into play. She cut her antagonist once at the elbow, again above the elbow, and a third slash on the fleshy part of the forearm. Somehow, by accident, Mr. Considine's right coat sleeve was also cut."

It took thriteen stitches to patch up Miss Goodwin. Mrs. Masterson was arrested but was released when Kitty, after a conference with Considine, refused to bring charges. That was not the last time Considine's name was to be associated with violence along the Skid Road.

Such non-professional activities made things lively south of Yesler Way, but they offended a number of good citizens. In 1894 the representatives of these respectables gained a majority of seats on the city council and set about abating the box-house nuisance. Their method was simple. They passed an ordinance forbidding the sale of liquor in theaters.

"Silence reigned in the music halls last night and not a bar of music nor a snatch of song were echoed from the walls of the dingy basements in which they are located," the *Post-Intelligencer* reported the day after the ordinance was passed. "License Inspector Taylor went round yesterday and saw each of the proprietors personally and advised them to discontinue. Last night Sergeant Willard made the rounds and found the order had been observed."

Considine toyed with the idea of running the People's purely as a theater, but he gave it up; things had been tough enough even with the profits from liquor and cards. He crossed the mounains to Spokane, where he put in three years as manager of a People's Theater, years that proved to be more controversial than they were profitable. The venture ended when the Spokane city council passed an ordinance barring women as box-house employees.

"I went to the mayor to ask him if I could be allowed to run," Considine said later. "I offered to close up all the upstairs and not let a man or woman go up there, to have no boxes, and to only have a few women on the ground floor in the open auditorium to sell drinks. He told me that so long as he was mayor he would permit no women to be employed in a variety theater. Word was sent to me soon after that I could not get a license from this council, and that was positive."

So, reluctantly, Considine gave up Spokane. He considered shifting his operations to Idaho, where the population had displayed a passion for rugged entertainment; but he decided to return to Seattle first and see how things were doing in his old stamping grounds.

When Considine had removed to Spokane in 1894 a few optimistic culture-vendors had tried to keep the People's Theater open without alcohol. "It was no use," according to a contemporary account. "At last the basement was given over to the rats and the cobwebs. Hobos found an entrance and soon they had the boxes, where wine had flowed freely in the old days, converted into sleeping apartments. With the passing of each day came an additional layer of dirt and filth, until the old cellar, which had been dignified by the name Theater, resembled a place where pigs hold forth."

The Klondike rush changed all that. Thousands of unattached males flocked to the town. While they waited for transportation north they were eager to spend the fortunes they were going to make. The box-houses reopened. The city council, which had closed the establishments because they were fleecing Seattle citizens, had no objection if the houses kept some of the visitors' money in town. Among the theaters that reopened was the People's. Mose Goldsmith and the Millar Brothers rented the basement, spent three thousand dollars cleaning it up, and, according to some estimates cleared three thousand in their first two weeks of operation.

So it was that when Considine returned to Seattle late in 1897 he saw at once that the good old days had never been so good. He would have to set up in business again. But where? Every likely basement south of Yesler Way was occupied. Then he had a profitable, if unethical, inspiration. As an old occupant of the People's basement he knew the owners were in San Francisco; he guessed that Goldsmith and the Millars might be operating on a verbal contract. He caught the next train for San Francisco.

When Goldsmith learned that Considine had visited the People's, he guessed what the visit might mean. He too started south, but too late. On reaching San Francisco he found that Considine had signed a year's lease on the People's Theater for two hundred and fifty dollars a month, starting in February 1898.

3.

To celebrate his return to the Skid Road, Considine imported the most famous variety performer of the day, Little Egypt, a dancer whose national reputation rested on the fact that she had been arrested in New York for dancing nude at a stage party at Sherry's. (She was acquitted when she told the judge that she just looked naked.)

The press was on hand when Little Egypt arrived in Seattle. In the great tradition of burlesque queens she proved to be "a charming woman, a pleasant conversationalist and one who is well informed on current topics of the day"—so said the *Times*. As for her dance being suggestive, Little Egypt assured the reporters that the people of Turkey became very angry when anyone laughed about it. She was dedicated to her work. It was art. She danced the muscle dance, the Turkish dance, and the Damascus dance. On a good night, she said, she combined all three.

Seattle's male population packed the People's to watch the pleasant conversationalist in action. According to a first-night observer they were not disappointed. "Little Egypt proved a hummer and she was greeted with tremendous applause in an extremely interesting dance."

The People's was soon the dominant box-house on the Skid Road, though never without rivals. In summertime, when the regular theaters were closed, a man looking for entertainment could find it only south of the Deadline. There, according to a somewhat supercilious observer, "every evening, week in and week out, the beauties of the drama are unfolded to the admiring gaze of audiences who are admitted to the best seats in the house for the small sum of ten cents."

While goldminers and gamblers, prostitutes and sports, soft-handed cheechakos and horny-palmed river pilots from the Yukon roamed the newly cobbled streets, barkers shouted of the attractions to be seen in the basements. Every night at the corner of Second and Washington musicians from the People's Theater clashed in a resounding duel with a brass band from a rival establishment. On July 30, 1899, a *Post-Intelligencer* reporter described the musical battle and its aftermath:

It is about 8 o'clock in the evening that the battle begins. About that hour the players of the brass band on the west side of the avenue file out from behind the swinging doors of some cool, darkened beer saloon and, removing their coats, hats and collar, prepare for the fray. . . . An admiring crowd quickly gathers. The selection ended, the leader of the orchestra lowers his cornet from his ruddy countenance, bows low to the crowd surrounding him and to his brave supporters.

In the meantime, the champions of the opposition have . . . taken their stations on a high platform built over the entrance of the People's Theater. There are three of them. The leader is armed with a violin, which he handles with the daredevil grace and ease of a plowman handling a six-shooter. Scarcely less deadly is his execution. Another dark-faced young man with a melancholy cast of countenance strums a huge harp. The third of the challenged musicians defiantly pipes away through a husky clarinet.

These three musicians have only been dallying during the bout of the brass-band men. Now they strike up a lugubrious melody. . . . A stalwart young fellow with lungs of leather adds his voice to their efforts of the instruments. "She stole nine thousand and six hundred," he bellows in the deepest of baritones. "Say, Babe, I know we will be happy after a while." . . .

The band across the street hesitates to return the fire. The crowd looks toward them for an answer. Suddenly around the block is heard the discordant blare of an untutored brass band and the voices of men and women upraised in a popular street ditty. But the words are strangely out of joint. They seem to have been adapted from a hymn book and misfitted to the tune. It is the Salvation Army!

Fifty strong, the uniformed Soldiers of the Lord swing into the street in front of the theater and march up toward their Yesler Way barracks, flags flying, torches smoking and sputtering, musicians playing like mad.

The approach of the Army settles it with the brass band. The [summer] heat is forgotten and with renewed interest the players await the signal. It comes, and pandemonium reigns. . . . The crowd cheers. The Salvationists are outpointed two to one in the contest, but on they march, happily unconscious of the fact, leaving the theater band to finish that enlivening melody, "There'll Be a Hot Time in the Old Town Tonight." . . .

On both corners lusty-lunged spielers shout the advantages

of their respective shows and, as the musicians file down the stairs into the theaters, the crowd divides and flows after them.

For a few moments the entrance hall is crowded, and dirty dimes, nickels, and quarters by the quart are poured out onto the ticket-seller's desk. The hubbub subsides and the show begins.

Gaily dressed girls and women, wearing abbreviated skirts, plenty of paste jewelry, and a superabundance of paint, powder, and false hair, come and go without hindrance to all parts of the house, soliciting patrons to buy drinks, upon which they make a commission.

"Beer is five a glass. Do you know the price, gentlemen?" shout the white-aproned waiters as they hurry up and down the aisles. "Any beer here? Yessir." Then in a louder key to the bartender in the rear of the theater, "Draw one!"

Over and over, the monotonous invitation to buy beer is repeated and often accepted. Many are the foaming mugs consumed by the audience on a hot night, and it is probably in order that the audience may buy more liquid refreshments that the theater is never closed before one in the morning and often remains open longer.

4.

The setup for a sporting man at the turn of the century would have been perfect, a Skid Road entrepreneur remarked to a reporter, if it weren't for the damned newspapers and the goddamned politicians. John Considine might well have breathed an amen to that remark. As proprietor of the best box-house in town he was an important figure not only in sporting circles but politically. The Fourth Ward, which took in the Skid Road, had more votes that could be delivered than any other section of the city. The men in position to deliver that vote were the gamblers, the saloonkeepers, and the box-house operators. Considine's control of a considerable block of Skid Road votes made him important not only to habitués of basement theaters but to nice people north of the Deadline. He had what they needed.

As he became settled in his power—the papers now referred to him as "The Statesman" and "The Boss Sport" —Considine developed a rather regal air. His suits were more expensive and more subdued, his ties more gaudy, his collars higher; he looked like a tough Herbert Hoover. Bartenders in saloons on both sides of Yesler became accustomed to serving him his favorite drink: ice water. He knew an increasing number of important people by their first names, and he chewed more gun—five sticks at a time. He gathered a retinue. His righthand man was his brother Tom, a burly fellow with a local reputation for toughness. Doc Shaughnessy served as his shadow, body-guard, and court jester; in addition to serving Considine, Doc opened a physical-culture institute where he offered to "Remove Fat Fast from Fighters and Men under Forty. For Those Over Forty, I'll Just Try." His clientele was drawn from both the business and the sporting elements.

Considine too branched out. He bought an interest in a saloon. He backed a gambling hall. He invested thought-fully in real estate. He got rich. And he got caught in the political crossfire between two rival Republican papers.

Politics and the press were pretty much the same thing in Seattle at the turn of the century. Political figures owned two of the three large papers, the *Times* and the *Post Intelligencer*. The *Star* was then, as later, relatively impartial, relatively incompetent, and wanly oppor-tunistic. Bayard Veiller, later to become well known as a playwright, worked briefly as a reporter on the *Star* and, years later, still reveled in an incident that was symbolic of the era.

Veiller says he uncovered the fact that a young naval officer had lost some two thousand dollars in a roulette game in the biggest hotel in town. He asked the proprietor about it. "Yes, that's true," the proprietor said. "But I didn't think anybody'd find it out." He went on, "I guess you're a pretty bright young man, aren't you? I've been looking a long time for a young fellow like you. Why don't you come here and live in a hotel? It won't cost you anything. You can get a paragraph into the paper every now and again, and that'll boost the hotel along."

Veiller knew what he meant. He reported the matter indignantly to one of the editors, who was very much interested. He asked, "Are you going over there to live? Did you take his offer?"

Veiller told him that of course he hadn't taken the offer. The editor looked decidedly relieved. "You're going to write the story, aren't you?" he asked.

"Certainly I'm going to write the story," said Veiller. "It's a good story."

The editor said he thought it was a good story too. It didn't appear in the *Star* that night though, or any other night. And the editor, who was unmarried and a lonely soul, promptly moved over to the hotel to live.

Such were the ethics of Seattle journalism in the post-Klondike era. Political ethics were no better. Honest Tom Humes was mayor of Seattle, and Humes, a fine-looking character with curly gray hair and a curly gray mustache (he bore a resemblance to Mark Twain and, according to his political opponents, sometimes thought he was Mark Twain) burned candles nightly before the image of an open town.

Humes' rise to political power had been made possible by the gold rush. During the depressed days of the mid-nineties, Seattle had a reformist government dominated by business leaders. The municipal politics of the day were openly partisan and the mayors were Republican. Consequently the men who wished to open up the town concentrated on gaining influence among the Republicans. When Frank Black, a Milquetoastish hardware merchant, was elected in 1896 he found, to his real surprise, that the Republican machine had made certain commitments in regard to the police force that he could not in conscience abide. Yet, not being a battler, he did not want to lead the fight against what he considered corruption. He made a deal. He resigned, and the Republican majority on the city council elected his hard-hitting friend, Colonel W. D. Wood, to the mayor's office.

All was serene with the forces of righteousness for a few

months. Then the *Portland* arrived with her cargo of gold, and soon after came the gold-hunters. It is probable that not even the redoubtable Colonel Wood could have held the line against a more interesting night life, but he would certainly have tried had he remained mayor. Wood, however, came from Forty-Niner stock. The lure of gold was strong upon him. He resisted the urge to gamble on a prospector's luck, but when friends offered to back him in a merchandising enterprise that could hardly fail (he was to take a load of hardware north and sell to prospectors in the field), he asked and was granted a leave of absence. On sailing, Wood left behind his resignation, to be accepted by the council if he was kept in Alaska by bad weather or good business. Wood wasn't back when his time was up and the council, now dominated by people who felt the city was duty-bound to lighten the load of Alaskans, prospective and bonafide, by taking as much of their money as possible, elected Humes mayor.

Tom opened up the town in the interest of good business. He ran on his record in 1898 and was elected again, this time by the people. He came sailing through in 1900. If he pried things even wider open after his re-election none of his supporters could honestly complain that they were not getting the sort of administration they had voted for.

On the surface everything was lovely for Seattle Republicans, but there was one little difficulty. Tom Humes wanted to be more than mayor. In 1898 he had coveted a seat in the United States Senate, but his ambition had been denied by the state's backwoods and open-plains voters, who considered him a city slicker. Now he wanted to be governor, and 1900 looked like a good year to run. Popular William McKinley, abetted by Rough Riding Teddy Roosevelt, could be counted to carry quite a few of the GOP faithful in on their presidential coat tails. Humes was no sooner re-elected mayor in March than he set his henchmen to working for his gubernatorial nomination.

He might have made it had it not been for a newcomer to Seattle, John L. Wilson, a dapper ex-senator from

Spokane, who, with the blessing of Jim Hill, the genius of the Great Northern, had purchased the *Post-Intelligencer* in 1899. John Wilson still had political ambitions of his own. He too had lost his Senate seat in 1898; now he was ready to settle for being the power openly behind the scenes, the kingmaker. Since Humes was already established as the leading political figure in Seattle, Wilson had nothing to gain by backing him. If he did he would merely be another Humes hanger-on. He set out to undermine the mayor and build up a candidate of his own.

Wilson blocked Humes' nomination. He persistently struck the theme that Humes was a political hog, intent on gobbling up all the good jobs. Not only did he stop Humes but he secured the nomination of his own candidate, a businessman named Frink.

Came the election. Mckinley was in. So were Republicans running for offices from congressman to constable, but not Frink. He failed to carry King County, though McKinley rolled up a substantial lead there. Wilson was sure he knew whom to blame.

The issue he chose to get back at the mayor was Humes' open-town policy, which indeed had become a little blatant. The *Post-Intelligencer* opened up with an attack on corruption in our fair city, which was detailed enough to call for some kind of action. Humes adroitly passed the buck to the chief of police, accepting that worthy's resignation before it was tendered. For his new chief Humes chose a well-connected young man named William L. Meredith.

A small, wiry, handsome man of thirty-one, Meredith was a native of Washington, D. C., the son of the head of the Bureau of Engraving. He had come to Seattle as the personal representative of W. C. Hill, an influential Eastern capitalist who had obtained much of the real estate the government reclaimed from Doc Maynard. After finishing his work for Hill, Meredith entered the customs service in Seattle, specializing in work with the Chinese; he quit the customs to join the police force as a detective, then quit the police force to work for John Considine, whom he had first met in line of duty. Meredith followed Considine to Spokane during the Boss Sport's hiatus in the wheat country, then came back with him to Seattle. For reasons which have never become clear, their relations cooled. Meredith quit Considine and went back to work as a detective. The break became complete in 1899 when Meredith had the temerity to arrest a pickpocket friend of Considine's. For the Boss Sport it was a matter of principle. He claimed that Meredith had taken protection money from the dip, then double-crossed him. How could you trust a detective who would do that? Not long after the arrest of the pickpocket, Meredith was transferred to a clerk's job. He blamed Considine.

When Meredith was made chief of police, Considine knew he could count on trouble. It was not long in coming. The law against using women in box-houses to hustle drinks was still on the books, and the police began to enforce the law on Considine's side of Washington Street, though nowhere else.

This unilateral clean-up failed to placate Wilson. It is doubtful that even a full-scale crusade against vice would have been good enough for him. His morning paper continued to whoop and holler about vice and the threat it posed to the good reputation of Seattle. Soon a Law and Order League sprouted; most of its members were men of the cloth and professional reformers, but there were also some of Wilson's political followers. The League, pure though its avowed purpose was, was really an instrument for Wilson's political ambitions, and it was effective. When the League presented an encyclopedia of charges against Mayor Humes and Chief Meredith to the city council the council decided that it should find out if Seattle really was an open town. The councilmen appointed a committee of six of their own members and instructed them to conduct hearings—secret hearings—on vice in Seattle.

The newspapers were indignant at this star-chamber tactic. If the hearings were secret, how could the papers keep the public informed—i.e., cash in on the scandal? The editors needn't have worried. Every secret leaked. All the testimony detrimental to Meredith made banner news daily in the *Post-Intelligencer;* the statements favoring the administration appeared in the *Times,* which under the editorship of choleric Colonel Blethen was against anything the *Post-Intelligencer* was for.

The hearing developed into a duel between Considine and Meredith, the weapons being libel at close range. Considine testified first. He told the committee that one of Meredith's henchmen had approached him and demanded a contribution of five hundred dollars, that he had paid the protection and, not being a trusting type, had followed the man and had seen him give it to Meredith. The *Post-Intelligencer* played this testimony for as much as it was worth, perhaps more.

A few days later the hearing produced testimony to the *Times'* liking. Meredith took the stand in the committee room. He said that Considine was not only a barefaced liar but a bad influence on young women. His campaign against Considine, Meredith said, was carried on to prevent other innocent girls suffering the fate that had overtaken Mamie Jenkins. He elaborated on that fate. Mamie Jenkins was a seventeen-year-old contortionist at the People's Theater who had been, in Meridith's words, "ruined by the *P-I's* favorite gambler." As a result of her fall, Mamie needed an operation, which was performed by one Dr. Boxie and paid for by Considine.

The day he told the committee this lurid slander, Meredith also moved against Considine on another front. He dispatched Captain John Peer to the People's with orders to tell Considine to stop selling drinks or be arrested for violating the box-house ordinance. Peer found Considine in a box at the theater.

"I haven't any closed boxes," Considine said. "It's legal to sell drinks in open boxes. I asked the city attorney and he told me to go ahead."

"I know that, but the orders were given to me," Peer said. "You know how it is."

"Look," Considine said, "this is a personal matter. You go back and tell that little son-of-a-bitch that I'll run my business. If they want me for anything at the police station they can send for me." Then he calmed down a bit and added, "Never mind. It will only be a few days before they get that shrimp anyway."

The following Friday the council reported to Mayor Humes that his chief was unfit for office. The committee's findings were that "Money has been paid to Meredith and Detective Wappenstein for the privilege of being permitted to conduct bunco and 'sure thing' games in the city undisturbed; that the fact of their existence was reported to the chief by officers of the force and private individuals; that no notice of these reports was taken; that for a time the fleecing of victims in an open manner was a matter of daily and nightly occurrence; that when the victims complained to the police they were usually told by Meredith or by Wappenstein that they had better be satisfied that they were not themselves incarcerated or detained as witnesses; that in some cases when victims insisted on some assistance from the police in recovering their money, the money was recovered without difficulty but that the perpetrators of the robbery or bunco were never arrested, and that there seemed to exist some understanding between them and the police that they should not be molested if the money was returned."

Mayor Humes looked surprised and pained. He stroked his gray mustache thoughtfully and said he would act on the matter at once. He sent word to Meredith that his resignation would be accepted.

The next morning, Saturday, June 22, Chief Meredith told Sergeant M. T. Powers to go to a secondhand store and buy a sawed-off shotgun they had noticed there a few days earlier. While Powers was off shopping, Meredith sat at his desk and wrote a difficult, almost incoherent letter:

Honorable T. J. Humes,
Mayor of Seattle.

Sir:

I herewith tender my resignation as chief of police to take effect on July 16, 1901. In so doing I desire to enter an emphatic protest against the star chamber investigation of the city council; that for your sake prompts me to do so. I was ever willing and sought a fair open American investigation.

> Respectfully,
> W. L. Meredith

Sergeant Powers returned with the gun, an ugly twelve-gauge with two barrels. It was barely a yard long from stock to muzzle.

"What are you going to do with this, Bill?" the sergeant asked.

"I'm going to get my man."

On Monday John Considine visited the offices of his legal advisers, Humphries and Boswick. They had gathered affidavits from all parties concerned with Mamie Jenkins' operation. The affidavits made Meredith out to be a scurrilous liar. Each document attested that Miss Jenkins had not been made pregnant by Considine but had, indeed, ruptured herself while performing her widely advertised "miracles of contortions" on the stage of the People's. After reading the affidavits, Considine told his lawyers to send word to Meredith that unless he wrote out an immediate confession of error and an apology and had them printed on the first page of the *Times*, Considine would sue him for libel.

Meredith wasn't at the police station, but the lawyers found him at home that evening. They delivered Considine's message. Meredith said, "I've already lost my job. Now this."

5.

The next day, Tuesday, June 25, John Considine rose early for a gambling man, about nine. He breakfasted with his wife and three children and left his house on Seventeenth Street about ten-thirty. It was a cool, clear spring day, and as he walked downtown he could see the Olympics across the bay, still heavy with winter snow.

Rainier stood clear against the eastern sky. It was a fine day to be alive.

Considine walked to Columbia and Sixteenth, where he talked to M. L. Baer, Meredith's attorney. He asked Baer whether Meredith intended to retract his statements about the contortionist. Baer didn't know. Considine said as he left, "I want you to tell that little sport that unless he retracts in the newspapers about Mamie, I will prosecute him for civil and criminal libel."

From the lawyer's office he went to his brother's house on Yesler Way. Together the Considines walked down the hill to Morrisons', a saloon, where Tom stopped off to shoot pool. John went on to the courthouse to discuss the problems of box-house liquor sales with the prosecuting attorney, but the official was out. As he left the courthouse a friend rushed up. "John, are you carrying a gun?" "No," said Considine. "Why?" "Meredith's after you. Get a gun, for God's sake." Considine said he wouldn't take any unnecessary chances.

After lunch John rejoined his brother at the pool hall and lost three straight games to him. Tom kidded him heavily about his poor playing on their way to the People's. John went to his office, which was on the ground floor, and wrote a couple of letters. He decided to go home early. He wasn't feeling well; his throat was sore. Before leaving the theater he took a .38 revolver from his desk and thrust it into his gunpocket, a buckskin pouch sewed into his pants where a watchpocket usually is. The day had turned gray and a chilly wind was blowing. The Considines started walking north along Second. Half a mile away Meredith was walking south on Second, festooned with weapons. In his arms he held a yard-long package wrapped in brown butcher paper. At his right hip was a .32 Colt in a .45 frame. In his right vest pocket there was a .38 caliber bulldog revolver, a weapon with a very short barrel. In his left vest pocket was a dirk. He also had four silver dollars in his vest pockets, perhaps for armor.

As he walked down the street Meredith met M. F.

White, a real-estate agent from Spokane. He asked if White had seen the Considine boys.

"No," said White, and then, with mischievous innocence, "Why? Are they friends of yours?"

"The town isn't big enough to hold us both," Meredith said and walked on.

He went south to Occidental and Yesler, where the Considines usually caught a streetcar up Yesler. There he met his attorney. The two men stood on the corner talking for nearly an hour. The Considines would have encountered him at that corner if John had not met Solon Williams, an attorney, who reported hearing a rumor that Meredith had resigned as chief. They walked down to First Avenue with Williams, who invited them to join him in a drink to Meredith's misfortune. Tom was for it, but John, a teetotaler, said he wanted to go to Guy's Drugstore at Second and Yesler to get something for his throat. The brothers walked along First to Yesler, turned up to Second, and crossed the cobbled street to the drugstore.

Meredith, a block away, saw them crossing the street. He started toward them, calling over his shoulder to Baer, "Stick here. I want to see you in a minute." Hurrying down the block, he encountered Tom Linsay, an old acquaintance, who started to speak, but Meredith brushed by him with the remark, "There's the son-of-a-bitch I want to settle with."

As the Considines started into the store, John first, a policeman, just coming out through the narrow swinging doors under a sign that read, "Erusa Cures Piles or $50 Forfeited," recognized them, grinned, and reached out to shake hands. Patrolman A. H. Merford had had no use for the chief of police ever since Meredith had suspended him briefly for pocketing half of a five-dollar protection payment he had been sent to collect from a pimp. Merford had heard of Meredith's resignation and wanted to congratulate Considine for ridding the force of such an unprincipled leader.

The men were unaware of Meredith, who had now come up behind them. He stopped next to a pillar that divided the outer entrance. With his foot next to a Coca

Cola advertisement and his elbow touching a black-and-gold sign for MacKenzie's Catarrh Treatment, he pushed the shotgun over Tom's shoulder and at a range of about two feet fired at John Considine.

He missed. The very nearness of the gun saved Considine; the buckshot failed to scatter. It passed over Considine's shoulder and knocked a shower of plaster from the ceiling. Unwounded but dazed by the muzzle blast, Considine staggered through wooden screens into the store. Meredith pushed past Tom Considine and Patrolman Merford, both of whom were stupid with shock from having the heavy gun go off almost in their faces.

Jonn Considine ran on rubbery legs down the closed horseshoe formed by the glass display counters. Meredith raised the shotgun, which was still wrapped in brown paper, and fired again. The swinging door hit his arm as he pulled the trigger. One pellet struck Considine in the back of the neck and flattened against the bone at the base of his skull. The rest of the blast smashed through the forearm of a Western Union employee who was having a glass of sarsaparilla at the counter. Dr. Guy, who was mixing a prescription at the back of the store, ducked behind the counter when a bottle of medicine shattered in front of his face.

Meredith dropped the shotgun, its paper wrappings now torn and burned. He hitched the revolver off his hip.

Considine was trapped in the corral formed by the showcases. "Tom! Tom!" he screamed. Then he turned and lunged at Meredith before his assailant could level the gun. He wrapped his long arms around Meredith and hugged him close, forcing him to keep the gun pointed into the air. Considine, outweighing Meredith by fully sixty pounds, pulled him toward the front of the store.

Tom Considine came out of his daze. He burst into the store and twisted the gun from Meredith's hand. He beat Meredith savagely on the head with it, fracturing his skull in two places. Sheriff Ed Cudihee and Detective A. G. Lane, who had been a block away when the shooting started, rushed in. Lane grabbed the gun from Tom, who yelled, "Give it to me! Give it to me! He's got another!"

Someone pulled John Considine away from Meredith, who reeled across the aisle and sagged against a counter. Tom with a sudden grab wrenched the gun away from Lane.

"Give it to him, Tom," John Considine shouted. Tom turned the gun on the people who were crowding into the drugstore. "Stand back, you sons-of-bitches," he yelled. Somebody grabbed him from behind.

Meredith had pulled himself almost upright and stood swaying near the showcase. His head was down on his chest and his hands were scrabbling aimlessly at his side, but he was on his feet, moving. John Considine broke free from the man holding him. He pulled out his .38 and stepped toward Meredith. He fired when he was about three feet away. The shot struck Meredith below the floating rib on the left side and passed through his liver. He reeled to his left. Considine fired again. The bullet went in just under the left nipple and smashed Meredith's heart. Meredith said, "Oh," and pitched forward. Considine was so close that his second shot set Meredith's coat on fire. He shot again as Meredith fell, the bullet entering below the collarbone.

Meredith fell on his back, his head toward the west. He was dead.

Sheriff Cudihee ran up to Considine. The gambler handed him the gun. "You're under arrest, John," Cudihee said. Considine nodded.

The whole fight, from Meredith's first shot to Considine's third one, had taken about ninety seconds.

6.

Five months after the shooting the State of Washington put John Considine on trial. The charge was premeditated murder—murder in the first degree. The sentence sought was death by hanging.

The trial overflowed into politics. Both Meredith and Considine were Republicans in good standing, identified with the locally dominant anti-reform elements. But the shooting changed Meredith's status. Dead at the hands of a notorious gambler and box-house operator, he became a martyr for those who wanted to tidy up the Skid Road and corset the bountiful damsels in the drinking establishments. The trial was more than a trial of John Considine: it was a test of open city versus closed city, of law officer (though resigned) against box-house operator (though personable), of the *Seattle Times* versus the *Seattle Post-Intelligencer*. The appeal was to emotions rather than to thought.

The prosecution argued that Meredith was fired on first and replied in self-defense. Before he opened up on Considine with his bargain-basement shotgun, the prosecutor said, somebody lurking in an alley had tried to pot him at long range with a pistol. The State marshaled a parade of witnesses who swore that they had heard six shots, not five; or, at least, thought they might have heard a sixth shot. Under cross-examination by William Norris, the defense attorney, their confidence, and their credibility, collapsed. The prosecution brought up the Argument of the Limp Hands, that after Tom Considine cracked Meredith's skull with the revolver, Meredith was helpless and could not attempt further damage to anyone, and that John Considine knew it.

The defense countered with the Doctrine of the Continuous Struggle, the purport of which was that things were happening so fast and so steadily that Considine had no opportunity to think things out but acted instinctively. Morris argued that if the State felt Meredith had been justified in being so miffed by Considine's testimony that he would carry a sawed-off shotgun and use it on sight, then surely Considine's uneasiness at seeing Meredith standing alone and unguarded by the castor-oil counter was equally understandable.

The State played hard on Considine's unsavory reputation. When Considine took the stand, the prosecuting attorney asked him if it were not true that he had shot a man in Chicago. Considine replied angrily, "No, sir. I never shot a man in my life until this trouble. I never shot at a man. I never shot a gun toward a man and I never paid a dollar's fine in my life for simple assault."

Most damaging to the State's case against Considine was Meredith's pre-duel gabbiness. He had killed Considine so many times verbally that the defense was able to round up a host of witnesses who swore they had heard him make statements that ranged from "This town isn't big enough for both of us" to "If he gets me out of my job I'll kill the son-of-a-bitch. They couldn't get a jury in King County that would convict me for killing Considine."

Political passions were aroused to such a degree that observers were unsure of the outcome until the very last moment. The *Argus* reported that betting odds were on a conviction. When the final arguments were presented, the Widow Meredith and her two children sat at the State's table. Mrs. Considine, her three children, and Considine's aged father sat beside the accused.

The jury went into deliberation at two-thirty on the afternoon on November 21, fifteen days after the trial began. An hour later they asked for a résumé of Judge Emory's charge. Two more hours passed, but few spectators left the courtroom. At five-thirty the jury filed in and took their seats.

The foreman handed the verdict to the bailiff, who in turn handed it to the judge, who inspected it briefly and gave it to the clerk to read.

John Considine leaned forward over the table; his eyes squinted and the muscles in his cheeks twitched slightly. The clerk droned through the paper, which gave no hint of the verdict until the last sentence.

As the clerk impassively read the phrase, "not guilty," there was a gasp from the table where the Considines were seated. John half rose from his chair. His wife threw her arms around him. Tom burst into tears and put his arms around John from behind. The old father looked quietly at the jury, not moving, tears rolling down his cheeks. John whispered to Tom; together they walked to the jury box and shook hands with the jurymen who were filing out.

The *Post-Intelligencer* was delighted at the verdict,

which it felt was a vote of no-confidence in Humes' administration. The *Times* commented sourly that it was a miracle the acting chief had not been shot, since open season had been declared on law officials. Down the Sound, the Tacoma *Ledger* had some pungent remarks about the outcome:

A jury declared Considine innocent. On the showing in open court the fact was made clear that Considine had repeatedly shot a man already dazed and helplessly wounded, a man who without this violence would have been dead in a short time. . . . Perhaps conduct such as this is the outcome of innocence. . . . It will, however, be acknowledged that innocence has on other occasions taken a less sanguinary way of manifesting itself. There have been plenty of real innocent persons never moved by the impulse to shoot a dying man.

Murder is a serious affair. Among the rights of the human being is the right to live. Society says he shall not be deprived of that right. . . . With all respect to the courts that they deserve, it will have to be admitted that in this instance they have declared homicide not to be a crime.

John Considine has been acquitted, after having killed a man. All who feel the impulse to congratulate him are at liberty to do so.

In a few months' time Considine crossed the Line and established himself as one of Seattle's most successful businessmen.

7.

The secret of Considine's success was the advent of the moving picture as a means of entertainment.

The first moving picture had been shown in Seattle in 1894. Four years later Considine had shown as part of the entertainment at the People's a veriscope reproduction of Ruby Bob Fitzsimmons' kayoing Gentleman Jim Corbett in Carson City. These showings were merely demonstrations of a novel toy.

The nickelodeon craze began to sweep the East in 1896, but it was five years before Seattle had its first movie house, La Petite, a hole in the wall on Pike Street. The nickelodeons were usually nothing more than stores converted into theaters by the addition of several rows of chairs or benches. La Petite had been in operation less than a year when a more enterprising establishment was opened on the second floor of the Times Building; it was run by the local distributor of Edison phonograph records.

Edison's Unique Theater boasted that it offered "Moving Pictures, Illustrated Songs, Dissolving Views and Colored Slides: Refined Entertainment for Ladies, Gentlemen and Children." The movies were mostly shots of important people, Teddy Roosevelt grinning, William Jennings Bryan shaking his mane, sporting figures like Jim Jeffries, or models displaying the latest in bustles and bathing suits. The illustrated songs were quite popular, though the audience, which was supposed to join in singing them, seldom did. *Washington Magazine* carried this description of a typical song, "done to words by H. K. Beal":

It opens with a very pretty picture in which he is apparently leaving her, his straw hat lifted from the bright curls that cluster 'round his fair young head, her eyes cast modestly down. Then he goes away and fights 'neath the Stars and Stripes forever, is pierced 'neath the blue coat by a cruel bullet from an unseen foe, falls 'neath the tropical sun, she miraculously comes upon the battlefield, covers his aching head 'neath her tresses, and as the lifeblood ebbed away, he unto her did say, "When I Left You 'Neath the Willows." Somehow it is always "neath" in the illustrated song.

Everybody except the snippy reviewer for the *Washington Magazine* seems to have loved the movies. The *Argus* reported wonderingly, "If you go to one of these theaters almost any time, you are bound to find somebody you know, whether you are a mechanic or move in the Four Hundred."

Considine quickly saw the possibilities in a type of

entertainment which drew all classes of people. He reasoned that with all the nickelodeons showing the same movies, the crowds would go to the one that offered the best live entertainment, just as that segment of society willing to be found in saloons went to the box-houses that offered the best variety acts.

For two hundred dollars and a promise to divert acts uptown from the People's, Considine obtained a half-interest in Edison's Unique in 1902. Not only was the Unique the first well-appointed nickelodeon in town, but it was the only one with a stage large enough to hold more than a monologist. For the first time in Seattle a real variety program was offered on the same bill as a movie. The routines designed to attract the Skid Road drinkers proved just as attractive to uptown teetotalers. The Edison prospered.

But it proved hard to get fresh acts. The better performers back East wanted big guarantees to cross the country, and Seattle, with a population of less than eighty thousand, could not always provide a big enough audience to pay the guarantees. Considine decided that a circuit of theaters would solve his problem. He opened houses in Victoria, Vancouver, Portland, in Bellingham, Everett, Yakima, and Spokane. With eight towns on his string, Considine could offer big-name entertainers substantial guarantees and long engagements, and rotate them around the circuit.

According to students of American entertainment, there was truth in Considine's boast that his was "the first legitimate, popular-priced vaudeville chain in the world: admission ten cents."

As his new venture prospered, Considine cut off most of his connections south of Yesler Way. If he continued to make money from alcohol and cards he kept it a secret. He contributed to the proper charities. He was elected president of a fishing and hunting club. In 1906 he and John Cort, another Seattle theater man, were elected delegates to the annual convention of the Fraternal Order of Eagles, to be held in New York.

The two theatrical Celts, Considine and Cort, had been together in 1898 at the conception of the Order. Its beginnings were rather unfraternal. The Musicians' Mutual Protective Union was on strike against three Seattle theaters—Considine's People's, Cort's Palm Gardens, and H. L. Leavitt's Bella Union. The managers and a few of their associates met on a waterfront dock, so union spies couldn't creep up on them, and organized to break the strike. Their plan was to disband their bands and make do with piano accompaniments for their variety acts. (The customers broke up the lockout by demanding more musical volume than could be furnished by pianos.) Having arranged strike strategy, the theater men decided to form a club. They called it The Independent Order of Good Things, and they selected a motto, "Skin 'Em."

The next time the Order assembled things were a bit more formal. The members got together front center on the stage of the Bella Union. A Seattle lawyer who did frequent business with theater people was initiated; he drew up some bylaws, which were adopted unanimously. The month-old name seemed somewhat unspecific for a group with bylaws. Cort, looking at a picture decorating the stage curtain, suggested they call themselves the Eagles. Agreed. Next they drew up a short, earthy declaration of principles: "Not God, heaven, hereafter, but man, earth, now." Under this mundane motto the Order prospered. Membership quickly expanded beyond theater people; aeries, as the Eagles called their lodges, were formed in more than a hundred cities by the turn of the century. Considine and Cort remained friends as well as fraternity brothers. (Leavitt dropped out of the Eagles and organized a lodge of his own, the Moose.)

When the founding fathers left Seattle for the National Convention of 1906, Considine was thinking of mixing theater business with aerie pleasure. He wanted to set up a booking agency in New York to locate talent for his circuit. He did much better than that. In Manhattan he met Big Tim Sullivan, the Tammany boss. The two large Irishman found they could do business. They formed a partnership in which Sullivan put up money[2] and influence and a nationally known name, and Considine contributed experience and his existing organization.

Considine ran the shows on the Sullivan-Considine circuit. He bought theaters in Portland, Butte, and San Francisco, built the Grand, a hundred-thousand-dollar showhouse in Tacoma, and set up a nationwide booking agency. He entered into a working agreement with a California chain, and he contracted to supply acts for theaters in Missouri, Ohio, Pennsylvania, Indiana, Michigan, Illinois, Wisconsin, Kansas, and Manitoba. He was a shrewd ingenious showman, always looking for angles that might increase attendance; as part of his Midwestern operations Considine air-conditioned his theaters by dropping blocks of ice down the ventilation ducts.

How much Considine made from his theatrical operations has never been revealed. At the peak of the circuit's operation, however, Big Tim Sullivan was clearing four hundred dollars a day on his seventy-five-hundred-dollar investment. Considine probably did as well.

But while Considine was expanding so profitably on the national scene, there appeared in Seattle the man who was his master as a showman: Alexander Pantages.

8.

Pericles Pantages, who started calling himself Alexander after he had been told the story of Alexander the Great, was born on a Greek island. He ran away from his native village at the age of nine and shipped out as cabin boy on a undermanned schooner. Three years later he was beached in Panama after contracting malaria; he stayed on the isthmus two years, swinging a pick and running a donkey engine in the ill-starred French attempt to dig

[2] Sullivan's financial contribution was not staggering. A New York political writer says Sullivan was in financial trouble at the time and gave Considine three post-dated checks for $2500 each, with instructions to wire him whenever he had to deposit one.

canal. He learned to speak "a sort of French," as a friend phrased it, and he got malaria again. A doctor told him he'd die if he stayed in Panama, so he shipped out on a brig bound for Puget Sound.

Young Pantages made a memorable entry into the Sound. As the ship entered the harbor at Port Townsend, he fell off the yard-arm into the chill water, a shock treatment that he later claimed cured his malaria. The free-and-easy atmosphere of Seattle's Skid Road (where Considine was in his first term as manager of the People's appealed to Pantages; he talked about jumping ship and settling there, but a companion persuaded him it would be better to go on the beach in San Francisco.

Pantages spoke half a dozen languages, "English as bad as any," as an acquaintance put it. He found a job as waiter in a German restaurant on the San Francisco waterfront; the owner liked him because he could always find a language in which to communicate with a sailor. Though multilingual, he could read "very little much more than my very own name," but he was a meticulous man with figures. When his boss decided to visit his homeland, he left Pantages in charge of the restaurant. Pantages seems to have run it efficiently.

For a time young Alexander thought that his future was in the prize ring. He appeared in some preliminary bouts in Vallejo, a booming fight center. Short—about five feet six inches—but husky, he fought as a natural welter-weight, 144 pounds. The ringside experts soon decided that Mysterious Billy Smith, the reigning welter champion, had nothing to fear from Pantages, and though it took him longer to make up his mind, he came to the same conclusion and hung up his gloves.

He was still looking for a quick way to fame and riches when the *Excelsior* steamed into San Francisco on July 26, 1897, with more than a million dollars in Klondike gold. Pantages felt that fate had nudged him. He withdrew all his savings—more than a thousand dollars, for though his pay was not large he was frugal—and started north. But fate put him aboard a ship loaded with some of the world's most adroit cold-deck artists. When he reached Skagway, a boomtown where coffee cost a dollar a cup and ham and eggs five dollars a plate, he had twenty-five cents in his pocket. He stopped worrying about getting rich and started worrying about getting food. He took the first job offered, as a waiter in the Pullen House, an establishment that had just been started by Harriet "Ma" Pullen, a thirty-seven-year-old widow who had arrived in Skagway from Puget Sound with four children, seven dollars, and a knack of making wonderful pies out of dried apples. Alexander failed to make anything like the money his employer did—his salary was board and room—but he did pick up enough information about the trail to the gold fields to be able to foist himself on a party of tenderfeet as a guide.

The party made it over the White Pass trail, escaping the dangers of the precipices and the infantile paralysis epidemic then raging. Pantages' role as guide had the advantage of permitting him to cross the Canadian border in spite of the fact that he had no grubstake or passage money to display to the Mounted Police, but the disguise also had its complications: a guide was expected to build a boat to take his charges down the Yukon to Dawson City. Alexander bluffed it out. He wandered about a riverside camp, watching the experts whipsaw lumber from the trees, arguing with the experienced boatbuilders, telling them what they were doing wrong, soaking up information when they explained why their methods were right. He learned enough to build a boat that looked like a boat, but when he put it in the river it listed dangerously. Quickly he hauled it ashore, explained, "Well, the job's half done," and made another. He lashed the two boats together and ushered his uneasy companions aboard. They made it to Dawson. Pantages later confided to a friend in Seattle that his method of shooting the rapids was to close his eyes and trust that he was too young to die.

Pantages had a quick enough head for figures to realize that while prospectors might get very rich, they were more likely to die or go broke. He abandoned his dream of finding gold in the creek beds and concentrated on removing it from the men who had already found it. He found a job in Dawson tending bar. He had never mixed drinks, but a sign over Charlie Cole's Saloon read, "Wanted, One Expert Mixologist. Salary $45 per day." The money convinced him he was an expert, and he soon became one, not only at mixing drinks but in such specialties of the Alaskan barkeep as pressing his thumb on the bar to pick up stray grains of gold and spilling a little dust on the ingrain carpet under the scales when he weighed out payment for drinks. After a good day a shaky man could fluff an ounce from the carpet.

It was at Dawson that Pantages first became interested in the financial possibilities of entertainment. He realized that, the drinks being equal, men would patronize the saloon that offered the most amusement. He suggested that Charlie Cole turn his saloon into something of a box-house, with a real stage and a regular orchestra. Cole did, and his place prospered.

When gold was found in the dark sands along the beach at Nome, Pantages rushed there with a group that has been described as "the liveliest, speediest, swiftest and most sporting Dawsonites, with everyone ready to do everyone else." Alexander was as greedy as the next Sourdough "to do" a rival or, if there were enough money in it, a friend. He had been trained in a tough school; many of his friends were pugs and pimps; the most legitimate people he knew were gamblers; he asked no quarter and he gave none. In the town of white tents on the dark and treeless beach he expected to start his conquest of the world of entertainment.

He spent the first winter working in another bar. It was so cold that he could hear his breath snap when it left his mouth, but he burned with an inner fire. Finally he found what he was after: a theater in financial trouble. Though the costs of operation were fantastic (a new violin string cost forty dollars), Pantages was sure the reason for the failure was bad management. He talked some entertainers into staking him and took over management of the enterprise.

Pantages did well; his associates did well to get their money back. Among those he was reported to have bilked was Kate Rockwell, Klondike Kate, the Queen of the Yukon. There were men who hated him until his dying day (in 1936) for playing fast and loose with the money lent him by Alaska's favorite dancing girl. Even if they hated him, they had to go to Pantages' Orpheum, where a seat cost twelve-fifty, if they wanted to see the best show in Nome.

The rush petered out before Pantages could make a millionaire's killing in Nome. What he gained was a grubstake and confidence that he knew what people wanted. In 1902 he sold the Orpheum and sailed for Seattle. He rented an 18×75-foot store on Second Street, fitted it out with hard benches, bought a movie projector and some film, hired a vaudeville act, and opened the Crystal Theater. He was his own manager, booking agent, ticket taker, and janitor. Sometimes he ran the movie projector. Instead of twelve-fifty a ticket, Pantages set admission at ten cents. He based his hopes on keeping ticket costs down and turnover up. He was seeking a mass audience and he found one.

"On Sundays there was no such thing as a performance schedule at the Crystal," a vaudeville fan has reported. "With people lined up at the box-office waiting to get in, Pantages would limit a vaudeville turn that usually was on stage twenty minutes to half that time, and the moving picture streaked across the screen so fast you could hardly recognize the scene. Turnover was all that mattered."

Pantages made enough from the Crystal to open a more pretentious establishment at Second and Seneca in 1904. He unblushingly named it The Pantages. Tickets still cost a dime and customers still lined up to wait for the next show. In 1907 Pantages opened a third theater in Seattle and began to expand his circuit southward along the coast. Big John Considine became aware that in the little Greek from Alaska he had a rival who might run him out of business.

9.

The duel between Considine and Pantages was intense. Each man wanted to break the other, yet in the moments when they were not trying to steal each other's acts and customers they got along well. Each knew the other was an able operator in a difficult field.

In their battle for control of vaudeville, first in Seattle, then along the coast, and finally in all points west of the Alleghenies, Considine had the advantage of Tim Sullivan's political and financial connections; Pantages had the advantage of genius. A man without roots, a man who knew six languages but could write in none of them, a man who had traveled widely and always among the lower classes, a man without illusions, tough with the cynicism that comes from rubbing elbows with pugs and pimps and gamblers, he had an unerring instinct for what would please most people. He judged any act by the act itself, not by the names of the performers. On a trip to New York he saw outside a theater an enormous electric sign which said simply, "John Drew." "Who's he?" asked Pantages. "What kind of act does he do?" His rivals scornfully repeated the story. How could a theater man not know the great star of the day? But that was one secret of Pantages' success: he wouldn't have booked a Barrymore for his name's sake.

Pantages and Considine took great pleasure in stealing acts from each other. Pantages probably came out ahead; he worked at it full time, often putting in an eighteen-hour day at his booking office—noon to six a.m. Whenever Considine announced a star attraction—a juggler, for instance—Pantages would not rest until he could hire someone better, say W. C. Fields, and put him on stage the day before Considine's man arrived. Performers, aware of the rivalry between the two promoters, would make tentative agreements with each and wait until they arrived in Seattle to learn which promoter offered more. Pantages fought fire with fire. While Considine's agents met the trains with a roll of greenbacks, Pantages' man met them with a moving van. The actors might sign with Considine only to find their equipment at Pantages', who of course wouldn't give it up. Eugene Elliott tells, as typical, the story of a xylophone trio that came to town in 1909. When Considine offered them twice the money, they argued with Pantages that their agreement with him was not air-tight and they preferred the schedule at the other house. Pantages got his stage manager on the phone. "Are those xylophones down there?' he asked. The stage manager said they were. 'Take them in the alley and burn them.' The wood-block virtuoso tore his hair. 'My life, my soul,' he cried. 'For twenty years I've played those instruments. You couldn't do that to me.' 'Burn 'em,' repeated Pantages into the phone. The trio appeared at his theater."

The two Seattle showmen fought each other in their home town and across the nation. Considine had entered the national entertainment scene in 1906 when he allied himself with Sullivan; the same year Pantages had begun to expand by buying out a six-theater circuit that had lost its principal showplace in the San Francisco fire. By 1911 the Sullivan-Considine Circuit had become the first transcontinental, popular-priced vaudeville chain in America and could offer performers seventy weeks' continuous work; Pantages, the same year, made agreements with three Middle Western chains that let him offer sixty straight weeks.

Better booking procedures won the day for Pantages in Seattle, and nationally. He simply booked better acts. Nationally he never made the mistake of relying blindly on New York booking agents. The New Yorkers were likely to send out talent that had succeeded on Broadway with the attitude that if the hicks in the sticks didn't like the act, the hicks didn't know what was good for them. Pantages shuddered at such efforts to uplift the national taste. He wasn't out to improve the customers' minds; he just wanted their money. He gave them exactly what they wanted.

Ten years after their personal rivalry started in 1904,

Pantages was clearly the victor. Considine was ready to quit. Sullivan had gone insane in 1913 and could no longer raise money or use his political influence to arrange for good theater sites. The circuit involved a great amount of real estate, but each new theater had been built by mortgaging one of the others. To keep things going, Considine had to travel a hundred thousand miles a year, and he wanted some home life.

The Considine and Sullivan interests sold out to Marcus Loew and a Chicago syndicate in 1914; they were to receive a million and a half for good will and two and a half million for the real estate—four hundred thousand in cash and the rest over a period of several years. Loew retained the right to call off the agreement on thirty days' notice. World War I disrupted vaudeville business by shutting off the international circuit and in 1915 Loew turned the chain back. Though Considine had Loew's down payment with which to finance operations, he was unable to get vaudeville going again. In 1915 he told the court he did not have cash on hand to meet a twenty-five-hundred-dollar judgment. The next year the New York Life Insurance Company foreclosed a mortgage on his most important property. The circuit fell apart and Pantages picked up the pieces.

By the end of the war in Europe, Pantages had the strongest circuit in America. He kept adding to it. At the peak of his operations in 1926 he owned thirty playhouses and had control of forty-two others. In 1929, just before the crash picked the pockets of the nation's audience and the talkies administered the coup de grâce to vaudeville, Pantages sold his circuit to Radio-Keith-Orpheum for twenty-four million dollars.

Throughout the struggle Considine and Pantages remained personal friends—not close friends, but amiable. Some years after Pantages had driven his rival to the wall, his daughter Carmen, who had been born in Seattle, married Considine's son, John Junior, in Los Angeles, where both families had moved after leaving the Sound country and where the Considines, father and son, did very well indeed as motion-picture producers.

Gold

Erastus Brainerd was a handsome Connecticut Yankee, solid and sandy-haired and conservative, a delegate to the Republican National Convention in 1904, a pillar of the Chamber of Commerce, a lover of the arts who once wrote a book on painting and served in his youth as curator of the Gray Collection of Engravings at the Boston Art Museum. Though his name is hardly known in Seattle today,[1] this author and editor, whose friends considered him to be touched with genius, probably did more than any other individual to annex the Territory of Alaska to the City of Seattle. Certainly he was the man most responsible for making Seattle the main port of the Klondike and Nome gold rushes.

Brainerd started his newspaper career as an editorial writer on the *New York World* and later served as an associate editor on two other good papers, the *Atlanta Constitution* and the *Philadelphia Press*.

In 1890 one of Brainerd's friends in Philadelphia, W. A. Bailey, bought the *Seattle Press* and persuaded Brainerd to go west to run it. The next year Bailey bought out the moribund *Times* and combined the two papers under Brainerd's editorship. The New Englander ran a literate paper, but his editorial tastes were a bit rarefied for the frontier.

---

[1] Though Brainerd was editor of the two surviving Seattle newspapers at different times in his career, the morgues of the *Post-Intelligencer* and the *Times* are almost bare of material about him. When I asked to see the clippings at the *P-I*, one of the librarians asked, "Brainerd? Brainerd? Is he a Communist or something?"

Times were bad again; so bad, in fact, that the new Baptist minister was advocating "the practical redistribution of wealth." The whole state echoed to the sound of crashing banks; in Tacoma alone, fourteen out of twenty-one shut their doors. The unemployed began joining Coxey's Army. Two thousand men converged on Puyallup, seized an unfinished hotel, commandeered food wherever they could find it, and demanded that the Northern Pacific give them train transportation east, to march with Coxey on the nation's capital. They disbanded when Governor McGraw threatened them with Army action. In the midst of all this, the people of Seattle found Brainerd's enthusiastic coverage of art, literature, and South American customs less than exciting. The *Press-Times* lost money steadily, and finally Brainerd resigned his editorship and accepted the post of state land commissioner, offered to him by Governor McGraw.

Land Commissioner was an important job. Jim Hill had just pushed the Great Northern through to Seattle and was trying to get control of the Northern Pacific, which had run out of money again. The railroad lines had tremendous holdings in timberlands, and as the first lumber moved east over the Great Northern, far-sighted lumbermen began to investigate the Northwest. Brainerd found his work interesting. In 1896, however, the Populists unseated Governor McGraw and within a few months Brainerd was succeeded by a land commissioner of the ruling party.

Times were still bad, and Brainerd had a hard time finding a job suited to his talents. He picked up pin-money by serving as the Paraguayan consul in Seattle, but there seemed to be little future for a Yankee in that country's diplomatic corps. Brainerd was still looking for work when on July 15, 1897, the newsboys chanted, "Gold discovered."

The ship *Excelsior* had just landed in San Francisco with half a ton of gold aboard. A second ship was due in Seattle with an even larger payload. The papers printed extras as each new bulletin came in.

Everyone read the papers that day, read them time after

time. The whole nation was excited, but Seattle was in a frenzy. People who had crossed the continent and waited months and years in the mud and the rain, hoping for their luck to turn, now felt that they had been led by destiny to the end of the rainbow. It was not just that Seattle was the nearest American rail-port to Alaska, though no one forgot that factor for a moment; the really exciting elements in the stories were the names. Among those who had struck it rich were men everybody in town knew. Jack Horne, an inept heavy-weight prize-fighter from Tacoma, was considered one of the unluckiest of the prospectors: he had come out with only six thousand dollars. T. S. Lippy, who had been a secretary of the Seattle YMCA, had gathered nuggets worth eighty-five thousand dollars. And, of course, the rumors ran ahead of the golden facts.

The next day a cutter with an Associated Press correspondent aboard spoke the steamer *Portland*[2] off Cape Flattery, and fact again sprinted ahead of rumor. This was the *Portland's* greatest voyage—in her hold was more than a ton of gold. At Seattle a huge crowd was awaiting her at the dock. The stories the prospectors had to tell were fantastic. A servant girl had found fifty thousand dollars in a week; a man had made twenty-four thousand in a day; a schoolteacher, in Alaska on her vacation, had taken out eighty thousand in a month. A Seattle boy had bought a claim for eighty-five dollars and without so much as turning a spadeful of dirt had sold it for thirty-five thousand dollars. A Fresno fruit-farmer had come back for one last try after repeated failures and had made a hundred and thirty thousand over the winter. A Negro who

[2] The *Portland* was perhaps the most notorious ship on the Pacific Coast. She had been built in 1885 and took to sea under the name *Haytian Republic*; she was seized four years later for carrying ammunition to rebels in Haiti during a civil war, and an attempt was made to sink her as she left Port au Prince. She began operating on the Pacific Coast in 1889 as a cannery boat, but government agents found a load of Chinese aliens and some packets of opium aboard her on one voyage; she was seized, condemned, and sold. Her new owners renamed her *Portland* and put her in the coastal trade as a passenger ship.

had been a slave made thirty thousand in three months, then left for Georgia to give his treasure to the woman who had owned him.

The tales told by the men on the Portland were unbelievable—until the prospectors staggered off under the weight of the canvas bags they carried. The gold talked convincingly, so much so that it soon became heresy for anyone to believe that a man could fail in Alaska.

Even before the *Portland* docked she was booked full for her passage back north: fifty first-class passengers (including former Governor McGraw) and ninety-eight second class. Seven other steamers were accepting bookings. Half of Seattle seemed to expect to make its fortune by going to Alaska, the other half by outfitting the prospectors. It was the same in the other coastal towns. San Francisco expected that it would naturally be the center of any gold rush; Portland hoped to capitalize on its quick transportation to the East; Tacoma had the Northern Pacific terminal; Nenaimo, British Columbia, trumpeted the fact that the gold was in Canada and so was Nenaimo. But Seattle had the natural advantage of being the northernmost American rail-port, plus the good fortune that Erastus Brainerd was in town and without a job to keep him busy.

The Chamber of Commerce appointed a committee to see that Seattle got more than its share of the Gold Rush trade, and the chairman of that committee was Erastus Brainerd. The man who had failed as a frontier editor proved to be the most resourceful publicity man on the coast. He might not know a good local story, but he did know most of the important journalists in the East by their first names. He knew magazine editors and advertising rates, and he knew what questions an Easterner would want answered about going to Alaska. The Chamber gave him a fat expense account to draw on, and in return Brainerd gave Alaska to Seattle.

First, of course, he advertised. He placed more inches of ads for Seattle than all the other ports together had bought. His biggest splurge was for six full columns in Hearst's *New York Journal*, which then claimed the highest circulation figure in the country. He placed ads in rural papers with an aggregate of nearly ten million readers. He put ads in all the major magazines, *Cosmopolitan* and *Century*, *McClure's* and *Munsey's*, *Scribner's* and *Review of Reviews*.

He thought up devices for getting free publicity. He wrote a series of "letters home," and whenever he heard of a newcomer to town he gave him one of the form letters and had him send it to the editor of his hometown paper. He wrote articles for Eastern papers and magazines, including *Harper's Weekly*, and then quoted his effusion in news dispatches datelined Seattle without mentioning that their author was Seattle's paid booster.

Anything to link the two words: Seattle and Alaska, Alaska and Seattle. He had a staff of stenographers write personal letters to every state governor and to the mayor of every community of five thousand or more. The letters gave information about the goods anyone would need in Alaska and mentioned that anyone wanting further information should write to Seattle. Thousands did. He asked officials to send estimates of the number of people from their communities who would be going to Alaska, so that Seattle could prepare to outfit them. Alaska and Seattle, Seattle and Alaska. He wrote an information booklet about the Klondike and the way to get there (only one way, of course), and persuaded the Secretary of State of Washington to print it and send it out in the name of the state government. The federal State Department sent copies to the governments of fifteen countries, and in many of these the information was reprinted in official bulletins and in the press. Alaska and Seattle, Seattle and Alaska.

Brainerd had folders of pictures printed, pictures of Alaska and the Klondike and Seattle, and sent them to every library in the country. Elaborate editions of the folders were sent as Christmas cards to every king in Europe and to the presidents of the South American republics. When their secretaries sent letters of thanks, Brainerd turned the letters over to the papers and more news stories went out mentioning Seattle and Alaska in the same paragraph. The best story of all came from Germany: the Kaiser's staff had been afraid to open the package containing the pictures—they thought it was a bomb.

When the *Post-Intelligencer* printed its special Klondike edition Brainerd's committee paid for nearly a hundred thousand copies and sent them to every postmaster in the country, to every library, and to five thousand public officials. Seattle and Alaska, Alaska and Seattle.

Amid the Brainerd-created clamor the other claimant cities barely made themselves heard. They kept trying, but soon almost everyone except residents of the rival coastal cities considered Seattle the gateway to gold. As the publicity went out, the prospectors came in—by the hundreds, by the thousands. The streets were crowded with men, hotels overflowed, and men rented out their barns. "Flop in the hay. Six bits." Prices inched up under the steady demand of men who with their life-savings in their pockets were outfitting themselves for a trip into the unknown. The innocents would buy anything. They were starting on a trip where they would have to climb mountains and float down rivers, but in Seattle they could be persuaded to buy a "still," large as a fifty-pound lard can, in which to purify water. The tenderfeet—the Alaskan epithet "Cheechako" was just coming into use—were suckers for heating equipment. Whatever they did not know about Alaska and Northwest Canada, they were sure it would be cold. One of the products offered in the Alaskan outfitting stores along First Avenue was a burner that would use coal, oil, or gas and fit into anything from an oil can to the largest range. A Cheechako ruefully recalls:

The sample burner kept going by the solicitors seemed to work all right. A lady who had been testing its oven qualities assured me it would "bake potatoes beautifully." As proof she held up a good-sized tuber that had been partially cremated. I bought the burner for $18. We set that coal-oil-gas burner up in our tent. It roared like a small Vesuvius in full eruption. Flames shot from every crack and opening in that stove.

I worked the pump with frantic haste—it was no use, the whole thing was going to blow up. I started for the door of the tent, but a lad who had seen the burners work before said, "There's no danger." He coolly took out his pocket knife, cut the lead connecting pipe, took the burner on a stick, and threw it outdoors. There were a good many suckers in Seattle those days.

The Seattle banks combined to set up an assay office to convert the prospectors' gold to cash, and Brainerd began a successful lobbying campaign to get Congress to assign Seattle a government assay office.

Though he conducted one of the most masterful publicity campaigns of all time on behalf of Seattle, a campaign that helped hundreds of his friends get rich, Brainerd did not cash in on the gold rush himself. Not that he didn't try. While propagandizing for Seattle he also organized a nationwide campaign to get Erastus Brainerd appointed as the United States Consul in Dawson, Yukon Territory. Twelve senators, nine governors, and numerous representatives, editors, bankers, businessmen, and collectors of etchings wrote to the State Department, urging creation of a Dawson consulship and Brainerd's appointment; but this was a Brainerd campaign that failed. He was left in Seattle to watch his friends and associates grow rich off the people and trade he had helped to attract.

Every business prospered. Real-estate values boomed. Papers increased their circulation. Anyone who owned or could lease a ship, no matter how old, no matter how unseaworthy, could find passengers. One captain hitched a series of rafts behind the ship, loaded two hundred passengers and a herd of cattle aboard the rafts, and started north. When a storm blew up in the Gulf of Alaska he had to be restrained from cutting the rafts adrift. When the party landed at Dutch Harbor he sold his passengers the cattle that had come with them—at a mark-up of a thousand per cent a head.

Ships were needed desperately, and Brainerd's friend, Robert Moran, who had been mayor at the time of the fire, went to work to meet the demand. Brainerd recalled later, "When I went to Seattle, Bob Moran simply had an ordinary boat-building establishment and a little marine railway on which he could haul up schooners and all that sort of thing. Shortly after that he took a contract to build a harbor tug for the Revenue Cutter Service, which he built successfully. Then he built a torpedo boat for the government. Then he built fourteen river steamboats for the Yukon River, the trade in that country being started then. And, by the way, he personally navigated those fourteen river stern-wheel steamboats of three and a half feet draft through the North Pacific Ocean and Bering Sea to St. Michael—one of the most astonishing feats that ever was done in the way of navigation." With Moran's success the Seattle shipbuilding industry was firmly established.

Of all the entrepreneurs who benefited by the gold rush, none did better than the operators of the saloons and the brothels and the dance halls along the Skid Road. With thousands of single men pouring into the city, men with money to spend and time to kill, the prostitutes were not far behind. Within two years after the strike in the Klondike, Seattle had become, according to a government report, one of the three main American centers of the white-slave traffic. There were more saloons in the business district than there were restaurants or drygoods stores. The town was wide-open and swarmed with easy-money men, some going, some coming, and some satisfied to stay in Seattle. It was along the Skid Road that the most famous of Alaska's bad men, Soapy Smith, rounded up the gang that eventually operated the town of Skagway as its private enterprise. Soapy Smith—like Erastus Brainerd—was a part-time genius. He took a weird bunch of individualists, men who went by the names of Fatty Green and Kid Jimmy Fresh, Yank Fewclothes and Jay Bird Slim, and organized them into a syndicate that not only ran all the gambling and robbery at the southern end of the gold trail, but even took over the United States Army Recruiting Station at Skagway during the Spanish-American War and assigned men to pick the pockets of the recruits who were taking their physicals. Soapy did not profit personally from his endeavors. When he was killed

in a duel with the civil engineer who had laid out the town
(and who, like Soapy, felt a proprietary interest in Skagway) Soapy's estate was a hundred dollars in cash and a
satchelful of marked cards.

As for Brainerd, he finally went to Alaska and worked
there as a "mining consultant." He did not prosper. Back
Outside, as Alaskans say, he went to Washington, D.C., as
representative of the Seattle Chamber of Commerce. In
1904 he became editor of the Post-Intelligencer and, as
representative of the Better Element, engaged in a historic
journalistic duel with Colonel Blethen of the Times, the
spokesman for an open-town policy. Brainerd lost. He
moved to Tacoma and died there on Christmas Day,
1922. His death did not make the front page of either of
the papers he had edited, and his obituaries did not men-
tion that he had made Seattle the gateway to the gold
rush.

The wealth brought to Seattle by the prospectors who
heeded Brainerd's carefully sounded calls helped finance
the work of another local genius, Reginald H. Thomson,
who was city engineer during the years of the city's
greatest growth. Without Brainerd, Seattle might not have
tripled its population in a decade, climbing from 80,671
in 1900 to 237,194 in 1910; without Thomson, it could
not have handled the newcomers.

An Indianan of Scotch descent, Thomson was twenty-
five years old when he came to Seattle in 1881. A precise,
schoolteacherish Presbyterian, he decided at once that the
town "was in a pit and that to get anywhere we would be
compelled to climb." But when he became city engineer
in 1891, instead of climbing, he dug. He dug a sewer
north to Lake Union, an enormous sewer, "far too large
for a city of forty thousand" some taxpayers complained.
Next he laid a pipeline over the hills from the Cedar
River and argued the City Council into eighty thousand
acres of land in the watershed to prevent pollution.
With sanitation and the water supply attended to,
Thomson turned his attention to the walls of the pit.

The pit was formed by hills that rose abruptly from the
bay. The most awkward of the hills were Denny Hill,

which blocked the city's expansion northward toward Lake Union; Dearborn Hill, which stood between the business district and expansion toward Lake Washington; and Jackson Hill, which cut off easy access to the White River valley. The grades on streets over the hills were twenty per cent in some places; they were impossible for horse-drawn vehicles. Thomson felt that the bottleneck formed by the hills was the only real threat to Seattle's continued growth. In 1898 he began to apply to the hills the sluicing methods used in Alaskan mining. He literally washed the tops off them.

Denny Hill went first; five million cubic yards of earth were sluiced down onto the tideflats and the maximum grade on the north-south streets was reduced to five per cent. Another three million cubic yards came off the Jackson Hill, and two million from Dearborn Hill. In all, sixteen million cubic yards were washed away, and when Thomson was through, traffic could move easily north and south. Ballard and West Seattle were brought within the city limits.

By 1910 the city was level enough to take advantage of the automobile, which greatly increased land transportation. Most traffic along the Sound had to flow through Seattle, and the city's dominance of the region was secure. Seattle was no longer a leading Washington city. It was the metropolis.

IV

Hiram Gill and the
Newspapers, 1910-1918

1.

The meeting of the city council droned on. The evening
was warm and the discussion routine. Hiram C. Gill, president of the Seattle city council, had removed his coat and
was sitting in shirt sleeves, toying with an unlit pipe. A
man hurried through the double doors at the end of the
hall, which had been wedged open, and came up to the
rail that shut off the councilmen's portion of the hall. He
motioned to Gill, and the council president came over to
the rail. The man whispered something. Gill nodded,
went back to the table, interrupted the speaker to explain that he had been called out on business, and turned
the gavel over to one of his colleagues.

The duty that called the council president away from
the meeting was connected with civic affairs: the police
had just raided the town's largest brothel. Gill, as the lawyer for the Skid Road brothelkeepers, was expected to arrange bail. After seeing that his clients were released,
Gill went back to attend to council business, and the
girls returned to the house to attend to theirs.

Gill's extracurricular activity during the city council
meeting brought some angry comment from the righteous,
particularly from a gaunt, long-maned Presbyterian minister named Mark A. Matthews, but no one was surprised.
There never had been any question where Hiram C. Gill
stood with regard to harlots, pimps, and gamblers. He was

a lawyer, they were potential clients. Society paid judges
to pass on the conduct of their fellow men and Hi wasn't a
judge.

Gill was a skinny man with a bulging forehead and
thinning hair. An Eastern reporter visiting Seattle described him as having a "pinched, triangular face, a nervous twitching mouth, and keen but shifty blue eyes." It
was an unkind description, but certainly Hi was no beauty. He knew it too. Physically undistinguished, he was
shrewd enough to adopt sartorial trademarks that made it
easy for voters to recognize him—a white string tie, a
Stetson hat, and a corncob pipe. He was a fake hick. He'd
been to law school in Wisconsin and his father had been a
colonel in the Grand Army of the Republic, but Hi assid-
uously acted the role of lubber. He was careful to appear
often in shirt sleeves; he was self-consciously casual in his
speech. "I'll be just the same as now if I'm elected may-
or," he told the voters after he filed for office in 1910. "If
Bill Taft comes to Seattle I'll wash my face and put on a
dress suit. But I'll smoke a cob pipe if I want to, as long
as I teach no one else the habit."

Gill believed in letting people alone. If a man wanted to
go to hell, Hi was unwilling to set up roadblocks. He
didn't believe morality could be enforced by legislation
and he didn't believe it was healthy to try to keep a town
closed, especially a seaport town on the frontier. Strict law
enforcement, he argued, merely drove prostitution and
gambling underground.

"Somewhere in this city," Gill wrote in a formal statement of his views, "occupying about a hundredth of one
per cent of its area, these unfortunates, whose lives are
gone, most of them beyond recall, will go. They will move
out of the resident districts and the apartment houses and
hotels of this city. They will stay out." In a off-the-cuff
campaign speech he phrased it more naturally. "What
Seattle needs is a mayor who will get a chief of police to
handle the restricted district, who will back the chief up
when the delegations of citizens call and protest—one who
will stand by the chief of police. And I'm the bird."

He was too. On March 7, 1910, the voters elected him

mayor of Seattle by five thousand votes. "I don't pretend to be a very good man," Hi said when he was sworn in, "but I know the law and will enforce it."

To enforce the law for Seattle's 230,000 inhabitants, Hi picked a peculiar instrument. As chief of police he named Charles W. Wappenstein.

2.

Gill's chief was the same Wappenstein whose grafting had led to William Meredith's resignation and, indirectly, to his death at the hands of John Considine. Wappy as he was almost invariably called by friend and opponent, was a mixture of frontiersman, tout, and Tammany politico. He was a softspoken man of considerable personal warmth. Physically he was short and a bit shaggy, with a scraggly mustache, a great wart on his left cheek, and owlish circles around his eyes. He affected tight pin-stripe suits and narrow-brimmed derbies. He looked, according to the *Post-Intelligencer*, which didn't admire him, "like a somewhat disreputable walrus."

Even that paper admitted that Wappy was an able policeman; when he wanted to, he could enforce the law with the best. But he had come of age in Cincinnati, when Cincinnati was perhaps the most corrupt city in the country, and when he migrated to Seattle in 1898 he found a wide-open town. He had no trouble adapting his morals to those of gold-rush Seattle; in fact he adapted them a little too well, with the result that he was kicked out by Mayor Humes. Wappy then went to work as an investigator for the Great Northern and became a protégé of J. D. Farrell, a highly political vice-president of the railroad. Farrell, though nominally a Democrat like his employer, Jim Hill, became something of a Republican boss in Washington State, dominating the votes of the Republican majority on issues affecting the railroads. In 1906 Judge William Hickman Moore, a milk-and-water reformer, was the Fusion candidate for mayor, running on a platform that called for a closed city and municipal ownership of utilities. Boss Farrell's brother worked in Judge Moore's law office; to the amazement of the reformers, Farrell threw his support to Moore. It turned the trick. Moore won the closest election in the history of Seattle's minicipal politics. All that Farrell asked in return for his support was the appointment as chief of police of his friend and protégé, Charles Wappenstein. Moore's reformist friends raised anguished objections, but the grateful mayor appointed Wappy, and Wappy gave the town what one of the reformers called "the best police administration Seattle ever had." In 1908 Judge Moore was defeated for reelection, and Wappy lost his job to a friend of the new mayor. Wappy was bitter. "You see," he told friends, "people don't really want a clean city. They just say they do." When Gill chose him to give Seattle the sort of police administration they had voted for in 1910, Wappy was ready to oblige.

The six months following Gill's inauguration must have been the happiest of Wappy's life. The mayor had said he wanted a chief who could run the restricted district, and Wappy knew just how it should be run: wide open.

On the afternoon of the day he was sworn in, Wappy strolled into Gerald's Bar Room and closeted himself with Clarence Gerald, the manager of the saloon, and Gideon Tupper, two of the more important figures in Seattle night life.

"There will be a chance for all of us to make some money," Wappy told them happily. Then he moved from the general economic picture to the particulars of supply and demand. He told Tupper to lease the Midway, a cribhouse of more than a hundred rooms, and to open up as soon as possible. Tupper did. Once the Midway was in operation, Wappy called Tupper to the police station, complimented him on his quick work, and suggested that it would be a good idea to open the Paris House on a similar basis. Tupper tried to oblige, but reported back that he couldn't get a lease; the owner of the building thought Tupper was not financially responsible. Wappy told the discouraged entrepreneur not to worry; he'd fix things. He got on the phone and told the hesitant landlord that Tupper was "all right" and that he himself stood ready to guarantee Tupper's financial integrity. Soon the Paris House was in business too.

Wappy had a politician's natural desire to be helpful to his supporters, but in his aid to Gerald and Tupper he was actuated by other considerations as well. As Tupper explained to a grand jury later, "He agreed on my paying him ten dollars a woman.... It was monthly. The first payment was made along, I think, about the first of May. It was one thousand dollars. I made the same payments every month ... in his office."

At ten dollars per month per harlot, Wappy was doing all right financially. There were at least five hundred women in the Skid Road establishments, and the Chief knew the whereabouts of each of them. He turned the talents which made him, even in the eyes of an enemy, "a master detective" toward seeing he was not short-changed on protection payments. The cops who patrolled the Skid Road were required to make periodic reports on the number of girls in each house. An occasional patrolman made trouble by raiding an establishment where protection had been paid, or by engaging in a shakedown on his private initiative, but such mavericks were quickly transferred to outlying residential districts or put to pounding beats along the windswept stretches of the waterfront. Wappy had everything under control.

His interest extended beyond putting Seattle's sex on a paying basis. While Tupper organized the bigger brothels under his supervision, Gerald, who ran the barroom where Mayor Gill and his cronies met for lunch, took over the city's gambling. He bought into the Northern Club, a gaming establishment, which under his direction became in the eyes of a national magazine "one of the greatest spectacles of the Pacific Northwest."

Several national magazines, most noticeably *Harper's* and *McClure's*, began to pay attention to the peculiar law-enforcement practices in Seattle. Reporters for *McClure's* had been raking through the muck of municipal corruption from one end of the country to the other, but one of *McClure's* case-hardened muckrakers found the size and openness of the Northern Club's gambling operations hard to believe. *McClure's* said flatly after the Northern had been closed:

No American city has ever seen anything comparable with it. The most hardened sports after a glimpse at the club's openly exhibited wonders would telegraph to their pals to come to Seattle and inspect it, if only as a curiosity.

In order not to lose any possible patronage, the Northern Club ran twenty-four hours a day, including Sunday, utilizing the services of three shifts of employees. At the door barkers were regularly stationed. "Gambling upstairs, gentlemen," they would call to the passing crowds. There were "cappers" located at convenient points who made a specialty of teaching high-school boys how to beat the game—instruction which, as these young men subsequently learned, was entirely misleading. Respected and prosperous businessmen frequently found their sons in possession of membership cards giving them entree to this institution. In the main, however, introductions were not required.

A few days after the club opened, a self-appointed committee of Seattle lawyers, curious to learn how Gill was redeeming his open-town pledge, made the rounds. They found the Northern Club filled to suffocation with two or three hundred of their fellow citizens, and from sixty to eighty attendants were solicitously providing for their needs. Everywhere the wheels were clicking and the bones were rolling. A particularly impressive sight was a heavily gold-braided police captain who benignantly elbowed his way in and out of the throng.

Seattle was wide open, all right. What of Hi Gill's promise that "these unfortunates" who lived with sin would "move away from the resident areas"? That promise was broken. The uptown joints didn't close. High-class whores remained in the high-class hotels. The more select gaming rooms in the business district stayed put. There was one noticeable difference after the restricted area began unrestricted operation: gambling games blossomed everywhere. *McClure's* reported:

The city seemed to have been transformed almost magically into one great gambling hell. All kinds of games simultaneously started up, in full view of the public. Cigar stores and barbershops did a lively business in crap-shooting and race-track gambling, drawing their patronage largely from school-boys and department-store girls. In the back of the billiard rooms, poker games were operating as openly as in a mining town. All over the city "flat-joints," pay-off stations, and dart-shooting galleries were reaping a rapid harvest. At one time it looked as if the whole of Seattle were going mad over faro, roulette, blackjack, and numerous other forms of entertainment provided in the thirty or forty gambling-places opened up under the administration of Hi Gill.

If Gill had kept his promise to open the Skid Road and close the rest of the town, he might have avoided serious trouble, for Seattle wanted a bit of a fling when it elected him. But as Gill put it himself, "I may have let things get away from me." Wappy's two associates, Tupper and Gerald, got farthest away; not content with their profit-making enterprises south of Yesler Way, they decided to establish a super-Skid Road on Beacon Hill. They formed a new corporation, the Hillside Improvement Company, and peddled its stock, successfully, on the Seattle market. Local buyers knew that the corporation's greatest asset was the cooperation it was certain to get from the city administration. The Improvement Company purchased several acres of land in the southern part of town and hired architects to plan a model red-light district. The central feature in the planned community was to be a five-hundred-room brothel, the biggest in the world. When construction was about to begin, the contractors found their work would be simpler if they were to build eighty feet west of the original site. There was one trouble: most of that eighty feet was occupied by a Seattle street, so the city council thoughtfully granted the Hillside Improve-

ment Company a fifteen-year lease on the thoroughfare. A
contemporary observer remarked, "American cities have
voted away their streets to gas companies, electric-light
lines, and street railways, but Seattle is the first one that
ever granted a franchise to a public thoroughfare for the
erection of a brothel."

The huge building was completed by the autumn of
1911, but it was never occupied by the tenants for whom
it was designed. Gill's boys had gone too far. The great
barn on Beacon Hill became a symbol of the administration.[1] Preachers and the press opened up on vice conditions, with the *Post-Intelligencer* hitting the hardest:

Gillism has allowed enforcers of the law to enter into lewd
partnership with breakers of the law. It has allowed gambling.
It has allowed and encouraged graft in the police department.
It has allowed a gang of pink-cuff vagrants to plunder the
fallen women of the city. It has encouraged drunkenness and
debauchery. It has permitted dance-hall orgies so shameless
in character that they would have shocked the maudlin
voluptuaries of the ancient capitals. It has licensed the
libertine to prey upon the innocent girlhood of the community. It has shielded sleek vultures who make chattels of
women. It has loosened the safe and reasonable restraints of
the law so that the criminal could go his wicked way un-
afraid because unmolested. It has demoralized the departments of the city and reduced their efficiency. It has fostered
and encouraged a species of governmental and official favoritism wholly at variance with the spirit and genius of American
political institutions and American law.

3.

It was "the spirit and genius of American political
institutions and American law" that made possible the
correction of Gillism.

In 1906 Seattle had inserted into its city charter an

[1] The building was destroyed in August 1951, when a B-50 from
Boeing Field crashed into it.

amendment permitting the voters to use, whenever the occasion should arise, the latest device of American democratic machinery—the recall. Its operation was simple. If you wanted to get a man out of office, you had to collect the signatures of one-fourth of the registered voters on a recall petition. When you got that number, a special election would be held between forty and fifty days after the recall petitions were filed with the city controller. The recall election was like any other election. The name of the official under attack would go on the ballot unless he refused to stand (in which case he forfeited office); other candidates could be named in the way they were nominated in an ordinary campaign. If the incumbent received more votes than any opponent, he was considered to be vindicated and the recall was defeated; if another candidate received a plurality, the official was recalled.

Gill had been in office only a few weeks before conditions got so bad that the first petitions for his recall appeared on the streets. The charges listed on the petition included "incompetence and unfitness" and "abuse of the appointive power," but the important ones were "refusal and neglect to enforce the criminal laws of the city; permitting the city to become a home and refuge for the criminal classes; and failure to enforce impartially the laws and ordinances." For these reasons, it was set forth, Gill's continuance in office constituted a menace to the business enterprises and moral welfare of the city.

For a time few people were willing to sign the petitions. Many voters, especially businessmen and city employees, were afraid to offend the city hall. Some voters who opposed Gill also opposed the newfangled elective device by which it was proposed to oust him; and nearly half of the voters wanted Gill to stay just where he was. The Times served as spokesman for this group; Colonel Blethen thundered and volleyed at the very idea that vice could be suppressed.

Gill was so sure the storm would blow over that he left for Alaska on a yacht owned by a prominent gambler. That was a tactical error. While he was away, the acting mayor, a conscientious person, suspended Wappenstein and named a committee to investigate the Skid Road conditions. Gill came steaming back, but the damage was done: the *Post-Intelligencer* spread the news about local vice all over page one. The recall drive began to do better. The churches sponsored it; Gill's old enemy, the pure and publicity-minded Dr. Matthews, fumed against Gillism and Graftitis in every sermon. From many pulpits one of the regular Sunday announcements was that at the close of the service the men in the congregation would have an opportunity to show how they felt about the Open City Excesses; standing beside the minister at the door would be a canvasser with an anti-Gill petition. The labor unions, the YMCA, and finally some of the department stores helped to circulate the petitions. At one stage there were four hundred full-time canvassers rounding up signatures. Then help came from an unexpected source.

In November 1910, while petitions were still being circulated, the men of Seattle voted to give Seattle woman the ballot, restoring the right they had lost in 1887. It was assumed that the female voter would be more moral than the male, and Gill's supporters feared what would happen if the women got a chance to vote on the open-city issue. Once it became apparent that there would be enough signatures to force an election eventually, the Gill people quietly threw their weight behind the drive: if there had to be a recall vote, they wanted it to come before the suffrage legislation took effect.

The anti-vice people weren't quite as amateurish as the professionals hoped: they merely refrained from filing the petitions until late December. Shortly before Christmas half a dozen men, led by the head of the Public Welfare League, marched self-consciously into the city controller's office. Each carried an armload of petitions. They passed them across the desk to the controller, who, in a photo taken at that historic moment, looked pained. It was the first time in the history of the Northwest, the second time in the history of the country,[2] that a public figure had been forced to account for his stewardship.

[2] The mayor of Los Angeles, faced with a recall election the previous year, had resigned.

Gill, a free-swinging orator of the old school, took to the stump to tell the people his side of the case. He didn't make any pretense of being perfect, he said, but he was better than the dogs, the skunks, the puppies, and the hypocrites who opposed him. "I want you to overlook my faults and give me credit for what I do," he told the voters. "Look at the number of arrests during my administration. Look at the revenue derived from the fines in police court." Both were admittedly higher than during the closed-town administration that preceded him. Anti-Gill people argued that higher fines meant a greater turnover in crime business rather than stricter enforcement.

"This proposition of holding office is a tough one," Gill assured the electorate, "but I will continue to be mayor. I don't care how large a majority is against me. . . . Public decency is not the issue in this campaign. What do you care for the detriment some cuss suffers from shooting craps?"

The Forces of Decency, as the reformers styled themselves, picked as their knight-errant a bland real-estate man named George W. Dilling, who was nominally a Progressive Republican. His chief appeal was that, except for a sole term in the state legislature, he had avoided politics. Nobody was sore at him—except, of course, choleric Colonel Blethen, who remarked in the *Times*, "Dilling is running on his record as a good husband."

The real invective came from Gill. As he warmed up to the campaign, he told his audiences that Dilling "hadn't got the brains of an underfed microbe." When he learned that a local millionaire had contributed some money to the reform group, Hi spoke of the donation as a "twentieth-century marvel," because the donor was notorious as "a tightwad by comparison with which the bark on a tree appears like the loosest Mother Hubbard."

The Reverend Dr. Matthews toured the Skid Road to get firsthand information on vice conditions. After the cleric had told his congregation of the horrors he had seen below the line, Gill asked, "What was the bachelor, that unmarried young man, doing in a place like that? How did he know where to go? He knew his way around. Don't believe anything that wizard oil artist tells you." When one of the minister's colleagues rebuked Gill for the implications of the speech, Gill called that divine "another tramp." A layman who defended both ministers was characterized as "a senile old dude," and the Forces of Decency in general he dismissed as "a lot of ringtails," while their consorts were "a bunch of magpies."

The latter epithet was aimed mainly at the Women for Dilling, an organization that campaigned vigorously for the recall. Its main job was to make sure that women registered in time to vote. The registration committee coined the artless logan, "Women—Get Out and Hustle." Not all the campaigning on the distaff side was on behalf of Dilling and Decency. The Skid Road maques herded their protégés to the city hall and registered them en masse. A spokesman for Dilling complained querulously that "a steady stream of fallen women are appearing to register, almost the entire female population of the tender loin signing up, many of them foreigners who do not even know the language, many of them imported into the town within the last few weeks from New Orleans and El Paso but claiming long residence. And what respectable man can prove them liars?"

On election day in February 1911, less than a year after Gill's inauguration, 36,000 men and 22,000 women voted. Gill was defeated. Political analysts of the day guessed that the women's vote had been decisive. Dilling's majorities were largest in the districts where the vote had increased the most, presumably those in which women had registered. The correspondent for the New York Tribune pointed out that "the downtown precincts gave Gill large pluralities, which were offset by the vote from the residence districts, where the influence of the women was mostly felt."

Gill, commenting on his defeat, told a reporter, "Wait a few months. Let 'em try to run this city closed. I don't think anybody can do it without direct intervention of the Almighty."

Mayor Dilling made an earnest effort to close the town. He removed Wappenstein as chief of police. Word went out to the brothelkeepers that in most cases no fix could be made. The exodus from the Skid Road was immediate. According to one account, nearly two hundred women left on one train. It was a strange spectacle. "A few of the girls were weeping but many were in their gaudiest finery. Some were accompanied by their pink-cuffed fancy men. A crowd of spectators had assembled to see them off and the girls took their pleasure in calling old customers by name and waving at respected men whose names they did not know." They bought tickets for towns as distant as Buffalo and as close as Tacoma, Everett, and Bellingham. Within a month after the election, police estimated that more than half of the Skid Road women had left town. Others took apartments.

Meanwhile a grand jury studied the organization of vice in Seattle under the Gill administration. After listening to the testimony of the town's most prominent gamblers and madams, the jury indicted Wappenstein and his two henchmen, Gideon Tupper and Clarence Gerald. To the surprise of nobody, they were tried, convicted, and sentenced to the state penitentiary. The jury also made one indictment that came as a shock to much of the community. The man was the editor and publisher of the *Seattle Times*, Colonel Alden J. Blethen.

4.

Alden J. Blethen was the dominant figure in Seattle's journalism. He may have been the most brilliant newspaperman ever to operate in Seattle, and he certainly was the most controversial. Few Seattle citizens found it possible to be non-partisan about him; he himself was one of the least non-partisan men who ever lived. It is quite possible that, as his enemies claimed, people bought the *Times* because they wanted to see "what the big-headed bastard is up to now"; but they bought more copies of his paper than they did of any other, and whatever the motives behind these purchases they enabled Blethen to grow rich and powerful.

Seattle journalism was thirty-three years old when Blethen came to town in 1896. The first issue of Seattle's first paper, the *Gazette*, had creaked off a battered Ramage screw press[8] on the second floor of Henry Yesler's office building at Front and Mill Streets (now South First and Yesler Way) on December 10, 1863. The *Gazette* was written and edited and put in type by James R. Watson, a frontier newspaperman who had found the competition too strenuous in the big town of Olympia; an Indian boy worked the ancient press whenever there was enough news and advertising matter to fill the four 9½-by 14½-inch pages. This was not often. In the depressed days of the early sixties there was not much to buy or sell, nor were there so many people in town that everybody didn't know everything that happened as soon as it happened. The *Gazette* suspended publication for the summer of 1864. In the fall, though, an event occurred that changed the pattern of pioneer journalism. The Western Union telegraph line reached Seattle.

At four p.m. on October 26, 1864, the wire clacked out its first telegraphic story. The dispatch was from Chattanooga and dealt with General Billy Sherman's progress in Georgia. (He was maneuvering against General Hood

---

[8] The *Gazette's* equipment was historic. The press was a model developed in 1796. Built in New York, it was shipped to Mexico in 1832 and from there to Monterey, California, where it was used for printing the proclamations of the Spanish governor. In 1846 it ran off the first newspaper in California, the *Californian*, a tiny sheet in Spanish and English, devoted mostly to American naval and military pronouncements about the Mexican War. (Since the equipment was Mexican, the editor was bothered by a type font that contained no W's, which—he told his readers—was why "vve must use tvvo V's." The press was moved to San Francisco in 1847, and there it was used first by the *Star*, then by the *Alta California*, the best of the early West Coast papers. When the *Alta California* needed more modern equipment, the press was shipped to Portland and was used for the first issues of the *Oregonian*. The *Oregonian* soon outgrew it, and the press again sailed north. In Olympia it printed the *Columbian*, the first paper in Washington Territory. Watson brought it to Seattle in 1863. It outlived the *Gazette* and was in on another birth, that of the *Intelligencer*. The old press is now in the museum of the University of Washington.

in the campaign against Atlanta.) Watson issued his first extra.

The Western Union wire meant that the paper could get news ahead of the populace, but tolls were high and Watson didn't have enough money to pay them. He thought up a frontier-style solution. Whenever the telegraph operator climbed the wooden steps to the *Gazette* office to say a war dispatch had arrived, Watson would visit the town's more prosperous merchants and collect two bits each from them. With this money he'd pay the collect charges on the wire; then he'd set the dispatch in type, pull a galleyproof for each man who had contributed a quarter, and save the type for publication whenever a new issue was possible. Even with such ingenious publishing devices the *Gazette* was unable to survive more than three years.

The pattern of desperate improvisation set by Watson was followed by later editors, usually with no more success. The most charming of the early-day failures was *The Figaro*, a lively one-sheet daily that survived a scant fortnight and in its final issue invited all non-subscribers, who were legion, to go to hell. It was more usual for a Seattle paper to expire with a whimper ("In view of the lack of response to our appeal for all those who owe us money to pay their just debts, we are forced to suspend ...") than with a curse and a bang.

The first paper to show stamina was the *Intelligencer*, which began as a weekly in 1867 and eleven years later was strong enough to add a daily edition. The *Intelligencer* absorbed the *Puget Sound Dispatch* in 1879, then in 1881 combined with the three-year-old *Post*. Through the eighties the *Post-Intelligencer* was easily the dominant paper in town, first under the editorship of Thomas Prosch and after 1886 under Leigh Hunt. Hunt ran an interesting paper, but he also ran up a lot of debts, and the panic of '93 forced him to sell. For half a decade the paper staggered along under editors who were either too literary or else so passionately anti-Populist in a Populist era that readers gathered below the office windows at Post and Yesler to sing lynching songs. Politically minded John L.

Wilson purchased the paper in 1899 with four hundred thousand dollars lent to him by Jim Hill. According to accepted legend, the railroad tycoon became interested in Wilson in 1896 when he sent Wilson a check for ten thousand dollars to be used by the Republicans in the election; Wilson sent it back with the prediction, which proved correct, that the state was hopelessly Populist and suggested that Hill might as well save his money. Hill replied with thanks for such foresighted pessimism and added that if Wilson ever needed anything to let him know. In 1899 Wilson heard that the *Post-Intelligencer* could be had for a down payment of fifty thousand dollars and sent Hill a wire letting him know. Hill wired back that the money had been deposited in Wilson's name in a New York bank. Wilson ran an interesting paper which, though it had a strong Republican bias, never engaged in the outright fabrications that sometimes graced the pages of its only dangerous rival, the *Times*. Wilson was handicapped, though, by having to siphon off money to repay Hill, almost half a million dollars in principal and interest.

The *Times* did not spring from such hardy or expensive stock as the *Post-Intelligencer*. It was the lineal descendant of the *Chronicle*, which was born in 1881 and, after achieving an Associated Press franchise, disappeared in 1886, when it was merged with the *Call*; the combined papers were renamed the *Press*. Soon afterward, the *Press* combined with a small sheet called the *Times* and for a while appeared as the *Press-Times*, with Erastus Brainerd as editor. Blethen bought the plant of the bankrupt *Press-Times* in 1896 for less than a tenth of what Wilson had to pay for his paper three years later at the height of the gold rush. He lopped off the first name of the hybrid and embarked on an editorial policy which was at once vigorous, spectacular, and bewildering. In six months he pushed circulation from three thousand to seven thousand, with corresponding gains in advertising linage.

Blethen was a stocky, powerful man with a leonine head which seemed larger than it really was because he wore his curly hair in a senatorial bob. When he came to

Seattle in 1896 he was forty-nine years old, strong, impe-
rious, and hot-tempered. Old newspapermen say that after
a telephone conversation in which Blethen learned of a
successful maneuver on the part of his greatest rival,
Wilson, he ripped the phone from the wall and hurled it
toward the P-I building, half a mile away. He had a
remarkable memory—he is one of the men who supposed-
ly could draw a line across a map of the United States,
and then name every county the line crossed—and he had
a considerable talent for invective. He concealed an almost unlimited vulgarity behind a façade of formal education. He loved children and soldiers and animals; he
sometimes wept when he watched the flag being lowered;
he never seemed to doubt that he was a hundred per cent
right. His colossal self-confidence is surprising in light of
his pre-Seattle career.

During the half-century between his birth in Maine and
his arrival on Puget Sound, Blethen had been compara-
tively unsuccessful as a teacher and as a lawyer. He had
served as principal of a rural school in Maine and had
practiced law in Portland for seven years before leaving
his native state. In Kansas City, where he deserted the law
for journalism, he made a Horatio Alger rise to the editorship of the Journal. In 1884 he left Kansas City and
bought into both the Minneapolis Journal and the Minneapolis Tribune; he sold his interests there in 1888 for a
quarter of a million dollars, then bought them back the
next year, only to be wiped out in the panic of '93. When
he reached Seattle he had a twenty-five-thousand-dollar
credit, unlimited confidence, and the rather synthetic title
of colonel.

Blethen was no military man. He had gained his title by
serving on the staff of the Governor of Minnesota in a
political rather than a military post, but which left him, in
the phrase of a Washington congressman, "confused with
Napoleon." He worshiped all things military and his attitude toward "our soldier boys" was at best maudlin and at
worst pathological. Not even Hearst fought the battles of

raising it on top of the Times Building; he put the flag at
the masthead of his paper too, and on the front page;
when his opponents objected that no man should use the
flag as a personal trademark he chided them for "resenting
the display of Old Glory." This trick of replying to an
attack with an attack was typical of his operations. He
never apologized, never side-stepped, and never defended
himself; he just ripped into anyone who opposed him. To
suggest that Blethen might be wrong was to prove yourself
an unpatriotic crackpot in the pay of red-flag anarchists.

Blethen believed in an open town—or, more precisely,
in an open but regulated restricted district. He was positive that virtue could not be legislated. He opposed prohi-
bition on principle, and he was against reformers by pure
reflex. But, on occasion, he attacked the Skid Road operators who he felt had gone too far or who had the backing
of people he didn't like. He was against John Considine,
probably because Considine was "the P-I's favorite
gambler." He was against John Cort too, because a police
chief Blethein disliked allowed Cort to run a box-house
north of Yesler Way. He was for Hi Gill and he fought
the recall bitterly, asking no quarter from the crackpot
reformers and giving them none. He had no more respect
for Dr. Matthews than he had for Karl Marx. He railed
against the "best citizens' who were upset about sin and
saloons with the same vigor that he attacked the Wobblies
who were upset about conditions in the lumber camps.

Human nature being what it is, some of the Better
People suspected that Blethen might have a financial as
well as an idealistic interest in the Skid Road vice. When
the grand jury under Foreman Charles W. Corliss, who
was a Republican and a Presbyterian and a closed-town
advocate, began its eleven-month study of the organization
of Seattle's vice, it checked on Blethen's real-estate holdings. Nothing was found to support the rumors that the
colonel had a number of houses south of Yesler Way,
but the jury learned that Blethen was part owner of
the Morrison Hotel, a large brick building that housed,
among other things, a gambling establishment. Since there
was a law against owning buildings used for illegal pur-

poses, the grand jury returned an indictment of the publisher.

When the case finally came to court high-minded Judge James T. Ronald, a reformer and a Democrat, felt the connection described by the government as existing between Blethen and the vice lords was too tenuous. He directed the jury to bring in a verdict for the defendant. Blethen did not even have to take the witness stand in his own defense. It was not until two years later, when the colonel became involved in a battle against a mayor he considered a red-flag anarchist, that the public learned the peculiar method by which he had intended to discredit the people who had brought him to dock.

5.

After the recall there was no peace for the wicked, but the righteous had their troubles too.

George Dilling finished out the time Gill would have served as mayor. In the next regular election in 1912 the voters had a clear-cut choice between good and evil—at the very least, between a closed town and an open town: Hiram Gill versus George Cotterill.

Cotterill was a solidly built, youngish civil engineer of forty-seven, a politician of liberal-reformist kidney. He had served as assistant city engineer under that cross-grained genius Reginald H. Thomson, and had helped to formulate the plans for reconstructing the water-supply system of Seattle and the topography of part of Puget Sound. Though Cotterill's first political leanings had been Republican (he came to Seattle from England by way of New Jersey), he became disgusted with the local GOP because, as the dominant party, it was being wooed and won by open-town advocates. William Jennings Bryan's cross-of-gold oration won Cotterill for the Democrats, and he usually supported them, though he had nothing against Populists, Silver Republicans, and Bull Moosers. In 1902 Cotterill ran against Tom Humes, "a race for principle, not for office," he later called it. In 1912 the reform element picked him to try again. This time Cotterill made it, defeating Gill, to the disgust of the *Times*.

Colonel Blethen was in a pet. All the sacred orthodoxies were being overthrown. The direct primary ended the party-convention system, and candidates in city elections ran without the official backing of political parties. Women had suffrage. The reformers captured the city government. The state not only cast its seven electoral votes for the Progressives in 1912, but the Republicans finished third, far behind the Democrats and a bare thirty thousand votes ahead of the despised Socialists. The Colonel got the Wobbly Horrors.

The Wobblies—the Industrial Workers of the World— were active in Seattle. Every night their speakers mounted soapboxes along the Skid Road and sometimes in the business district—even in front of the Times Building. One spring afternoon in 1912 they marched through town in a parade, the red flag flying next to the Stars and Stripes. The police didn't stop them, but the crowd did. There was a small riot as spectators fought the Wobblies for possession of the red flag. From that time on Blethen campaigned against Mayor Cotterill on the issue of "red-flag anarchy." Blethen contended that the mayor, by permitting the Wobblies to talk, was endangering the safety of the community; he argued that, law or no law, the Wobblies should be suppressed; permitting them to carry on their activities was not liberty but license. Cotterill believed that to deny someone the right to speak or to carry a banner when no law prohibited such speeches or banners was "to evade the rule of law and was therefore no way to suppress anarchy. Indeed, such actions would be anarchy."

The dispute came to a climax on a sultry August evening in 1913. Josephus Daniels, the Secretary of the Navy, had been invited to Seattle to speak as part of the Potlatch Days celebration, a jamboree arranged to draw visitors to town during the dog days. After being introduced by Mayor Cotterill to the dignitaries assembled at the ultra-respectable Rainier Club, Daniels made a routine patriotic address, a set speech he had delivered some weeks before in Erie, Pennsylvania. Most of the men present were political opponents of the city administration and they cheered with unusual fervor when Daniels spread the eagle.

While the business community was demonstrating its sympathies at the Club, Mrs. Annie Miller, a pacifist, delivered a speech to a Skid Road crowd from a portable platform she set up on Occidental near Washington Street. As she talked a trio of sailors on leave from Whidbey Island joined the crowd. They heckled the speaker, and she in turn called them drones and burdens on the working class. The crowd was pro-Miller. When she left the stand, one of the sailors mounted it and made a speech too, probably just as patriotic as the speech delivered by the Secretary of the Navy, but it was received with jeers. After a while Mrs. Miller tried to get her stand back from the sailors; it was rented, she said, and if she didn't return it now she'd have to pay overtime. A sailor told her to shut up and raised his fist. Then, according to the sworn statement of several witnesses, "a large well-dressed man, with a diamond ring who bore no resemblance to the typical IWW broke in. 'You would strike a woman!' he shouted, and struck the sailor with his fist a number of times."

Some soldiers rushed to the support of the Navy. The military were roughed up thoroughly before the police came to their rescue. Three of the men were treated at the hospital, but all were released in time to make it back to their stations. Up to this point it was just another street-corner brawl, but then M. M. Mattison, the political reporter for the *Times*, went to work on it. He gave his story the full political treatment:

Practically at the very moment a gang of red-flag worshippers and anarchists were brutally beating two bluejackets and three soldiers who had dared protest against the insults heaped on the American flag at a soap-box meeting on Washington Street last night, Secretary of the Navy Daniels, cheered on by the wildly enthusiastic and patriotic Americans present, flayed as a type the mayor of any city who permits red-flag demonstrations in a community of which he is the head.

Warming to his topic, the Secretary proceeded with a merciless denunciation of the cowardly un-American, who, occupying the highest position in the gift of an American city, fosters anarchy in the streets by permitting the display of the red flag and the demonstrations of its adherents. . . ."

After reporting a version of the street fight in which Mrs. Miller was described as an IWW and was accused of swearing at the sailors and insulting the flag, Mattison closed his account with a series of quotes:

"The participants in last night's outrage ought to be rounded up and driven out of town," said a National Guard regimental commander. A leader of the veterans of the Spanish-American War was quoted as saying that his men would parade past the IWW headquarters "armed with everything from bolos to head axes." And "underground channels" were said to have notified police that a large force of enlisted men would circulate in town that night, ready to "decisively answer any insult."

When the sailors appeared in the evening and smashed up Wobbly headquarters, Mattison was there. After the riot he retired to the *Times* office and wrote his story:

Anarchy, the grizzly hydraheaded serpent which Seattle has been forced to nourish in its midst by a naturalized chief executive for 18 months, was plucked from the city and wiped out in a blaze of patriotism last night. Hundreds of sailors and artillerymen, who carefully planned the entire maneuver yesterday morning, led the thousands of cheering civilians to the attack and successfully wrecked the Industrial Workers of the World headquarters and "direct action" Socialist headquarters in various parts of the business district. . . .

Fired with patriotic enthusiasm and armed only with small American flags, the men in uniform wrecked the Industrial Workers of the World headquarters on Washington Street, demolished the news stand of Millard Price at Fourth Avenue and Pike Street, cleaned out the Industrial Workers of the World office in the Nestor Building on Westlake Avenue and the Socialist halls at the Granite Hotel, Fifth and Virginia, and in an old church at Seventh and Olive Streets.

They also broke into Socialist headquarters and messed things up a bit, then wrecked a gospel mission in the Skid Road; when they discovered their mistake in the latter spot, members of the mob made one of their number kneel and kiss the flag. The active mob, estimated at from a thousand by the *Sun* to twenty thousand by the *Times*, was watched by a huge crowd that had gathered for a Potlatch parade. According to Mattison's story, everyone was happy; Mattison obviously was—his delight echoed in his prose:

The smashing of chairs and tables, the rending of yielding timbers, the creaking and groaning of sundered walls, and above the rest the crash of glass of the windows on the east side all blended together in one grand Wagnerian cacophony. And all the while the crowd outside just howled and cheered. It was almost more joy than they could stand.

It was definitely more than Mayor Cotterill could stand. He felt that the *Times* had stage-managed the riot, and, while it had passed almost without bloodshed—one Wobbly got a broken nose—a resumption of the battle, with the Wobblies ready and the town packed with holiday visitors, might bring on real anarchy. Cotterill assumed personal command of the police and fire departments. He ordered the second platoon of firemen, the men ordinarily off duty, to help police the town. He issued orders that the liquor stores must remain closed on Saturday and Sunday, and that all street meetings and public speaking be suspended. He ordered the chief of police to see to it that no copies of the *Seattle Times* were circulated within the city limits until the following Monday, "unless the proprietors submit to me the entire proofs of any proposed issue and that it be found and certified by me as containing nothing calculated to incite to further riot, destruction of property and danger to human life."

Chief of Police Bannick stationed a force of twenty-five policemen around the Times Building, to see that no copies of the *Times* leaked out, then went to the colonel's office and handed him a copy of the proclamation. When Blethen calmed down enough to be articulate he telephoned his attorney. The lawyer called Judge Humphries at his home—it was a Saturday morning in August and Humphries was the only jurist in town—and asked him to hold court. The judge wrote out bench warrants for Mayor Cotterill and Chief of Police Bannick, ordering them to appear in court at once.

It was early afternoon before the warrants were served and the officials brought before the bar. Judge Humphries, a ponderous man of profoundly conservative views, asked Cotterill what he meant by such interference with freedom of the press. The mayor, using Blethen's own favorite phrase, said that stories as inaccurate as the one that touched off the Potlatch Riot were not an exercise of liberty but of license. The irony of Blethen's paper being suppressed on the ground that it was creating anarchy in its advocacy of suppressing anarchy was lost on Judge Humphries. He was not amused. He issued an order restraining Cotterill from interfering further with the *Times*. (His phrasing indicated that he considered the mayor's action to be in restraint of business rather than a violation of freedom of the press.) But having told Cotterill to remove the police from around the *Times* plant immediately, Humphries proceeded to scold him for almost an hour for overstepping his authority, a lecture the mayor rather enjoyed because as long as he was in the courtroom listening the Times Building was blockaded.

The police were withdrawn by midafternoon. The *Times* hit the streets with an account of the riot and a story about its troubles with Cotterill. It referred to the mayor as "an advocate of anarchy," "the leader of a red-flag gang," and "a loathsome louse," but in general its tone was mild. No one was incited to further riot. The last evening of the Potlatch celebration passed quietly.

On Sunday the *Seattle Sun*,[4] a newborn reformist paper, carried a long statement by the mayor, reviewing his action. He stood four-square on civil liberties for everyone with the possible exception of Colonel Blethen:

From the time I became mayor of the City of Seattle, I have directed constantly that in the making of arrests without warrant no person shall be thus arrested unless the officer making the arrest has information of his own knowledge or evidence from some other person upon which to base a definite charge for the violation of some law or ordinance. So far as I have controlling influence, there has been and shall be no dragging of people to jail for detention and release without charge, or for nominal charge unsustained by evidence or expecting dismissal by the police judge.

. . . On occasion when the *Seattle Times* has printed quoted treasonable statements alleged to have been made by some speaker, I have demanded from the reporter or city editor that they support by evidence a prosecution in the particular case which they claim to have heard. Such request has been refused.

I can not lawfully, nor will I arbitrarily, attempt to suppress or curtail free speech anywhere on suspicion or rumor or *Seattle Times* lies.

In cases where anarchy was openly advocated, as Cotterill felt it had been in the *Times*' story of Daniels' speech and the Skid Road brawl, he would take action. He defended his move in depriving Seattleites of alcohol and Blethen editorials for the duration of the Potlatch as being in the public interest. "I applied every power at command," he said, "to preserve the peace and prevent renewed rioting and threats to life and property. . . . If I can be blown down by a putrid blast from the *Seattle Times*, I have no right or desire to publicly serve."

It was neither the cool civil-libertarian logic nor the hot

[4] The *Sun*, a well-written paper with a first-rate plant, was started in 1912 by men who felt Seattle needed a non-Republican daily. It built up a fair circulation but failed to get much advertising and died in two years.

rhetoric that attracted the most attention in Cotterill's statement. What Seattle buzzed about was his reference to some photographs, doctored and dirty. There had been rumors of these photographs but now the story was out in the open. In May 1912, according to Cotterill, he had gone to Blethen's office to talk over his troubles with the *Times* and to see if some agreement could be reached. But "Blethen was bitter in his denunciation of Dr. Mark A. Matthews, Prosecuting Attorney Murphy, and others connected with the grand jury which had indicted him," Cotterill wrote. "With singular boldness he forced upon my attention two disgraceful photographs bearing the heads of the two gentlemen upon human figures in indescribably loathsome relations. He—Alden J. Blethen—explained in detail how and why he had conceived the idea of these vile photographs, secured foundation pictures by searching out some indecencies from a Paris collection, engaged one of our best Seattle artists to combine them with perfect photographic skill with the heads and faces of Dr. Matthews and of Prosecuting Attorney Murphy. The name of the photographer and the price he paid for making these faked exhibitions of degeneracy was part of the Blethen recital."

The townsfolk looked toward the Times Building for further developments. Blethen's answer was not long in coming. In a front-page editorial the colonel admitted that he had had the fake photographs put together. His purpose, he explained, was purely educational. When the grand jury had indicted him for association with the city vice lords, he had heard a rumor that the prosecution proposed to introduce "a piece of testimony . . . of a most damnable character, an alleged photograph, faked for the purpose, but representing the editor with a lewd woman under extraordinary circumstances." So, to demonstrate to a jury how easily such documentation could be faked, Blethen had ordered similar photos involving Murphy and Dr. Matthews. "The sole purpose, as Cotterill knows, was to demonstrate the viciousness of the Corliss-Burns gang, and to what ends they would go to convict an innocent man of crime." But since the judge had directed the jury to bring in a verdict for the defendant without Blethen's taking the stand, he had not needed to use the photographs in court. He had shown them to Cotterill merely because he thought the mayor would be interested.

The fight reached the halls of Congress. Representative J. W. Bryan of Bremerton, a Republican who had bolted to the Bull Moose and won election as delegate-at-large, read into the *Congressional Record* a long critique of the colonel's actions, including the complete text of Cotterill's statement. Representative Humphreys of Seattle replied on behalf of Blethen. He said, "As to the action of my colleague in attacking various persons in private life here upon the floor of the House, where he has the protection of the Constitution thrown about him and can not be called to account elsewhere for what he may say, one of the highest privileges that the Government can confer, I do not care to comment." Bryan hurried back to Seattle. In a speech before five thousand sympathizers in the Dreamland Auditorium he repeated the charges without benefit of congressional immunity from libel. The meeting adopted by acclamation a resolution censuring the *Times'* "terroristic tactics" and agreeing to boycott not only the paper but the "advertisers who make its existence possible."

The boycott failed dismally. The *Times* continued to prosper. The affair of the Potlatch Riots dwindled off into a series of lawsuits—the *Times* against Cotterill, Bryan against the *Times*, Blethen against Bryan—none of which was ever pushed to a conclusion.

6.

The real beneficiary of the confusion arising out of the Potlatch Riots was wiry and wasp-tongued Hiram C. Gill. In the serenity of the sidelines, the deposed mayor figured out a remarkable political maneuver by which he turned the riots to his own advantage.

Gill had written his own political epitaph after his defeat by Cotterill. When a reporter had asked him if he would run again, he said, "Hell, no! I'm one dead 'un who knows he's dead." But when he looked at the list of candidates in the mayoralty primaries in 1914 he felt it was time for his resurrection. Cotterill, his eyes on a Senate seat (which he did not achieve), had declined to run for re-election. Seven clean-city candidates offered themselves at once. Nobody admitted believing in an open town. On the last day for filing, Gill appeared at the city hall. He paid his filing fee with one-dollar bills and told reporters, "Frankly, I'm getting into this because I know politics well enough to recognize a soft touch when I see one."

Gill's re-entry into municipal politics was a surprise to many, but his campaign was a shock to nearly everyone. He announced that he was a reform candidate, the only candidate with the ability to run a closed town effectively. Gill said he was running "to seek vindication" and to prove to his children that he was a good man. His little boy had come home from school crying one day not long after the 1912 election; his playmates had said that his father was so bad he had been kicked out of his job. Now, said Gill, he just wanted to prove to his son that all he had been doing was the job as he had promised to do it. The people had elected him in 1910 on his promise to give them an open town; nobody could deny he kept that promise. The people had changed their minds about an open town and as a result they "dis-elected me." Well, he had changed his mind. He agreed with the voters. He believed in a closed town and, with all the knowledge he had gained about vice operations in his previous administration, he could run a better closed town than any uniformed reformer.

He sounded convincing. Even the Reverend Dr. Matthews felt it might be a good idea to give Gill a chance. When the primary votes were counted, Gill polled two-fifths of the total. He ran two to one ahead of his nearest rival, a businessman named James D. Trenholme. "Why, that man was unbeatable," Cotterill said later. "He *had* all the vice votes. They didn't take his reform seriously and they had no one else to vote for anyway. But he got a lot of our votes too." Gill agreed. "I told you I wouldn't have run if it wasn't a particularly soft spot," he said.

Gill remained a gentleman through the month of the final campaign. Gone was the candidate who in 1912 had lashed out at Cotterill as "politician who sold the souls of young women to dive-keepers for votes." In his place was a gentle campaigner who said of his opponent, "I think James D. Trenholme is personally a fine man; he is a man of excellent moral character." As an afterthought he mentioned that Trenholme was backed by the Seattle Electric Company, which was then in very bad odor.

On a rainy March day the voters of Seattle elected this new Hiram Gill mayor by the largest margin by which anyone had ever won the office. Among those wiring congratulations was John Considine. He suggested that the mayor-elect appear on a vaudeville show and deliver a five-minute monologue. He offered five hundred dollars a week and said Gill could have it until he took office. Gill declined, saying that Considine had paid Sarah Bernhardt seven thousand a week and "I being younger than the Divine Sarah should not consider an offer of less than ten."

When he took office Gill ran a closed town. He offered the post of chief of police to one of his political foes, Judge Austin E. Griffiths. Judge Griffiths didn't want the job but took it when Dr. Matthews asked him to. Within a few months there were pictures of Hi Gill smashing kegs of whisky in illegal saloons and breaking up gaming devices with a sledgehammer. Within a year Colonel Blethen was demanding Gill's recall on the ground that he was too easy on Wobbly agitators. "An advocate of anarchy," said the colonel.

Blethen died in 1915, and Gill was elected again in 1916. His third term was his worst. Chief Griffiths had resigned to run for Congress; his successor resigned as chief after being indicted by a grand jury. Gill said he hadn't known what was going on. Dr. Matthews thought this probable and spoke out for him. Talk of another recall was dropped, but in 1917 Dr. Matthews and Gill and all Seattle were told what was going on. The Skid

Road was wide open again. Military authorities noted that the venereal-disease rate at the major Army post of Camp Lewis was skyrocketing and placed Seattle off-limits to troops.

Again Gill reformed. He named a strapping seven-footer, Jim Warren, a former United States marshal, as chief of police, and closed things down again. But he was dead politically, and this time he didn't know it. He ran for re-election in 1918 and was badly beaten in the primaries. He had not made the most of the chance he had once asked the voters to give him—the chance to tell his grandson that he had been mayor of Seattle, had made a mistake, had been kicked out, but had come back to be the best mayor Seattle ever had.

In the finals that year Seattle elected a red-headed reformer named Ole Hanson.

Strike

A general strike, by dictionary definition, is a strike in all industries of a locality or nation, generally in sympathy for a smaller group of workers. Theoretically it brings about complete cessation of business.

The first strike in the United States to meet that definition took place in Seattle. It began at ten a.m. on Thursday, February 6, 1919, and lasted until February 11. Sixty thousand workers went off their jobs, and they did bring about an almost complete cessation of business. When the strike ended no one was sure where it had led, but the effects were far-reaching. The strike led the mayor of Seattle to dream of becoming President of the United States; it started a young Seattle woman, Anna Louise Strong, who had been a member of the school board, along a path that led her to Moscow—and back; it gave impetus to a series of Justice Department raids in which young J. Edgar Hoover first showed aptitude in rounding up radicals; it frightened millions of Americans into believing that revolution was just around the corner, and it cheered thousands with the same thought; it gave labor a sense of power and a sense of frustration; it disillusioned a young truck driver named Dave Beck. The general strike influenced the thinking of a generation in Seattle. It framed the world in which they lived.

The strike started in the shipyards. Seattle's shipbuilding industry had expanded enormously during the war. Though the fighting had ended, the war was not legally

194

over and a Shipbuilding Adjustment Board—established by agreement among the United States Shipping Board, the Navy, and the presidents of the ship-building crafts—still supervised the shipyards.

Shortly after the German surrender, the Shipbuilding Adjustment Board announced a new, uniform, nationwide wage scale. Western workers were outraged. The cost of living was "slightly higher west of the Rockies" and previous agreements had allowed them higher wages than in Eastern yards. They appealed to the board for a revised scale, and they asked the shipyard owners directly for higher wages and shorter hours. They asked $8 a day for skilled workers, $5.50 for unskilled workers, and a 44-hour week. Their demands were turned down.

Feeling among the workers ran high, especially after they learned—through the delivery of a telegram, intended for the employers' Metal Trades Association, to the workers' Metal Trades Council—that the employers were willing to raise wages but were threatened with cancellation of their government contracts and loss of steel priorities if they raised the scale without the board's permission. The Seattle Metal Trades Council called for a strike vote among its seventeen member unions. The delegates from one of the unions voted against the strike; six unions voted for it but not by the majority required in their constitutions; ten approved without qualification. So by a vote of 10 to 7 the strike was approved. On January 21, 35,000 workers walked out.

The next day the Metal Trades Council asked the Seattle Central Labor Council to call its members out in sympathy. The council put it up to the individual unions. Most of the local union leaders were against the strike. The national policy of the American Federation of Labor was against the use of the strike as a political protest. Many locals had good agreements which they would jeopardize if they went out, and the national headquarters of the unions were solidly opposed to "political adventuring." But many local labor leaders were in Chicago attending a rally for the release of Tom Mooney, and in

their absence the rank and file voted. In union after
union they voted for a strike.

The carpenters, perhaps the most conservative of all
unions, voted to strike. So did the typographers. So did
the musicians and the longshoremen, the stagehands and
the millworkers, the hotel maids and the teamsters. One
after another, a hundred and ten unions voted to strike.
The Wobblies were not represented on the Central Labor
Council, but they sent delegates to applaud the strike
votes; the Japanees unions, kept off the council by racial
restrictions, sent delegates to say they'd strike too.

A general strike was approved overwhelmingly, but no
one knew how to run one. It was one thing to walk off the
job at some plant and try to keep strike-breakers from
walking in. It was altogether different to stop the industrial life of a city of 300,000. It had never been done in
America. No one was sure how to go about it.

A General Strike Committee was formed. It was made
up of three delegates from each striking union, plus three
from the Central Labor Council. The committee, with
more than three hundred members, was too large to func-
tion. Its first meeting, on Sunday, February 2, lasted all
day. After sixteen hours of uninterrupted talk, the committee delegated power to an executive committee, known
as the Committee of Fifteen, and adjourned until Thursday evening—the night after the strike was to start.

The Committee of Fifteen became the center of power
in Seattle. It decided who would work after Thursday and
who wouldn't. Here is a list of typical requests received by
the committee and recorded by the strike historian:

King County Commissioners ask for janitors for City-County
Building. Refused.
F. A. Rust asks for janitors for the Labor Temple. Refused.
Co-operative Market asks for janitors because of the food they
handle for strike kitchens. Granted.
Teamsters Union asks permission to carry oil for Swedish
hospital. Approved.
Retail Drug Clerks ask for instructions in view of medical
needs of city. Referred to public welfare committee which

decides that certain prescription counters remain open, but the drugstores are not to sell any other merchandise.

Telephone girls requested to stay on the job temporarily.

Longshoremen ask permission to handle government mails, customs, and baggage. Permit given for mails and customs but not for baggage.

Plumbers Union given permit to keep seven plumbers on duty for emergency calls. Streetcar workers given permission to appoint six watchmen to safeguard car barns.

C. R. Case, chief of street department, and backed by mayor, requests that street lighting be allowed "to check hooliganism and riots." Confused discussion over this due to the technical difficulty of separating light from power: City Light finally allowed to run.

Robert Bridges, who was elected to presidency of the public port by votes of progressive workers, appeals on behalf of farm products in cold storage, saying, "The big companies store in private warehouses, getting power from Seattle Electric which your strike cannot touch. Do not ruin the small farmers, who store in the public warehouses with power from City Light." This also influences retention of City Light in full operation.

There were hundreds of details for the Committee of Fifteen to arrange. They made sure there would be milk for children and for the hospitals, that the hospitals could get laundry, that water pressure would be kept up. They set up strike kitchens and arranged for food to be supplied; anyone could buy a meal, but strikers got cut rates. They set up an auxiliary police force of "labor guards" to help the city police. All this they did with considerable foresight, but one thing they did not do: they did not state their aims. They did not state them because they did not know them. They were not sure how long the strike was to last, whether it was merely a gesture of solidarity with the shipyard workers, whether it was a move toward educating the workers in the problems of running a city, whether it was an attempt to touch off a nationwide general strike.

No one knew whether the gun was loaded.

But at ten a.m., Thursday, February 6, exactly on schedule, America's first general strike started.

Mayor Olie[1] Hanson was a friend of labor. He said so himself, loud and often. When the strike was first called he asked some of the labor leaders to lunch and over coffee he said, "Boys, I want my street lights and water supply and hospitals. I don't care if you shut down all the rest of the city."

He got his street lights and water supply and hospitals; he got many other services designed to prevent hardship, and he also got a chance to make a national name for himself. As a friendly reporter once said of him, "There are really two Ole Hansons—the one who talks and the one who acts; as a talker he is often erratically radical, but his actions are always rational." That was correct. Holy Ole, as his foes called him, might look like a political whirling dervish as he spun from the Republicans to the Progressives to Wilson and back to the Republicans, but he kept his eye on the ball. He had been in Seattle sixteen years when the general strike started, and by any standards he had done well for himself.

Ole was a small man with red hair parted just a little left of center and a high voice that seemed tinged with hysteria when he made a public speech. "He just seemed to be wound up too tight," a political associate of Hanson's said years later. "I never heard anything like Old Ole until Hitler came along. He'd get so worked up he'd be almost screaming. He sure sounded sincere." He had great vitality and an ambition that almost tore him apart; if he ever doubted that he was on the way to political success he did not show his doubts. There is no question about his courage.

Hanson was working in Butte, Montana, in 1900 when he injured his spine; doctors doubted that he would ever walk again. But Ole's hero was Teddy Roosevelt, and Roosevelt had conquered illness by exercise. Hanson bought an old covered wagon and rigged up a combina-

[1] Pronounced "Oley."

tion harness and sling, which he fastened to the rear of the wagon; it enabled him to walk behind the prairie schooner. With his wife driving the wagon Hanson trudged along behind. He walked the seven hundred miles from Butte to Seattle and reached the Sound country physically fit.

When Hanson and his family camped their first night on Beacon Hill and looked down on the lights of the Skid Road and the business district, Ole made his first political speech. He later recalled telling the idlers who had gathered to inspect his covered wagon that he would be mayor of Seattle some day. But first there was the problem of earning a living. He bought a grocery on Beacon Hill, sold it "after learning that the grocer is the king of philanthropists," went into the insurance business and left it when a real-estate man told him that no insurance agent in Seattle owned his own home. The real-estate man owned his house, so Ole became a real-estate agent.

As a dealer in property, Hanson never eclipsed the big holders but he did well enough to be able to turn his talents to politics. He was a reformer and he found his first issue in race-track gambling. The Seattle race track had been getting a bad press. An embezzler had gambled away a firm's funds there; a young man killed himself after losing his inheritance; the track was a hangout for gamblers and pimps and hoodlums. Hanson picked the track as his private political issue, ran for the state legislature on a "Ban Race-track Gambling" platform, and won. It was proof of Holy Ole's energy that as a freshman representative he was able to have his anti-race-track bill the first one in the legislative hopper and the first major law to be passed.

Hanson ran first as a Republican. He worshiped Teddy Roosevelt and named his second son for him. (It was a Seattle joke that Hanson named his six boys after the men he most admired, in declining order: Ole Hanson, Jr., Theodore Roosevelt Hanson, William Taft Hanson, Eugene Field Hanson—after the poet and columnist—Bob La Follette Hanson, Lloyd George Hanson.) He "moosed it"—his own expression—with Teddy, then swung to Wilson in 1916 because "he kept us out of war." But once the United States declared war on the Central Powers, Hanson became a home-front belligerent. In 1918 he told the voters with a straight face that he was running for mayor as "a patriotic duty." Ole Junior was old enough for the army but not healthy enough, and Hanson imagined he could hear his own parents saying, "Our country is at war. Others are going to the front, but you can serve at home. Do your duty."

The voters also did their duty as Hanson saw it. They elected him mayor to succeed Hi Gill, and on the March day that Hanson was elected mayor, the first female member of Seattle's school board was recalled. The issue was pacifism and radicalism.

Even more than Hanson, Anna Louise Strong was a newcomer to Seattle. A handsome women in her early thirties, she was of pre-Revolutionary stock on both sides of her family. She had been graduated from Bryn Mawr and had taken graduate work at Oberlin and her Ph.D. at Chicago. After a brief term as assistant editor of a Fundamentalist weekly and a period recovering from a nervous breakdown brought about by her love for a married man, she organized a venture known as the "Know Your City" Institute—a type of exhibition dedicated to telling Western newcomers about their communities. From that she moved to child-welfare exhibits in various cities, only to have more skillful promoters organize her out of a job. She worked for a while with the United States Children's Bureau, then in 1916 came to Seattle to make a home for her widowed father, a minister, who had moved west from Nebraska some years before.

Actually she spent little time making a home. She was a passionate mountain climber and organized cooperative summer camps in the Cascades. She led the first winter climb of Mount Hood. She guided parties across the glaciers on Mount Rainier. She quickly attracted the attention of Seattle, and less than a year after she came to town she was prevailed upon to run for the school board. She was a natural: the only woman candidate, the only candidate with a Ph.D., the only candidate to have published a book (she'd written a play, a novel, and a book of poems), the only candidate with practical experience in education. Labor was for her—her father was a progressive; the Municipal League, which was then a liberal organization, and the Commercial Club, a lively group of small businessmen who had organized in opposition to the Chamber of Commerce, both endorsed her. Women were for her, and she won easily.

Once on the board, however, she found there was little she could do. Her concern was with the theory of education; board meetings took up such practical matters as plumbing fixtures. She found her official duties "the most completely boring of my life." She was not bored long.

The year of her election was the year of the Everett troubles. The AFL Shinglewcavers were on strike in Everett, thirty miles north of Seattle and the IWW was supporting them. Late in August the Everett police rounded up the Shingleweaver pickets, took them to a narrow trestle, and beat them up. The next day there was a riot in which the police routed the strikers. The Wobblies decided to reinforce the Shingleweavers (who had not asked for their support) with a free-speech demonstration. It was a Wob political tactic to send so many soapboxers into towns that restricted free speech that the jails couldn't handle the crowd; but this time the demonstrators, forty-one of them, were arrested, taken to the city limits, and made to run a gauntlet of deputies armed with clubs and slug-shots. A week later the Wobblies tried again. They chartered two Seattle boats, the *Verona* and the *Calista*, and on Sunday, November 5, 1916, 280 demonstrators sailed for Everett. Pinkerton agents in Seattle wired that they were coming. When the *Verona* tied up at the Everett dock, the sheriff and 200 deputies were waiting. The sheriff asked the Wobs to point out their leaders. They refused. Somebody started shooting. Before the *Verona* cast off and moved away, five of the demonstrators and two of the vigilantes were dead, thirty-one demonstrators and nineteen vigilantes wounded. When the two ships got back to Seattle, everyone on board was arrested.[2] Seventy-four were charged with murder. On March 5, 1917, the first of the defendants, Thomas Tracy, was put on trial for his life. Anna Louise Strong covered the trial for the New York Post, and the testimony she heard changed her life.

Years later she summarized her dispatches by saying, "The news was that at every stage the Everett police and private lumber guards took the initiative in beating and shooting workers for speaking in the streets. The lumber guards on the dock had begun the shooting and continued firing as the Verona pulled away; yet none of them was arrested. The men on trial for murder were not individually shown to have even possessed a gun; it was enough that someone on their ship, a comrade or agent provocateur, had fired."

Tracy was acquitted. Judge Ronald dismissed the charges against the other seventy-three defendants.

Anna Louise Strong came to have deep sympathy for the Wobblies as she listened to the trial. She thought of them as "direct inheritors of the fighting pioneer," who were "engaged in the struggle of men once free and expecting freedom but now slowly, inexplicably, irretrievably enslaved . . . waging a stark, bloody fight for elementary human rights." Her growing partisanship for the tough "class warriors" of the Skid Road merged with another new cause that had come to dominate her thinking: pacifism. The agitation for American entry into the war horrified her. Her father was a religious pacifist; she shared his moral scruples about killing and to them added her economic conviction that war was merely a way of making the rich richer and the poor dead. She joined every group she heard of that opposed American participation. She fought conscription, believing it to be a device for forcing the poor to fight the battles of the rich. When the United States finally did go in, she felt that the country she knew and loved was dead. She ran away to the mountains. There, after a summer of brooding nights and

[2] Mayor Gill denounced the vigilantes as murderers, ordered improved treatment of the prisoners, and held his position against threat of another recall.

days of desperate climbing, she came across some copies of a small Socialist weekly, the *Seattle Call*. Its anti-war sentiments were her sentiments. She rushed back to Seattle and became a reporter for the paper.

As a Socialist propagandist she worked herself to the point of exhaustion. But the paper was small and almost no one noticed that the female member of the school board was preaching pacifism in a radical weekly. It was not until Hulet Wells, a Socialist and the former president of the Central Labor Council, was put on trial for obstructing the war effort that Miss Strong's political position attracted citywide attention. Even then she might have avoided trouble had she been so minded. The principle charge against Wells was that he had circulated an anticonscription leaflet. Professional witnesses appeared against him to swear it was paid for by German gold. Miss Strong went to the defense attorney, George Vanderveer, an able man who had abandoned a lucrative private practice to defend left-wing causes. She told him that as secretary of the group that had originally sponsored the leaflet she could name the prominent Seattle people who had subscribed to its sentiments and who had contributed funds for its publication. To do this would make her many enemies among the people who had changed their views; it would also expose her as an ally of the far Left. But her testimony would be valuable because she was "the best known of the respectable women in town." ·

Vanderveer realized how much she had to lose. "Young lady," he told her, "my advice to you personally is that you need a guardian to keep you out of this. But my statement as an attorney for the defense is that you offer us our best chance of winning." She testified. The best the defense could get was a hung jury. Wells was tried again and convicted. A recall petition was started against Anna Louise Strong. It languished at first but gained impetus when she sat beside an anarchist friend, Louise Olivereau, during her trial on the charge that she had sent anti-war leaflets to soldiers. Miss Olivereau, a clerk-typist for the Wobblies, refused to defend herself. She was convicted and the school-board member stood convicted of being her friend. The recall petitions quickly got enough signatures to put her name on the March ballot.

Supporting the recall were most of the middle-class groups that had originally backed her: the Parent-Teachers' Association, the University Women's Club, the Municipal League. Opposing it was a new alignment in Seattle politics, an alliance of organized labor as represented by the Central Labor Council, the depressed population of the Skid Road as represented by the Wobblies, and a sprinkling of maverick intellectuals. This alliance, the clearest political grouping along class lines since the heyday of Mary Kenworthy, was not enough to defeat the recall; but the "viper in the bosom of the school board" was scotched by a slim 2000-vote margin out of a total of 80,000.

She was soon out of another job. A mob raided the shop where the *Call* was printed and broke up the press. The paper suspended publication, but its place was taken by the *Union Record*, a daily, supported cooperatively by a group of unions. Anna Louise Strong became an editor for the new paper. In January 1919 she went with the Central Labor Council delegation to cover the Chicago labor rally on behalf of Tom Mooney, and she shared the surprise of the Seattle delegates when they learned by telegram that the general strike was called. She hurried back to Seattle to work for its success.

Like almost everyone who supported the strike, she didn't know what it was intended to accomplish. Two days before the strike she wrote an editorial in the *Union Record* saying so. It became the most quoted editorial in Seattle's newspaper history:

THURSDAY AT 10 A.M.

There will be many cheering, and there will be some who fear. Both these emotions are useful, but not too much of either. We are undertaking the most tremendous move ever made by *Labor* in this country, a move which will lead

NO ONE KNOWS WHERE
LABOR WILL FEED THE PEOPLE

Twelve great kitchens have been offered, and from them food will be distributed by the provision trades at low cost to all.

LABOR WILL CARE FOR THE BABIES
AND THE SICK

The milk-wagon drivers and the laundry drivers are arranging plans for supplying milk to the babies, invalids, and hospitals, and taking care of the cleaning of linen for hospitals.

LABOR WILL PRESERVE ORDER

The strike committee is arranging for guards and it is expected that the stopping of the cars will keep people at home.

* * *

A few hot-headed enthusiasts have complained that strikers only should be fed, and the general public left to endure severe discomfort. Aside from the inhumanitarian character of such suggestions, let them get this straight:

NOT THE WITHDRAWAL OF LABOR POWER, BUT THE POWER OF THE WORKERS TO MANAGE WILL WIN THIS STRIKE.

* * *

The closing down of Seattle's industries, as a mere shutdown, will not affect the great Eastern combinations of capitalists much. They could let the whole Northwest go to pieces as far as money alone is concerned.

But, the closing down of the capitalistically controlled industries of Seattle, while the workers organize to feed the people, to care for the babies and the sick, to preserve order—*this*

will move them, for this looks too much like the taking over
of power by the workers.

• • •

Labor will not only shut down the industries, but Labor will
reopen, under the management of the appropriate trades,
such activities as are needed to preserve public health and
public peace. If the strike continues, Labor may feel led to
avoid public suffering by reopening more and more activities,

UNDER ITS OWN MANAGEMENT

And this is why we say we are starting on a road that leads—

NO ONE KNOWS WHERE!

At ten o'clock Thursday morning whistles sounded in
the mills and on the ships at the docks. With that signal
the industrial activity of the city came to a halt. Streetcar
service stopped. Schools let out. Banks locked their
doors. Restaurants shut down. The movies closed. Presses
and linotypes went silent and lead cooled in the pots.
Clerks left the groceries, the drygoods stores, the markets.
Elevator boys shut the gates of their lifts. Maids stopped
making the hotel beds. From Georgetown to Ballard
things quieted down.

That was the greatest surprise of all—the quiet. The
whines of the saws, the clatter of streetcars and trucks, the
honk of taxi horns, the creak of the winches, the shouts of
newsboys, the pecking of typewriters, the rattle of elevator
chains—all were silenced. People suddenly heard the
chirp of sparrows and the moaning of the doves that
nested in downtown buildings. It was so quiet, a striker
remarked, you could hear the grass grow; it was so quiet
that people were unnerved.

Many people had expected riot, even revolution. The
night before the strike Mayor Hanson sat in his bedroom
in his new fourteen-room house and worked on "plans for
defense, including securing cartridges, shot guns and ma-

chine guns, and drawing a map showing the places where men were to be stationed, and massing our forces at what I considered strategic points." At dawn that morning a convoy of trucks had rumbled in from Camp Lewis with fifteen hundred soldiers aboard; they were stationed at the armory, alert for trouble. There was no trouble.

After the ten o'clock whistle sounded merchants and lawyers and tradesmen and workers stood anxiously in front of their shops and offices, waiting for what was to come. The minutes stretched into hours and nothing happened. A hearse rolled slowly down the street, carrying a placard which read, "Exempted by the Strike Committee." An occasional laundry wagon or private car appeared, and there was a clatter of hoofs on the red-brick streets as a few farsighted commuters rode home on horseback. Heavily armed policemen stood at the street corners, passing jokes with people they knew. Labor guards, wearing armbands but vested with no real authority, patrolled the industrial district; whenever a crowd gathered, they asked the members to "break it up, fellows" or mentioned that it was a fine day to be home planting potatoes. Late in the afternoon the streets were almost deserted.

In the quiet rumors spread. There were no papers and, of course, no radio. One rumor was as believable as the next. The word spread that Mayor Hanson had been assassinated, that the Army was driving the strikers back to work at the points of bayonets, that the strike was spreading across the country, that the workers had announced the confiscation of private property, that the power company's dam had been dynamited, that the Central Labor Temple had been dynamited, that on the far side of town the water supply had been cut and firebugs were at work, that the water system had been poisoned, that homes on the outskirts were being pillaged, that the strike leaders had been shot, that the strike leaders had set up a soviet. As night fell the police station switchboard was flooded with calls from women pleading for protection.

The night passed without incident and the second day

started as quietly as the first. But there was a difference: the fear of the unknown was past. This was a situation, a thing within bounds; it could be understood and managed. Probably the first man to understand the implications of the orderly first day was Ole Hanson; he must have seen that there wasn't going to be violence, that the strikers did not intend to seize property. He must have understood something the strikers had not even admitted to themselves: that the general strike was not a means to an end but an end in itself. There was nothing concrete the strikers could achieve. The shipyard operators could outwait them; the strike might show sympathy but it would not win raises for the men in the shipyards. Nothing else could be done without violence, and the labor leaders had no stomach for bloodshed; even if they had wanted to seize the factories, they had no arms. All the strikers could do, sooner or later, was go back to work.

In a way Hanson smashed the strike. He smashed it every day for four days in stories he gave to the local United Press bureau, which in turn gave them nationwide play. He exorcised the strike as "a treasonable Bolshevist uprising," and when the strike died a non-violent death after five days, he went into business as the Savior of Seattle, the Suppressor of Red Rebellion.

His actual contribution to the end of the strike was a "Proclamation to the People of Seattle" and an "Ultimatum to the Executive Strike Committee." The proclamation, written on the second day of the strike, said:

By virtue of the authority vested in me as mayor, I hereby guarantee to all the people of Seattle absolute and complete protection. They should go about their daily work and business in perfect security. We have fifteen hundred policemen, fifteen hundred regular soldiers from Camp Lewis, and can and will secure, if necessary, every soldier in the Northwest to protect life, business and property.

The time has come for every person in Seattle to show his Americanism. Go about your daily duties without fear. We will see to it that you have food, transportation, water, light, gas and all necessities. The anarchists in this community shall not rule its affairs. All persons violating the laws will be dealt with summarily.

OLE HANSON, Mayor

The ultimatum was a warning to the strikers that if the strike was not called off at once the mayor would "operate all essential industries." Hanson sent his secretary to the Labor Temple to read aloud the ultimatum and the proclamation. During the recitation, Hanson declared, "the faces of the very men who had been loudest in egging on the workers turned pale, for they knew we were prepared to go the full limit in defeating their nefarious and un-American aims." The strikers' version is that they thought Hanson's ultimatum was just another publicity puff from a blow-hard politician.

Either way, the strike was in trouble. Its very success worked against it: the town was so quiet, there was so little activity, that the strikers lost their feeling of unity. There was nothing doing. There were no martyrs. No pickets had been beaten up. Nobody had been arrested. It was hard to stay angry. In the absence of specific strike aims the men soon wearied of the Iron March of Labor to "No One Knew Where." They had shown they could shut the town down tight. Now they wanted to get back to work and draw some pay.

The international officials of the unions wanted them back on the job too. Men from national headquarters began arriving the day the strike started; every train brought more; they all agreed that the strike was a mistake, that it jeopardized contracts that had been hard to get. On the third day, the Committee of Fifteen, by a vote of 13 to 1, recommended to the General Strike Committee that the strike be called off. The parent group voted down the recommendation, but the backbone of the strike was broken. The strikers learned of the dissension in the ranks of their leaders.

On the fourth day a number of unions failed to answer the roll call at the Labor Temple; their members were back on the job. Streetcars were running; beds were being made; presses were rolling. Hastily the General Strike Committee drafted a request to all the workers that they should form ranks again for one final day; after that everyone would go back to work. Some unions agreed, others stayed on the job. The strike petered out. On Wednesday, February 12, Lincoln's Birthday, the first general strike in America was over.

Ole Hanson celebrated his victory at a desk heaped with flowers, telegrams, and photographer's proofs. The flowers and telegrams had come from all over the United States. The proofs were from Seattle. Ole had gone out the day before and had the photographs taken. Now he was trying to pick out the best two. It was a serious business. He was going to have a hundred prints made of each and send them to newspapers all over the country so that everyone could see the man who had put down the traitorous bolshevist rebellion and saved America.

A reporter for a national magazine found him studying the pictures. Ole was frankly delighted about the publicity he was getting. "I guess you've got to grab it when it comes along," he said. "I'm a great man. I win. In six months I lose and it's all over—till the next time. I thought I had a mighty good labor record in the Legislature but Labor fought me when I ran for mayor. I told 'em that in six months they'd say I was the best mayor they ever had, and sure enough they came around and made me an honorary member of their biggest union, and gave me a membership card engraved on silver. Now they're giving me hell again. But that's just the regular thing in public life if you're doing anything. Every six months you have a different crowd of followers. This particular time it's about ninety-five per cent. But that doesn't fool me. I'm taking whatever fame there is in it for me right now."

There was plenty of fame. Four national magazines wrote him up. He was on every front page for two or three days. Finally he was asked to go on a lecture tour, an offer that was too good to turn down—all that money, all those audiences, and the Republican nominating convention only a year away. Ole resigned as mayor of Seattle and toured the country, explaining how the "loathsome monster of anarchy had roamed the streets of my fair city" and how he had saved the day. He wrote a book about it too, *Americanism versus Bolshevism*, and it went on sale a few months before the presidential nominations were made. The Republicans chose Harding. Hanson returned to Seattle, sold his property, and moved to California.

Anna Louise Strong was assigned by the Central Labor Council to write a history of the strike. She was at her desk in her father's house one afternoon not long after the men had gone back to work when the telephone rang. Harry Ault, the editor of the *Union Record*, was calling. "A deputy is here in the office to arrest us," he said. "You'd better hurry down and get it over."

She took a taxi to the Labor Temple, where a deputy handed her an indictment charging her with sedition. The charge was based on her editorials in the *Union Record*, especially the "No One Knows Where" editorial. She signed the receipt for the indictment and went to the district attorney's office to wait while the Boilermakers Union rushed to the bank to get her bail.

The arrest of the *Record* editors, Labor charged, was primarily a political move. Ole Hanson was propagandizing against the national administration, charging it with softness toward anarchists. "We have had enough of weakness, conciliation, and pandering," Ole thundered. "We must run the United States of America primarily for the United States of America. America First!" There was a crack-down on the strike leaders. But politics cuts both ways. A local Democrat hurried back to Washington to explain in anguish, "My God, those folks are backed by forty thousand votes, the votes that changed to Roosevelt and then to Wilson. Do you want to lose them all to the Farmer-Labor Party?" The case against the editors was quietly dropped.

It had not been a strong case at best. Of all the editorials "inciting to anarchy" that the *Record* had printed, Miss Strong's were the best known. Ole Hanson had quoted her "No One Knows Where" editorial time and again, always implying that the phrase "No One Knows Where" really meant "Straight to Moscow." Against the background of a city on strike, with the workers actually feeding and policing the people, Hanson's interpretation had emotional conviction, but in a courtroom the editorial had a different sound. It advocated nothing. It was unconsciously—or unconscionably—clever in the way it avoided threats. It said, "This looks too much like the taking of power," but it did not say that the workers would take power or should take power. It said, "Labor may feel led to manage more activities," but the word was "may" not "would" or "should." The defense could argue that the editorial meant exactly what it said, that it was a frank admission that the leaders of the strike could not read the future.

Actually, the editorial meant more than that. It had caught the real mood of the general strike, the mood of confident hope, the belief that if only the workers were united, if only they could close down the town, everything would work out for the best. It was this confident hope that led them to confuse the means with the end, the strike with the goal to be achieved. They were sure that if all the unions went on simultaneous strike, a better world would be born. Miss Strong's editorial was an incantation of affirmation, chanted before the image of the general strike.

When she returned to her task of writing the story of the strike, Miss Strong and her assistants on the history committee tried to analyze what had gone wrong so that the "workers of the world may learn from our mistakes as well as from our successes." They decided that they should have stated their objectives more clearly, but they still could not agree what their objective should have been.

Reaction set in. Labor candidates for the city council lost in the 1919 municipal election. The Seattle shipyards were the first to be closed in the postwar slow-down; times were hard, and many of the most militant—the single men who had no stake in the community—roamed away to greener pastures. Those who remained kept looking back to the strike and blaming one another for what had gone wrong.

In 1920 Labor nominated a candidate for mayor—Jimmy Duncan, president of the Central Labor Council, a tough, irascible radical who several times cast the lone dissenting vote against Sam Gompers at national AFL elections. Duncan's candidacy was a defense of the general strike. He was defeated by a Republican lawyer, Hugh M. Caldwell, 50,875 to 33,777. The militant Left was discouraged; the conservatives sighed with relief. "Seattle is safe against the dictatorship of the proletariat," a commentator wrote. "No man and no group of men can dictate to this town."

Not long after the election Lincoln Steffens, a leader among the muckraking reporters, came to town on a lecture tour. After his formal talk Miss Strong took him to Blanc's—a basement café popular with Seattle radicals and bohemians—for dinner and "the real story." At first she asked him questions about Russia, for he was just back from Moscow, but Steffens was one of the world's great reporters and soon he was asking the questions. He wanted to know about Seattle and the general strike.

"All the old comradeship is torn to pieces," she told him. "All the old friends are calling each other traitors."

"When did it start?" asked Steffens.

"It's been getting worse for months," she said. "The Central Labor Council meetings that used to have such fine speeches from workers all over the world have turned into nasty wrangles between carpenters and plumbers for control of little jobs. I think it began when the shipyards closed and the metal trades workers began to leave. These workers' enterprises we were so proud of began to go to pieces. And everybody who took part in them got blamed. Now some of the members of our staff are attacking Harry Ault, our editor, most horribly. One of them told me that if I didn't join the attack they would rub my name in the dirt. That from a man I used to like."

She went on with the tale of bitterness that grows from defeat. Steffens told her that she would have to choose sides; she would have to go with one group or the other,

with those who felt the fault lay with not going far
enough or with those who felt the fault lay with having
gone too fast.

"I can understand both sides somewhat," she protested.
"I must help them get together. They were such good
comrades before, and we all went ahead so rapidly. They
must be good comrades again."

"Never," the bearded reporter exclaimed. "Never. The
gulf will grow wider. It is growing all over the world." He
talked of what it had been like in Moscow where, it
seemed, the issues were clearer.

"Oh, I'd give anything if I could go there," she said.

"Why don't you then?" said Steffens.

She did. Twenty-nine years later, when the friends in
Moscow turned against her and expelled her as a turncoat
and a spy, she returned to Seattle. Her home town had
changed. It was a middle-class town now, a town of high
wages and white collars, a prosperous town dominated by
a fat, bland, tough labor leader named Dave Beck, who as
a young truck driver had learned better than anyone else
the lesson of the general strike.

V

Dave Beck: Labor and Politics, 1918-1960

1.

It is the year 1951. In a big, quiet office that is paneled with lustrous dark wood and luxuriously carpeted, a large, bald, blue-eyed man of fifty-six sits behind a desk of Philippine mahogany. He talks pleasantly with his secretary, who has been with him for a quarter of a century, leafs rapidly through a stack of correspondence, and dictates decisive notes to his subalterns and flowery letters to his peers. Every few minutes he picks up the phone and tells the switchboard girl to get Indianapolis or Denver or Washington, D.C., or San Francisco. His voice is high, almost boyish, but his tone is one of command. He is the big boss.

His memo pad is full of the names of people who want to ask his favor or his advice, who hope he can make their way easier or more profitable. He speaks at service-club luncheons on such topics as "Americanism" and "The Second Half of Our Century"; he listens to speakers on similar subjects. He raises money for the Community Chest, helps promote the sales of apples and apricots,[1] and distributes football tickets to servicemen stationed at

---

[1] A Teamster once complained that when Beck was trying to win the favor of the eastern Washington apple-growers, "We all ate apples till we damn near busted; then Dave got sore at those jokers across the mountains and we caught hell if anyone found an apple-seed in our pocket."

Fort Lewis and Fort Lawton. He has served on the State Board of Terms and Paroles, on the wartime Rubber and Oil Conservation Committee, and, though he did not finish high school, he became president of the Board of Regents of the state university, a non-paying position that his secretary estimated took one-fifth of his valuable time. (He resigned from the Board in May 1951 in protest over a raise in student fees.)

He likes to run things. He may talk over his problems with his doctor, whom he sees almost daily, or with his trusted lieutenants, or even with other businessmen, but he thinks it poor policy to consult workers about a decision unless he has to. "I'm paid twenty-five thousand a year to run this outfit," he told a reporter some years ago. "Why should truck drivers and bottle washers be allowed to make decisions affecting policy? No corporation would allow it." More recently he told a visitor, "I am a firm believer that the administration of a local union should be responsible to the members, but it should also have responsibility. It must be able to make decisions. That's what the officials are for, to sell what labor possesses, its own labor. Now to do that they must use business methods. That takes specialists. You can't take a vote on each question and you can't just haul a guy in off the street and let him negotiate with a high-powered lawyer. You can't even ask him to do office work. Truck drivers can't do those jobs. But they can decide whether we are getting them what they want and re-elect the officials who do get them what they want. When we get the best conditions for the men, and they re-elect us, then we are accomplishing what we are set up for."

Dave Beck executive vice-president of the Teamsters and the dominant personality in present-day Seattle, is a plump and efficient businessman who cornered the local labor market during the thirties. He's a lot of other things too. He is the poor boy who made good; the kid who had to quit high school to earn a living and is now president of a three-and-a-half-million-dollar corporation. He is the man who took the Teamsters Union and made it into a better mouse trap. He is a self-made man, all right, and the finished product could have been turned out only in Seattle. Beck's pattern of thought, his conception of the role a labor leader should play, his ruthlessness, his ostentation, all are tinged by the Seattle experience—by the boom-and-bust of the gold-rush days, by the corruption of the Gill administration, by the success of men like Considine and Pantages, and of other men like Jim Hill and Frederick Weyerhaeuser, by the toughness of the Wobblies, by the failure of the general strike.

Like a majority of Seattle residents, Beck was born elsewhere; in his case, in Stockton, California, on June 16, 1894. His father, Lemuel Beck, a carpet cleaner from Tennessee, worked hard and prospered not; Dave has referred to the old man as "the world's worst businessman." The Becks moved to Seattle in 1898, drawn by the glint of Klondike gold. They were to see precious little of it. Unable to pay passage to Alaska, Lemuel went back to carpet cleaning and odd jobs; his wife worked in a laundry and little David—he dislikes the name David, preferring the diminutive—hawked papers on the street after school hours. In his junior year at Broadway High School he dropped out to go to work, driving truck for a laundry.

The young redhead held the job for five years. He thought about changing things so no one would have to work as hard as his mother did for so little; he thought about how nice it would be to live like the people in the big wooden houses with the view of the bay and the Olympics.

Twenty-two-year-old Dave was still jockeying a truck and dreaming of a better life when two events changed his life. The first was a strike: the laundry drivers went out for more pay. The strike lasted three weeks and the union's gains were meager. It was the only big strike Beck ever took part in as a worker, and he hated it. "You lose more in pay than you get from the raise in years," he complained later. Others argued that the employers lost too, that next time they would be easier to deal with, but for Dave it was a pure matter of dollars and cents. He wanted stability, not strikes.

The other event was the war. Dave joined the Navy; he

got a rating as machinist's mate and went overseas, to England, where he rode in Curtiss seaplanes that patrolled the North Sea against German Zeppelins. He must have done a lot of thinking about his future during this period. When he returned to Seattle after the war he acted like a man who knew exactly what he wanted, and how to get it.

Beck wanted money and he wanted a responsible position in the Teamsters Union, a position where he could shape policy. He wanted to work for stability, not strikes. Seattle, when Dave shucked his Navy blues, was a city tight with the tension raised by the general strike. Beck thought the strike had been wrong, criminally wrong; it had been impetuous, it had been pointless; it had brought disrepute to Labor and had won nothing. He was disgusted with the idealists who had dreamed it up. He was disgusted with the Wobblies who had preached general strike. He would no longer answer when the Wobblies greeted him as a "fellow worker."

Back on the laundry run, Beck went all out to get customers. When one of the drivers remarked that the boss got a bigger cut from each new customer than the driver did, Beck is reported to have said, "He ought to. It's his business."

Dave was soon making a hundred a week on his laundry run, good money in 1920. When he wasn't selling housewives on the merits of his laundry, he was selling other drivers on the merits of Dave Beck. They elected him business agent of Laundry Drivers' Local 566. He was on his way. He took extension courses in public speaking and economics; he dressed like a young businessman, made speeches before any group that would listen, warned business people against radicals, warned workers about the danger of being unorganized. "Organize! Organize!" was his favorite topic; if you were organized you won without striking. By 1924 he was secretary of his union. Dan Tobin, the national boss of the Teamsters, had his eye on him. San Francisco's Bloody Mike Casey, who had organized the Teamsters of the other great West Coast port, thought the hefty, businesslike redhead had the stuff. After the Teamsters held their national convention in Seattle in 1925 Dave was hired as an organizer. The next two years were a time of prosperity for the city, the nation, the union, and Dave Beck, but it was the depression that made the Teamster boss the ruler of Seattle.

2.

In the early thirties Seattle lay gray and sullen under the shadow of the great depression. The mills were shut down and piles of lumber slowly rotted in the open sheds. The wharves were almost deserted; a fleet of ghost ships rode at long anchor in Lake Union, rusting to uselessness. It didn't pay the men who owned the trim boats tried up at Ballard docks to make a fishing run. Vacant storefronts dotted Third and Fourth Avenues. A man could get a full meal for twenty cents in any of a dozen joints south of Yesler Way, but many went hungry. Hundreds of men sat glumly on the curbs along the Skid Road, or elbowed one another around the blackboards in front of the employment agencies, or prowled the alleys looking for food and salvage; those who found something good might eat it on the spot, or they might scurry back to the shacktown that had risen on the site of an abandoned shipyard at the southern edge of the Skid Road, a new community known as Hooverville.

No civic association has erected a plaque with the names of the latter-day pioneers who raised the first shacks on the flats between the Connecticut Street dock and the Central Terminal of the Port of Seattle. It is improbable that pageants will commemorate their landing or that civic dignataries will discourse on the pioneering impulse that led the men of the thirties to build homes in the wilderness. Yet the unheralded pioneers of the depression days were impelled by motives similar to those that had moved the men who had settled at Alki. They wanted a place where they could live a life of their own. Their settlement grew much faster than early-day Seattle had; it expanded so rapidly that the city administration, like the

Salish Indians, became worried; in the interests of the
health of the established community, the administration
ordered the police and fire departments to destroy the
shacktown. Hooverville was burned to its damp founda-
tions, but pioneer determination was in its makers. Like
the men of '89 after their fire, the shacktown citizens re-
built "before the ashes grew cold."

When the Denny party built its community it was hind-
ered by a lack of tools and capital but was aided by the
bounty of the forests, which stood thick to the edge of the
clay cliffs. The pioneers of the depression were even shorter of capital, just as shy of tools, and they had no forest
to which they could repair for lumber; there was not a log
cabin in all Hooverville. The shacks were constructed of
materials rustled from the docks, the railroads, the dumps:
tin and tarpaper and packing-box boards, that's what
Hooverville was made of.

In 1934 a young sociologist from the University of
Washington, gathering material for a thesis, came to live
in the community. His name was Donald Francis Roy,
and he did not tell his neighbors his mission, though
eventually they found it out. In his sprightly document,
Mr. Roy gives a good picture of life in the community.[2]
The houses ranged from roofed dugouts, like the native
barabaras some of the old-timers may have seen in Alaska, to a cottage, built by an unemployed carpenter, that
boasted a kitchen, a dining room, two bedrooms, a
storeroom, and a front porch. One residence was two
stories tall; the others followed the contour of the tideflats.
In a few of the shacks the only furnishings were bed-
clothes: a heap of gunny sacks, three old overcoats, a pair
of mattresses, one to be slept on, the other under. The
sociologist was startled to find that one man had made a
bed out of a coffin. Another slept under a verdant strip of
artificial lawn stolen from a window display.

Nearly all the shacks had cook stoves, which varied
from second-hand ranges to oil cans with holes punched in

[2] Donald Francis Roy, *Hooverville: A Study of a Community* of
Homeless Men in Seattle. (Unpublished Master's Thesis, University
of Washington, 1935.)

them. The stoves doubled as furnaces but, the saying went, "the only way to keep warm is to work up a sweat hunting fuel." The men spent hours combing the beach for bark ("fishermen's coal") and driftwood; they paced the railroad tracks in search of bits of coal; they raided woodpiles. The stoves quickly warmed the tiny shacks but smoke was always a problem. The smoke hurt the men's eyes and discouraged reading on the long, wet, winter nights—and so did the men's educational background. Few had been exposed to much formal education. Of 632 men living in Hooverville when Mr. Roy took an informal census, twelve per cent had never attended school at all; eighty-nine per cent had not finished the eighth grade. There was a superstition in the thirties that all the hobo jungles were alive with Ph.D.s, but only five of the 632 had been graduated from college. Another five had taken classes for a year or two. Of the ten college men, four were Filipinos.

Mr. Roy had as neighbors 632 men and 7 women. The men ranged in age from fifteen (a young homosexual) to seventy-three (a destitute physician); in nationality from a majority of whites of North European extraction to a Chilean Indian and a pair of Eskimos. There were 292 foreign-born whites, 120 Filipinos, 29 Negroes, 25 Mexicans, 2 Japanese, 2 American Indians, and 3 Costa Ricans.

A third of the men in Hooverville had worked in the lumber camps, but the total range of their occupations, as listed by Mr. Roy, reads like an ode by Walt Whitman to the builders of a nation:

Logger, fire fighter, foreman,
Section hand and brakeman;
Civil engineer, bridge carpenter, shovel runner, powder
    monkey,
Miner, coal miner, gold miner, hard rock miner;
Fisherman, farmer, seaman, petty officer, and ship carpenter;
Camp cook, dishwasher, bullcook, waiter, flunkey.
Painter and steamfitter, electrician and machinist helper;
Pipefitter and paperer;

Barrel-head maker.
Millwright, street grader, blacksmith, stonecutter,
Shoemaker, molder,
Bricklayer, structural iron worker, tinsmith.
Storekeeper, salesclerk, butcher, nightwatchman.
Restaurant owner.
House-to-house salesman.
Truck driver, teamster, longshoreman,
Street car conductor.
Racehorse groom, animal trainer, dairy instructor in a Swiss college.
Missionary to the Indians.
Sewer digger, schoolteacher, dope peddler, sewer cleaner.
Laborer.

They had done everything, but now they had nothing to do. Their common bond was poverty. Almost half of them were drawing relief: 188 had papers permitting them to patronize the breadline, 86 received weekly commissary vouchers of $1.20, 25 got $6 a month from the county, 10 worked in the county woodyard six days a month for $3 a day. Some had part-time jobs uptown. One man, a carpenter by trade, built skiffs for sale to owners of fishing boats. The rest touched householders for food or raided the garbage cans behind the markets. They were proud of their ability to stay off relief.

It was not safe to accumulate property, at least movable property. A man who had the foresight to choose a Chinese lottery ticket worth $300 did not have the foresight to lock his door; he was found bludgeoned to death in his tin-plated shack. A Negro bragged that he had made $11 in one week, gathering and selling wastepaper. Two men, ignorant of the fact that he also earned money as a heavyweight boxer, tried to expropriate his capital. The man of means put down this share-the-wealth movement with a right-cross and a left hook.

Yet by the large Hooverville was orderly. Certainly the citizens were not revolutionists. They were old and tired and hoped they had found a place where they would be let alone. While a majority blamed the economic system for their problems, their real antagonism was directed toward the relief officials with whom they most often came in contact. Many of the older men firmly believed that the interns at the county hospital "used the black bottle"— that is, poisoned aged men from Hooverville who came to them for treatment. They were afraid of the city police and the health authorities. They lived under the constant threat of having their homes burned again as a sacrifice to the health of the larger community.

A six-man vigilante committee helped enforce the sanitation code in Hooverville. (The code regulated traffic to the six privies set over the beach and reached by rickety catwalks.) In the pioneer tradition the committee had no official power but it was respected. It had been elected at a community caucus, attended by only one-fifth of the residents, and the Hooverville committeemen, like their councilman brothers in the County-City Building uptown, deplored the low vote. Members served until removed by death or prosperity. Two whites, two Negroes, and two Filipinos were chosen to the committee. Political domination in Hooverville swung to the man with the greatest lust for power, a Texas cowpoke who just hankered to run things. He served as ex-officio mayor. Since no elections were held after the first caucus and no recall system had been outlined, his election was permanent. The principal challenge to the Texan's political ascendancy came when a neighbor got drunk on denatured alcohol and announced that it was his intention to behead the entire council, including the mayor. The Texan met this revolt by rallying his fellow office-holders and capturing the agitator; after beating him up, they deported him to the Seattle jail, tore down his shack, and distributed the boards among those whose houses needed patching. During the battle the mayor stopped a coffee mug with the top of his head but didn't bother to seek medical attention. As a badge of office he wore a towel-turban for two weeks. He also kept the community radio, a battery set donated to Hooverville by a relief agency. It was the most conspicuous spoil of office, and it sat on the porch of the mayor's house. He kept it turned on loud so that each and every one of his constituents could learn daily of the torments suffered by people like "John's Other Wife."

The men of Hooverville, like the earlier men of Seattle, had one great problem: no women. Only 6 of the 600 were living with women they claimed as their legal helpmeets; only 95 men in the entire community had ever been married. These were the men who, a generation earlier, had become Wobblies, had answered the IWW call to the homeless, the voteless.

"The rest of the men are living without the domestic companionship of the opposite sex," the young sociologist observed. "Their transient association with women might better be described under the head of Recreation instead of Family. Such social contacts are necessarily limited in the main by economic considerations. Some of those who occasionally come in possession of legal tender through odd jobs or junking invest small sums in the more economical brothels of the Skid Road. Now and then 'squaws' from uptown participate in little firesides at the homes of popular Hooverites. When sober, these older and less attractive battleaxes offer their services for sums ranging from ten cents to thirty-five cents. When they are properly intoxicated, or are presented with the prospects of becoming so, cash is not necessary. . . ."

Uptown elements suspected the citizens of the tideflats of staging orgies, but orgies were among the many things these men could not afford. The most popular pastimes were reading, cards, bull sessions, and cheap drunks. The books featured sex; the card games were poker and black-jack and fan-tan (almost never bridge) for low stakes or none; the bull sessions ranged from sex to politics and back to sex; the drunks were staged on denatured alcohol— "dehorn" to the initiated. The nearest thing to orgies would be friendly fights, quickly broken up by the vigilante committee, or community sings, or arguments (sings and arguments being distinguishable in their early stages), or walks to Pioneer Square to study the posters in front of the three bump-and-grind houses operated by latter-day Considines. These men were too poor and dispirited to be flamboyantly depraved; most of them were too old. "I never expect to work again," the men of Hooverville often said. "They all say I'm too old."

There were a few rebels in Hooverville, but their sparks set no flames. There were a few Communists, but they could do little more than pass out literature and inject some dialectics into the bull sessions. These were men who had reached the end of the trail.

In the Skid Road proper, and farther uptown, things were different. The economic system that had spewed up Hooverville-on-the-Tideflats was rousing discontent. A great many people agreed that "there must be a better way," but there was little agreement on the details of the better way. Communists and Trotskyists, Socialists and Silver Shirts, Single-Taxers and Wobblies, advocates of all the standard-brand remedies talked up their economic antidotes and found willing takers. Other medicine men were dreaming up home cures. The Seattle Unemployed Citizens' League offered a self-help palliation that was tried by thousands.

"The Republic of the Penniless" was what a sympathetic advertising man called the Unemployed Citizens' League and the phrase was exact. It was a community within the community. The League was an outfit with no dues and no paid officers, a self-help organization of workers without work. It was formed in the fall of 1931 and at its peak had more than 50,000 members in Seattle and as many more scattered throughout the state. Its members lived by a barter economy. They ran their own shoeshops and barbershops; they sewed one another's dresses and repaired one another's jalopies; they fixed plumbing and patched roofs; they fished and cut wood and dug potatoes and picked applies; all on a barter basis. Each member worked at what he knew; each received what he needed most. "In this Republic of the Penniless," wrote an observer, "honorable employment was all that passed for currency." During the fall and winter of 1931, 120,000 pounds of fish, 10,000 cords of firewood, eight carloads of potatoes, pears, and apples were furnished for unemployed relief by the unemployed themselves. The League demanded and received the right to distribute relief food supplies purchased with county and city funds. No money went to pay salaries, so the entire amount was available for food: $2.16 a week for a family of four.

Nobody was getting rich off relief, but the existence of a large body of citizens—enfranchised, mind you—who were experimenting with a production-for-use economy upset many businessmen. How, they asked, can merchants sell their goods if a considerable portion of the population is permanently kept from the market by a production-for-use scheme? Late in 1932, as the national economy scraped the bottom of the depression, a reporter climbed the steps to the headquarters of the League, which were in a big, bare loft formerly occupied by the High Hatters Cabaret, to ask the League's president what the ultimate aim of the organization was. And J. F. Cronin, a tired man of sixty-nine, who had been a newspaperman himself until he was laid off in his old age, said he didn't know where the League was headed but that it would keep going as long as there was need.

"We're dreadfully close to this problem and the outlook is dark," Cronin said. "We fail to understand how men in dominating political, financial, and industrial positions can ignore the necessity for fundamental change if the present worldwide breakdown is to be corrected. We're doing our best to meet a situation not of our own making. We have unworthy ones in our ranks, yes, but they are less than five per cent of our total. Most of our members are good people. Good people! I never knew until I got into this work how good people can be. Most of us in this work are near life's halfway mark or beyond. What happens to us doesn't matter very much. But it's hard for the youngsters to understand. Human life is terribly short and tomorrow comes soon. We'd like to see it dawn a little brighter for the children."

How to brighten the dawn? Some thought it could be glorified by political action.

The Unemployed Citizens' League went into politics. A few months after the League was formed it asked the city council for use of the Civic Auditorium to hold a mass meeting. The request was denied. At the next city election a trio of candidates unofficially supported by the League ran one-two-three in the race for councilman; and that was followed by a new vote in which the city council not only granted the League the use of the Auditorium but instructed the municipal streetcar system to supply free transportation the evening of the meeting. This simple demostration of the power of the ballot encouraged League officials to think of entering politics. A state federation of Unemployed Citizens' Leagues was formed. Its first purpose was to arrange for an exchange of services between the unemployed in farm and urban communities, a barter of food for goods turned out in co-operative workshops. The federation also made it possible to take political action on a statewide basis. Some dreamers talked of filing an Unemployed Ticket, with jobless candidates running for every office from governor to county coroner.

The federation held a state convention in Tacoma. Delegates arrived on foot, on the rods, in their own jalopies; one rode in on a mule and, on arriving, told a Tacoma newspaperman that he had neither food nor shelter and that while he could last out the depression, he was afraid it would kill his mule.

At the convention the unemployed decided that instead of running their own people it would be more effective to throw the support of the League to candidates filed under more orthodox banners. The jobless—and the rest of the voters—had some odd candidates to choose from that year, and they elected a number of the weirdest. A candidate who ran on a one-plank platform against hot foods was defeated, but a man who conducted the latter phases of his campaign from jail, where he had been placed on a charge of raping a twelve-year-old girl, was elevated to public office. A brilliant young lawyer named Marion Zioncheck won his first political race. So did John C. Stevenson, a professional radio orator. A collection of utopians and Communists and reformers, some of them good men and some awful, won seats in the State Legislature. A donkey was elected as a Republican precinct committeemen. But of all the odd ones who clamored for the attention of the electorate, the oddest by far was a dapper young man with a thin waxed mustache and an air of raffish dignity, Victor Aloysius Meyers, the joke that backfired.

Vic Meyers operated Seattle's most celebrated night spot, the Club Victor, and led its best dance band. He was a glib, personable master of ceremonies who suffered the usual occupational disabilities of his professions: he was often broke and sometimes in trouble with the federal authorities charged with enforcing the Volstead Act. He was a favorite with reporters. His name was news. Everybody knew Vic and he was always good for a laugh. It was worth a two-column picture when the government noticed that people were drinking at the Club Victor and padlocked the joint as a nuisance. It was copy when he won a radio contest as the coast's most popular M. C. It even seemed funny and worth a picture when he fell off a stepladder and broke his arm.

One dull afternoon in January 1932 a group of newspapermen were talking about the collection of fatuous has-beens and never-wases who were seeking to become mayor of Seattle. The only colorful figures in the race was John F. Dore, a stumpy little trial lawyer with a rasping vocabulary and a gift for saw-toothed phrases, but Dore was running under wraps; he was the businessman's candidate, and not even Irish Johnny could be lively on the subject of efficiency in municipal government. The rest of the candidates were hardly worth quoting. Somebody remarked that Vic Meyers was better copy than the whole kit-and-kaboodle. The remark set Doug Welch to thinking happy thoughts. Doug was an assistant city editor on the *Times* [3] and the most efficient humorist then practicing in the Northwest. The idea of Vic Meyers as a candidate for mayor appealed to him; Vic would be a good peg on which to hang some satirical feature stories about the other candidates. After clearing it with the higher brass,

[3] It sometimes seems to outsiders that everybody on the *Times* is an assistant city editor. I once asked a former a.c.e. about it and he said, "It's a job reporters work up to and friends of the Blethens work down to."

Doug phoned Vic and told him that if he'd hustle down to the County-City Building and file for mayor, the Times would give him an eight-column bannerline on page one and follow that up with daily pictures and features for the duration.

Vic thought it was a lovely idea, and so did the Times' readers, for with Welch and every happy cynic in the city room thinking up gags, Meyers put on a wonderful campaign. His slogan was a straight-faced parody of all the short, meaningless slogans dreamed up to fit on advertising placards: "Watch 'er Click with Vic." He announced that he would campaign in shirt sleeves, to prove he was not a representative of the vested interests, but later he took to wearing tuxedo, silk scarf, top hat, velvet-lapeled overcoat, and kid gloves. "Somebody," he explained, "has to give this campaign a little class."

Meyers drove a beer wagon around town. His band played "Happy Days Are Here Again," and Vic parked the wagon at intersections and harangued the townsfolk on topics of the day. There was the usual argument about daylight-saving time and Vic took a firm stand. "I don't believe in it. Seattle should have two-four time, allegro." He burlesqued the economy speeches that John Dore was making. "I'm not very economical and thrifty myself, but you ought to see my wife! As soon as I am elected, I will turn over the city to her. In two weeks Edinburgh will appoint a commission to come and study the economies my wife will put in." Dore was against waste, and so was Vic: he suggested putting flowerboxes around all the fire hydrants to utilize any water that dripped out.

Vic came out four-square in favor of graft. "There's not going to be any cheap chiseling on city contracts while I'm mayor," he said. "I'm going to take it all myself." On other topics he was less flat-footed, explaining that he had noticed that mayors who said "yes" ran into a lot of trouble and those who said "no" had even more. So he was going to be the nation's first "Maybe Man."

Sometimes a serious citizen would ask Vic how he stood on some topic. When he couldn't think of a wisecrack Vic would roll his eyes thoughtfully heavenward, wait a moment, then nod, smile, and lean forward. "I'm okay on that," he would assure his questioner.

He had more gag writers than a radio comedian and they delighted in thinking up stunts for him. All the candidates were promising to do something about Seattle's streetcars, which were ancient and ugly and flat-wheeled. Vic suggested hostesses, and when Laura La Plante, a reigning blonde in Hollywood, visited town, Vic took her for a streetcar ride. He generously gave her credit for the suggestion that the hostesses supply cracked ice on the late evening cruises.

When all the candidates were invited to speak at a luncheon of one of the service clubs, Vic arrived dressed as Mahatma Gandhi, leading a goat. He sat at the speakers' table sipping goat's milk and munching raw carrots and looking at his rivals over the top of his gold-rimmed spectacles. His very presence made all the speeches ridiculous.

It was good fun. Nobody took it seriously except the *Star* and the *Post-Intelligencer*, which sniffed disdainfully about degradation of the electoral process, and Vic himself. As the campaign wore on and he listened to more of his rivals' speeches, Vic arrived at the opinion the reporters had started with—that he was as good as any of the other bums in the race. From the time that notion assailed him Vic was a problem to his gag writers. He wanted to talk about issues. He was the comedian hellbent on playing Hamlet. Toward the end of the campaign he announced that the comedy was over; from here on in he was out for votes, not laughs. For many this statement seemed the ultimate in deadpan hilarity, but Vic was serious. He finished sixth in the primary field of ten. The *Times*, in his name, demanded a recount. Vic suggested that the FBI study the fingerprints in all the polling booths. Then he went back to leading his dance band—but only briefly. After a few months in which he failed to gain an inch of front-page space, Vic phoned Doug Welch and suggested another campaign, this time for governor. Welch said the gag had worn thin; anyway, once was enough. Not for Vic. He decided to run unsponsored, drove down to Olym-

pia, and appeared at the state capitol, ready to file. He
was less ready when he learned the filing fee was sixty
dollars. "That's too much," said Vic. "What do you have
for twenty?" "Well," said the clerk, "you could file for
lieutenant governor. That's twelve." Vic hesitated. "I can't
spell it," he said thoughtfully, "but I'll take it."

Vic worked hard at his campaign. He used the gags
Welch had dreamed up, but he had the swing of it now
and made up some for himself. He beat tom-toms on an
Indian reservation and expressed surprise when told that
wards of the government had no vote. He played his
saxophone at a lumber camp. He again wrapped himself
in Gandhi's mantle. He assured the voters he was okay—
but he also came out for pensions, children's welfare
measures and unemployment compensation. None of the
professionals took him seriously, not until the September
primaries. In the privacy of the voting booth, Washington
citizens scanned the long list of candidates for lieutenant
governor and found there the familiar name of Vic
Meyers. Enough voters pulled the lever or marked the
"X" beside his name to make him the nominee of the
Democratic Party.

The joke had gone far enough. It looked as though
1932 would be a Democratic year, and the last two Democratic governors had died in office. Clarence D. Martin,
the nominee for governor, was a gaunt gentleman who
looked none too durable. Republicans—and many Democrats—asked the voters, "Do you want a man like Vic
Meyers just a heartbeat away from the governorship?" On
election day 286,402 of them did, which was 40,000 more
than wanted Vic's Republican opponent.

So Vic had the last laugh.[4] He announced that he
would hold a coming-out-of-the-red party for his credi-

---

[4] It is a laugh that still echoes in Washington politics. In 1951
Vic has a year to go in his fifth term. He has survived two elections in which the Republicans won the governorship. The Times
has frequently carried exposés on the activities of its former protégé,
the most recent having to do with Vic's use of a state Cadillac while
on a vacation trip to the Southwest. "What's the fuss?" Vic asked.
"Sure it's the state's car but I paid for the gas."

tors; he also expressed hope that someone would tell how
to do whatever it was a lieutenant governor did. Editorial
writers throughout the nation shuddered in print for the
fate of the state.

Meyers' election by itself might have been a meaningless absurdity, made possible by the voters' preference
for a familiar name in the primary and by the Roosevelt
landslide in the final; but into office throughout the state
went other representatives of discontent, symbols of protest against the orthodox and the respectable.

Three months after the election, with the lumber industry prostrate and the number of jobless at an all-time
peak, the Unemployed Citizens' League announced a protest march on Olympia, a maneuver designed "to call the
attention of the representatives of the owner class to the
need for drastic action." There were those who seriously
hoped, and those who wildly feared, that the march would
touch off a social revolution. Not since the general strike
had there been violent talk. Wobblies and Communists
and Socialists all struggled to dominate the League and to
control the protest march. An oragnizer for the American
Vigilantes, a fascist organization of the day, appeared in
Olympia and instructed citizens in the way to handle
demonstators. "Temper your serverity to suit the occasion," the Vigilantes were told. "If forced to fight, don't
forget that nothing so swiftly sickens a mob as brutal,
stomach-wrenching, soul-sickening force, fearlessly and
judiciously applied."

The marchers and the Vigilantes met at the top of the
hills that surround Olympia; there was no violence. Most
of the demonstrators turned aside, which was, perhaps, a
symbol of a new era, for after March 1933 there was
less talk of violent revolution and more of a revolution
through due process. Nationally the first Roosevelt administration was starting its Hundred Days of reform, and
locally the radicals recently elected were learning to distin-
guish one another and were starting to form ranks in an
almost united front.

The Washington Commonwealth Federation was made

up of unions (though the Central Labor Council frowned on it), public-power advocates, Townsendites and other pension planners the remnants of the Unemployed Citizens' League (which rapidly lost strength as national relief measures became effective), Communists, ex-Wobblies, some Socialists, unaffiliated radicals, Technocrats, and a large body of liberals. The common denominator was desire for change.

The Federation's program was flexible and opportunistic, sometimes sounding like the New Deal, sometimes like the Communist Party, but there was no question that it was the most radical movement to approach power since the Populists captured the governorship in 1896. The Communists, though by no means in absolute control of the Federation, were in position to influence its day-to-day operations; most of the key shifts in Federation policy paralleled shifts in Community policy. These changes were often abrupt, especially the ones involving foreign policy, and along with the shifts in domestic viewpoint—shifts which made Roosevelt alternately saint and devil—they eventually confused and alienated much of the Federation's mass support.[5] But in the rosy days of the mid-thirties the radicals were joined in happy federation, united against the forces of entrenched conservatism—in their eyes, united against evil. A new world was a-borning.

The birth pains were sharpest, perhaps, at the 1936 state Democratic convention in Aberdeen. Technically the Commonwealth Federation was independent politically, endorsing candidates already filed in other parties; actually it operated as the left wing of the Democratic Party. In

[5] The basic shifts can be interpreted pretty well through the changes in title of the Federation's paper. It was first called the *Commonwealth Builder*, then the *Sunday News*. The name was next changed to *The New Dealer*, but in 1940, when Roosevelt was a "warmonger" and the Commonwealth's president the only delegate to the Democratic convention who wouldn't vote for his renomination, the paper became *The New World*. *The New World* collapsed in 1949, most of its staff and some of its circulation going over to *The People's World*, the organ of the Communist Party on the Pacific Coast, published in San Francisco.

1936 the Federation delegates stampeded the Democratic convention. When the conservative opposition, who controlled the convention machinery, tried to use parliamentary tactics to neutralize the voting strength of the "wild men from Seattle," the assembled radicals, led by a former drama critic, a former history professor, and a former barber, simply marched onto the platform, took over the agenda, voted themselves power, and carried on. The chairman splintered four gavels before the convention ended; the delegates broke political precedent with even greater frequency. When the shouting died down and the Democrats read the minutes, they found the Party was on record as favoring the nationalization of all banks, public ownership of all utilities and natural resources, and production for use; but it was not on record as favoring the re-election of President Roosevelt.

Having rewritten the Democratic platform to its own highly seasoned taste, the Commonwealth Federation endorsed the Democrats it considered deserving. Among them were Marion Zioncheck for re-election to Congress, John C. Stevenson for governor (against the Democratic incumbent), and Vic Meyers for lieutenant governor. These choices were not altogether fortunate. Vic was a joke, though perhaps a good one; Stevenson a plausible phony; and Zioncheck was mad, quite mad, and about to prove it.

Marion Zioncheck was perhaps the ablest radical Seattle ever produced. He was a brilliant, tough young Pole who had been brought to America at the age of three. He grew up on the Skid Road. He was poor, grindingly poor; at various times he worked as logger, fish peddler, rat catcher (ten cents a head), dishwasher, cowboy. He decided he wanted to be a lawyer and enrolled at the University of Washington, dropped out for four years to keep his folks in food, but came back, older and tougher. The fraternity system galled him. He organized the independents into an anti-Greek coalition and in 1928 he was elected president of the student body. As soon as he was in office he started investigating the way the athletic department was spending money; a mysterious fire destroyed some of the records, and a posse of football players captured Zioncheck, shaved his head, and tossed him into Frosh Pond. Twenty-one years and two Rose Bowl teams later, the students got the recreation building Zioncheck had recommended.

Admitted to the bar in 1929, Zioncheck barely had his diploma in place on the wall of his crackerbox office before he was mixed up in another good fight. He led a movement to recall Seattle's mayor, Frank Edwards, who was playing with private power people against what Zioncheck considered the best interests of City Light. The voters agreed, the mayor was recalled, and young Zioncheck was a political power.

He ran for Congress in 1932. "I am a radical," he would say at the start of a speech. "I guess I always have been. I hope I always will be." He won, and he won again in 1934. No congressman worked harder than young Zioncheck. (He was thirty-two when he was elected for his first term.) He was tough and hard-minded and diligent. He tried to read every bill considered by the House; he refused to compromise; he fought whatever he felt was wrong—racism, the Silver Shirts, the use of the National Guard to break strikes. He said, "People aren't paying taxes so that the National Guard can see to it that scabs get in there and break strikes." He was against big military expenditures; and though the Bremerton Navy Yard was one of the great payrolls in his district, he voted against increased naval appropriations. He thought the Townsend Plan was a fraud and he told the old folks so, while others hedged. He was tough and arrogant and he sometimes said, "I'm the best congressman our state ever had." The voters in his home district adored him—or hated him; some observers thought he would become the dominant political figure in the Northwest, but nationally nobody noticed him, not until New Year's morning, 1936, when he rolled into the lobby of a fancy Washington, D.C., apartment house, plugged in all numbers on the telephone switchboard and wished all the occupants a happy New Year. He sobered up in jail. "The police department is lousy," he told his captors.

A few weeks later the cops had him again. He wanted to know what he'd done this time. "You were driving seventy miles an hour on a crowded street," he was told. "It couldn't have been me," said Zioncheck. "I'd have been doing eighty." He borrowed money to pay his fine.

Rubye Louise Nix, a WPA typist from Texarkana, thought his exploits cute and on an impulse telephoned him. Zioncheck liked her voice, asked for a date, got it, and married her the next day. He borrowed the two-dollar license fee from a court clerk.

The Zionchecks gave an interview to the press (he was wearing an Indian suit and drawing a long bow) in which Rubye explained that she hoped to reform him. They started south on a honeymoon trip in Zioncheck's second-hand, twelve-cylinder convertible. They outran some cops, were caught by others. In Florida, Rubye bought Marion a kiddie car and told reporters she'd do all the driving in the family; but in Puerto Rico, Marion borrowed a car, sideswiped a truck, drove through a locked gate, was challenged to a duel, took part in a student riot, threw coconuts out of his hotel window, and finally demanded that the Marines be sent to protect him. He went next to the Virgin Islands, where he was noticed lapping soup from his plate at a swank hotel and biting the neck of the chauffeur assigned to pilot his car.

On his return to New York he went wading in the Rockefeller Center pool, judged a beauty contest in a night club, scuffled with the boy friend of one of the losers, and gave a rhumba exhibition. When the Zionchecks got back to Washington their landlady told them they'd have to move. Marion threw her out. The cops came again. Zioncheck posted bail of twenty-five dollars and complained of persecution. The next day Rubye disappeared. Marion accused Vice-President Garner of kidnaping her; as a protest he delivered empty beer bottles to the White House. Then Rubye returned.

At last someone realized that his actions weren't publicity gags and he was hustled off to a sanitarium. His enemies wrote his political obituaries. On the Fourth of July 1936 he escaped from the sanitarium, returned to

Seattle, and announced that he would run for re-election. His friends failed to talk him out of it. Then he changed his mind and withdrew from the race, changed it again and started his campaign.

On a lovely day early in August he drove with Rubye and his brother-in-law, William Nadeau, to the Arctic Building. While the others waited, Zioncheck went "to get some papers" in the fifth-floor office he had rented as campaign headquarters. Rubye and Nadeau waited ten minutes. Nadeau was nervous, for Zioncheck's psychiatrist had told him that same day, "You'd better keep an eye on Marion," so he went up to the office. The door was locked and Zioncheck didn't answer when Nadeau knocked. Nadeau got the janitor to unlock it. Zioncheck was sitting at his desk, writing. He was flushed and seemed nervous.

"Come on, Marion," Nadeau said, "or we'll be late for your speech."

Zioncheck shook his head and continued to write. Nadeau called him again. Zioncheck threw down his pen, pushed the paper to the floor, and got to his feet.

"You have a hat, haven't you?" Nadeau asked.

"It's on the shelf," Zioncheck said, nodding toward the anteroom.

"I'll get it," said Nadeau. He found the hat and came back to the room. As Nadeau came through the door, Zioncheck ripped off the light gray suitcoat he was wearing and dived headfirst through the office window. Nadeau grabbed for him and almost caught his foot. Zioncheck fell five stories, his body turning like a stick, and landed on his head in front of the automobile in which Rubye was sitting. He was killed instantly.

Nadeau picked up the note Zioncheck had been writing. It was scrawled on the stationery of the House Naval Affairs Committee, and it read: "My only hope in life was to improve the condition of an unfair economic system that held no promise to those that all the wealth of even a decent chance to survive let alone live . . ."

The Washington Commonwealth Federation had withdrawn support from Zioncheck a few days before his suicide, but it stuck with another questionable candidate right up to the day of the primary. John C. Stevenson was a husky, bald-headed mystery man who first attracted attention in the Northwest as the unctuous voice of the Painless Parker chain of advertising dentists. His salary was reported to be $1000 a week, and he lived up to it; his house was one of the finest town, he flew a $20,000 plane, he piloted a cabin cruiser on Puget Sound. While proclaiming the luster of his patron's lifelike dentures, Stevenson built up a large radio audience; he liked being an oracle and soon was hawking political nostrums along with dental floss. He had the technique down pat: he criticized specific wrongs and proposed vague remedies. In 1932 he filed in the Democratic primary for King County commissioner. He ran as "Radio Speaker John C. Stevenson," and in a field of nobodies he couldn't miss. He was radical enough to appeal to Seattle's great mass of unemployed and underpaid; he was plausible enough to appeal to the farmers who normally shunned the type of soothsayer who found favor on the Skid Road. From the day he was elected, he was the most important commissioner any county in the state ever had. He was, as the saying goes, "a comer," and the Washington Commonwealth Federation was delighted to sponsor him.

But there was more to Stevenson than met the ear. He had materialized out of nowhere, like the great Gatsby, and there were odd rumors about where he got his wealth. When he was about to be sworn in as county commissioner, a citizen arose to protest that Stevenson wasn't a citizen, that he had flown in the Royal Canadian Air Force and was a Canadian. Stevenson admitted he had flown for Canada, denied that he was a Canadian, and refused—on grounds of possible self-incriminaton—to reveal the name he had been known by in Canada. He was allowed to take office.

A few months later Governor Lehman of New York informed authorities in Olympia that Stevenson was known back East as John P. Stockman and was wanted for fraud in connection with a fake stock sale. Stevenson said he was Stockman, all right, but that he was innocent; he fought extradition. Governor Martin was in an uncomfortable spot. Should he, or should he not, turn over to New York a man who was at once an influential Democrat and a serious rival? He refused extradition and eventually the charges against Stevenson were dropped. Any gratitude that the Radio Speaker felt did not last beyond 1936. In the summer of that year Stevenson felt he was ready to take the state away from Governor Martin and filed in the Democratic gubernatorial primary. The voters were faced with a complicated choice between the rich, honest, unimaginative, conservative incumbent and his rich, opportunistic, brilliant, radical opponent.

The Commonwealth Federation supported Stevenson, ardently at first, then less enthusiastically when it became apparent that he was going to lose. What went wrong with the Radio Speaker's campaign was an experimental election device—the state is always adopting such devices, to the confusion of professional politicans—the blanket primary. Under this system voters can shop around and vote for one candidate for each office, no matter which party he is running for. Any Republican who felt like it could vote for Governor Martin in the primary, and since the Republican nomination was in the bag for moss-backed ex-Governor Roland Hartley, thousands of Republicans joyously indicated they would help the conservative Democrats beat Stevenson in the September primary.

Nobody trusted the public opinion polls very much, but when the gamblers started giving two-to-one on Martin, the Commonwealth Federation bosses decided it was time to cut and run. At the last possible moment they held a quick caucus and announced they were filing a write-in ticket of their own for the November finals. The Commonwealth candidate would be Howard Costigan, a former barber and mural painter, who had talked his way into the position of executive secretary for the Federation. This tactic was based on a correct interpretation of the way the primary votes would run, but it infuriated Stevenson and his supporters and it helped split the Federation.

Stevenson lost the nomination by 40,000 votes. Any joy

Governor Martin felt in his victory over the Radio Speaker must have been chilled by the fact that the voters who rejected Stevenson renominated Vic Meyers, by the greatest vote any candidate ever received in a Washington primary. Vic got more votes than Martin in the final too, though both were landslide victors. And the Commonwealth exulted in Martin's discomfort. "Just let the governor leave the state," Howard Costigan remarked one day, "and Vic'll show him how a state ought to be run."

Governor Martin had realized four years earlier that if he left Washington, Vic would be acting governor and could, if the urge were on him, open the gates of the state penitentiary, or call the Legislature into session, or mobilize the National Guard. The governor had spent his entire four-year term within the borders of his state, and now the voters had given him another four-year term as the lieutenant governor's political prisoner. It was embarrassing. A governor ought to get to Washington, D.C., once in a while, if only to milk a few extra million dollars of pump-priming funds from the federal government; going to Washington and coming home with word of a federal grant was always good politics, but it was a comfort Clarence Martin felt he must deny himself. His frustration became more active as the country slid into the recession of '38. The administration started priming the economic pump again, and Martin ached to see the boys.

Martin's chance came when Vic Meyers left the state for a vacation in California. The governor decided he could pay a flying visit to the capital. As soon as the Commonwealth Federation learned he was gone, a hunt for Vic was begun; all they could learn was that he was on a fishing trip somewhere along the California coast. Radio stations up and down the coast were asked to page him. A day later Vic learned that he was wanted; he got to a phone and called Howard Costigan at Commonwealth headquarters. Costigan told him "to get the hell up here and be governor." Vic didn't even bother to change shoes; he started north in fishing sandals. He picked up a police escort, which cleared the road as he raced for a train.

While Meyers rushed north, the Commonwealth Federation leaders drew up plans for a special session of the State Legislature to be called by Vic. They thought the recession would give them a good chance to pass relief measures that Martin believed too generous.

Martin's men learned that Meyers was on his way. They phoned the governor back East and warned him. But no commercial flight would get him home in time to head off Vic, and once a special session was called there was no way to un-call it. Martin phoned an airline and learned it would cost him more than a thousand dollars to charter a plane. "Get me one," he said and rushed for the airport.

Meyers made it into the state first, but it was at night. He would have to wait until eight a.m. to file his notice of the special session with the secretary of state. The Commonwealth Federation had all the papers ready. At five minutes after eight Vic rushed into the capitol and handed Secretary of State Belle Reeves the formal statement summoning the State Legislature into special session.

But Vic wasn't governor any more. Thirteen minutes earlier, at 7:52 a.m., Clarence Martin's chartered plane had come down outside Spokane. Meyers was lieutenant governor again, and a lieutenant governor can't call the legislature into seassion. Vic protested to the State Supreme Court but the jurists did not see things his way. Martin was unhappy too. He had won the race but he knew now he would not be able to leave the state again until either he or Vic was out of office. The airline sent him a bill of $1,308 for use of its plane.

Goings-on like this led Postmaster James Farley, after a visit to Seattle, to remark, "There are forty-seven states and the Soviet of Washington." Against this background of Hooverville and hocus-pocus politics Dave Beck fought his way to domination.

3.

In 1933 the National Recovery Act was signed by President Roosevelt. Section 7-a stated that "employees shall have the right to organize and bargain collectively through representatives of their own choosing, and shall be free from interference, coercion, or restraint of employers of labor or their agents." Across the land the great drive to unionize the workers began.

Dave Beck was ready and waiting, willing and able. He had by this time rounded up everything on wheels in Seattle. He was perfecting his technique of unionizing a plant by "organizing the boss"—convincing him that he could make more profit by paying higher wages and thereby creating stability. Where other union leaders were calling the bosses names, Beck soft-soaped them. "Some of the finest people I know are employers," he kept repeating.[6] He was too shrewd to rely mainly on propaganda. Behind the sweet words was the economic force of the Teamsters, who could refuse to haul supplies to any outfit that fought Beck. Professional bullyboys made it unhealthy to drive anything for pay if you didn't wear a Teamster button. Trucks were sideswiped and overturned, men who voted wrong at the Central Labor Council were beaten up. People heard the apocryphal Teamster slogan, "Vote no and go to the hospital." Judge James T. Ronald of the Superior Court studied the organizing tactics and declared them "so shameless and disgraceful as to parallel the lawlessness witnessed at times in certain saloons in pioneer days. If such is unionism, which I am unwilling to believe, then the world is witnessing the beginning of the end."

Such stories didn't hurt the Teamsters; they discouraged opposition. It was effective Teamster propaganda when one of the union's lieutenants, Al Rosser, was sent to the penitentiary for hiring men to burn down a box factory that refused Teamster services. Other hesitant employers—and workers—had an object lesson in how far some of the boys might go.

Beck, of course, never believed in labor violence as an end in itself. He stood for law and order and, above all,

[6] A Teamster remarked recently, "Dave used to say some of his best friends were bosses. Now I'll bet he tells the bosses some of his best friends drive truck."

stability. The Teamsters threw their weight around only as long as it was necessary for them to prove they could be tough. Once the fact of Teamster power was firmly in the public mind, the boys were well behaved. Even so from time to time there were reminders of what opposition might bring. The Teamsters once hired Leo Lomski, the Aberdeen Assassin, a perennial contender for the light-heavyweight championship of the world, to serve as business agent during a strike; and when the CIO was stressing the need to "educate the workers," Beck hired a jiu-jitsu expert to educate his Teamsters. "What we are after," he explained, "is a big strong union."

The Teamsters were strong, all right, but it took William Randolph Hearst, the publisher, and Alfred Renton ("Harry") Bridges, the longshore boss, to make them respectable. The year of the great transformation was 1936.

4.

Seattle had three papers in 1936 and none of them liked Dave Beck. The dominant papers, the *Times* and *Post-Intelligencer*, which Hearst brought in 1921 had a running feud to see which hated him the most. In May of that year the Newspaper Guild began a drive to organize the *Post-Intelligencer*. Two of the most active members in the Guild chapter were Everhardt Armstrong, the drama editor, and Frank Lynch, the chief photographer; they were good men who had been with the paper for more than fifteen years. Shortly after they let the management know they were in the Guild, Lynch was fired for "inefficiency" and Armstrong for "insubordination."

The Guild tried to negotiate for their reinstatement, but the management refused to talk about it. The Guild filed an appeal with the National Labor Relations Board and also put the matter before the Central Labor Council. Beck dominated the council, and it voted to put the *Post-Intelligencer* on the unfair list. That meant strike. Beck ordered the Teamsters to join the picket line and the union men turned out in force. To everyone's surprise, so did hundreds of unorganized citizens who didn't care for the paper or for William Randolph Hearst. There were housewives in trim frocks, faculty members from the University of Washington, lawyers, clerks, and at least four ministers of the Gospel on a picket line that jammed the streets for a block in each direction from the plant. The typographical unions refused to pass the picket line. A few non-Guild reporters slipped through and covered their beats by telephone; they pecked out copy in the echoing city room, but without the backshop men no paper could be printed, and even if one were printed it would have been difficult to distribute.

The executives of the *Post-Intelligencer* appealed by phone to the owners of the *Seattle Star*, who said that if the *P-I* sent them the copy they would print their rival's paper. But how could they get copy to the *Star*? There was a call for volunteers, and a chubby young reporter stepped forward. He'd carry the news through the picket line. He stripped down, wrapped the copy around his body and legs, dressed, and slipped safely through the crowd around the building.

The *Star* plant was across the street from the Labor Temple. As the reporter neared his goal he ran into one of the strikers, who was accompanied by a pair of large men with cauliflower ears, wearing heavy shoes, brass-studded belts, and shiny new Teamster buttons. "What you doing up here?" the striker asked. The reporter was up to the occasion: "I was just going to the Labor Temple to sign up with you guys." So they took him to the Temple and enrolled him in the Guild. Afterward, happy in the success of his stratagem, he slipped into the *Star* building; but the *Star* printers refused to set the type on the ground that to do so would constitute a lockout of the *P-I* backshop. When the four-month strike ended the Guild fined the reporter five dollars for each meeting he had missed, and the meetings had been daily.

The *Times*' attempt at assistance was purely editorial but it backfired just as loudly. General Blethen—the son of the late Colonel—dictated a hot editorial that closed with some explosive (and expensive) rhetoric. "How do you like the look of Dave Beck's gun?" he demanded. "Oh, the shame of it!" Beck sued the *Times* for libel. He asked $250,000 and settled out of court for $10,000.

Hearst took to the air. He brought in a battery of public-relations men, bought hours of radio time, and filled the radio channels with sound and fury. Beck was pictured as a racketeer and—of all things—a Red. Beck sued the *P-I* and the stations for $500,000, and later settled out of court for $15,000. The Hearst orators shifted their attack; they argued that freedom of the press was endangered and that a labor dictatorship was being established. The Guild had no money to buy radio time but it had plenty of supporters, so it organized some of its well-wishers into a telephone brigade. Whenever a station carried a pro-Hearst broadcast, the telephone brigade swamped the switchboard with indignant demands that the Guild's side of the story be told. Station managers began to give the Guild free time to reply to charges made on purchased time.

The Hearst people formed a Law and Order League, which started to take an inventory of firearms owned by its members; there was talk of an armed phalanx which would crash through the picket line around the plant. That talk died down after a mass meeting of Guild supporters, at which not only ministers but the mayor and the prosecuting attorney spoke on behalf of the strikers. Warren G. Magnuson, the handsome young prosecuting attorney of King County, carried a Teamster card in his wallet and had the Commonwealth Federation endorsement for the late Marion Zioncheck's seat in Congress. Magnuson cited laws guaranteeing the right to strike and the right to picket. Those laws must be obeyed, he said. The mayor, John F. Dore, once friend of the businessman, told the cheering crowd of five thousand that if the Law and Order League appeared with guns, the city police would take the weapons away from them in the interests of law and order. "I don't care if the *Post-Intelligencer* ever publishes," he said, "and I think it would be a good thing for the town if it didn't."

The emergence of John F. Dore as the four-square friend of the workingman (Central Labor Council variety) was Seattle's most enchanting political somersault since Hi Gill ran as a reformer. Dore had been elected mayor in 1932 (the year of Vic Meyers' political unveiling) on a cut-the-costs-and-reduce-the-taxes program. He had trimmed the budget, fired everybody he could fire without getting in trouble with Civil Service, lowered the taxes, kept the city well in the black—and then lost the 1934 election to an amiable young lawyer named Charles Smith, whose administration devoted itself largely to getting national publicity for Seattle by staging diaper-changing contests, put-out-the-cat contests, and icemen-racing-for-housewife's-kiss contests. Dore was disgusted. He felt that his sponsors had let him down. He had delivered economies for the businessmen, the businessmen had not delivered votes for Dore. That was a hell of a way to do business. Dore began to shop around for a new political sponsor and found one in Dave Beck.

When Dore ran for mayor again in 1936, this time with the backing of the Teamsters, he won handsomely. "Brother Dave Beck was the greatest factor in my election," he told the State Federation of Labor after the vote was counted, "and I say again that I am going to pay back my debt to Dave Beck and the Teamsters in the next two years, regardless of what happens."

Beck's political flank was guarded; neither police nor private guards were going to disrupt a Teamster picket line. The P-I strike settled into a siege. It became apparent that ultimate victory might hinge on the state and national election results. The Republican gubernatorial candidate was campaigning on the issue of the P-I strike. "If I were in Olympia," ex-Governor Hartley said, "I'd smash that strike." Nationally the Hearst chain was pouring out editorials in favor of Alf Landon; the Democrats made no secret of their delight that one of Hearst's spigots was plugged. Both sides waited for the political decision in November. The Republicans lost and Hearst surrendered. He wrote an editorial praising Roosevelt as the possible successor of Andrew Jackson, and a little later he announced that the *Post-Intelligencer* would resume publication with Roosevelt's son-in-law John Boettiger, late of the *Chicago Tribune*, as its new publisher. Hearst said that Boettiger would have a completely free hand.

The handsome young publisher arrived in town with Anna Roosevelt as helpmeet and assistant publisher and editor of the homemaker page. The President's son-in-law was not unmindful of the role Dave Beck had played in his rise from the editorial ranks to that of publisher. Boetigger told the assembled dignitaries at a welcoming banquet that he considered Seattle a "model industrial community." Never again did the *Post-Intelligencer* attack Beck, and when Westbrook Pegler or one of the other syndicated columnists made unfriendly remarks about the Teamster leader, *P-I* editors protected the public by deleting the heresy.

Nor did the *Times* find anything wrong with Beck after 1936. Its editorials, which once had equated Beckism with bolshevism and the Teamsters with terror, suddenly became models of restraint. It was not that General Blethen loved Beck the more; it was that there had appeared on the labor scene a man he loved much less. He was Harry Bridges, president of the Pacific Coast Longshoremen's Union, CIO.

The tough little longshoreman was the perfect foil for the bland and businesslike Beck. If anything could make the Teamsters look attractive to employers, Bridges could, and did. Beck was born in America; Bridges was a foreigner who hadn't bothered to become a citizen. Beck was a member of the American Legion and an active Elk; Bridges was an avowed radical. Beck was plump, well groomed and dressed conservatively; Bridges was angular as a chunk of coal, his linen was sometimes less than fresh, he wore cheap suits and dark shirts, and when he did try to dress up he looked, according to one of his admirers, "like a retired pimp."

Intellectually they were just as far apart. Beck understood the desire to accumulate money, Bridges never seemed to give a damn about a dollar. Beck told a reporter, "We recognize that labor cannot receive a fair wage unless business receives a just profit on its investment." Bridges, answering a question after a speech at a University of Washington luncheon club, said, "We take the stand that we as workers have nothing in common with the employers. We are in a class struggle, and we subscribe to the belief that if the employer is not in business his products will still be necessary and we still will be providing them when there is no employing class. We frankly believe that day is coming."

Behind Beck and Bridges were two great labor organizations, the old and conservative American Federation of Labor and the new and experimental Committee for Industrial Organization. The groups stood for opposing principles of union organization. The AFL had flowered late in the nineteenth century, before the rise of mass-production industries; its structure was centered around craft unions, local unions of specialists, which formed central unions within each city and federations within each state, which in turn formed national and international trade unions. This structure was not ideally constituted for dealing with mass-production industries, where the output was the product of many hands, some skilled, others unskilled.

For years men within the ALF had argued for "vertical" unions made up of all the workers within an industry, no matter what their craft. Jimmy Duncan of the Seattle Labor Council, one of the leaders of the general strike, had spoken up in national convention for the One-Big-Union concept so often that he was nicknamed "Resolutions" Duncan, but shift to industrial unionism would have disrupted the existing organization of the AFL. It might have endangered the control of the leaders of the craft unions, and few men in history have voted themselves out of power.

In 1935 John L. Lewis and leaders of unions operating in the mass-production fields set up a Committee for Industrial Organization. The group said it would work within the framework of the AFL, but the AFL executive council objected on the ground that it feared industrial unions would eventually get into jurisdictional disputes with craft unions. The Lewis committee was told to disband. It refused, and the AFL executive council expelled its members. Lewis and his followers turned their committee into the CIO. They took with them one-third of the membership of the AFL, and they at once began a nationwide drive to organize the workers on an industrial basis.

Harry Bridges was the oustanding CIO leader on the West Coast; Dave Beck dominated the AFL in the same area: their unions were bound to clash. Battle was joined all along the coast, but it was most savage in San Francisco and Seattle. In both ports the pattern of the struggle was the same: Bridges controlled the beach and Beck dominated the hills. They fought for hegemony over the men who worked in the warehouses that lay in no-man's land. When the organizers and agents and rank-and-filers of the rival unions met at the warehouses fights broke out, brutal and spectacular. Truck drivers and dock-wallopers tend to be hardy; they also run large; much of the fighting was in the heavyweight division.

Behind the union men, who fought as a sideline to their regular duties, were some goons, specialists in rough-and-tumble tactics, who served as paid stormtroopers and were thrown into the battles when the going got rough. One of the Teamster fighters, Tony Harn, is now a legend along the Skid Road. He was injured so badly in a battle that his left arm calcified into a club. Once back in action, "Stonearm" Harn delighted in braining sailors with the weapon they had given him. Teamsters without Harn's natural advantages usually went into battle armed with sawed-off softball bats that had been trimmed to fit inside the sleeve of a coat. The stevedores used their cargo hooks, and the sailors—who were on Bridges' side—turned their fists into war clubs by wrapping them with metal tape.

During the most violent period Mayor Dore again delivered for his supporters. The city police looked the other way when the Teamsters were winning their riots, broke them up and arrested the CIO men when the Teamsters were getting licked.

Red-faced Johnny Dore paid a high price for keeping a political promise. Prices were rising and the voters were sick of goon squads and labor violence. Though the Teamsters gave Dore their all-out support in 1938, he was defeated in the primary, running third; the finalists were Arthur Langlie, a conservative young lawyer whose platform called for honesty and impartiality, and Lieutenant-Governor Vic Meyers, who retained his state position while campaigning as the CIO-Commonwealth Federation man on a social reform ticket. Vic's only memorable wisecrack of the campaign came when Dore called him a Communist: "Who the hell ever heard of a Communist with a middle name of Aloysius?"

Many businessmen did not rejoice in Beck's political rebuff. The Argus, a slick-paper weekly with an editorial tone that echoes the conversation in the sedate Rainier Club, warned its readers that nothing good would come if Langlie kept his promise to be impartial. "Langlie ... will make Seattle an open labor town and allow the Lewis and Bridges elements to enter unhampered. That would promptly result in a new period of labor turmoil and in the undoing of all the progress that has been accomplished ... in creating harmony and economic cooperation in Seattle." The Argus needn't have worried. The Teamsters had the town well in hand. "This town is going to be organized," Beck warned the businessmen. "Choose me or Bridges." He organized the bosses. Except along the waterfront, the laboring force of Seattle was his, to have and to hold and to use.

Dore died soon after losing the 1938 election and Dave Beck helped carry him to his grave. Though Beck had lost an election and a faithful political servant, he must have found consolation in the realization that he had won the city. He had captured the hearts of the businessmen in his home town. He had sold himself as the lesser evil.

5.

Dave Beck's system for Seattle has been called by many names. The Commonwealth Federation described it as "labor fascism." The Los Angeles Times, which didn't like Beck any more than the radicals did, used his name like a four-letter word and called Teamster organizing policies "beckism." For a time people in Seattle called Beck's system "Dave's Little NRA," because, after the Supreme Court had outlawed the National Recovery Act and its price-fixing agreements, the Teamsters seemed nearly as effective in preventing price-cutting as the federal government had been. But after a few years under Beck's system, Seattle no longer spoke of it or questioned it: Beck's stabilization tactics were accepted, like the rain.

Charges of price-fixing would bring a flush to Dave Beck's pink face: price-fixing was illegal. The only time his Teamsters were ever charged in court with conspiring to fix prices—and that was back in 1928—they were acquitted. One of Beck's lawyers in that suit was Lewis B. Schwellenbach, who later won a seat in the Senate and was appointed Secretary of Labor by President Truman. Beck said repeatedly that he "never sat down with industry and discussed a price." His critics pointed to a contract he negotiated in 1927 with a laundry association, under which laundry-wagon drivers were to be paid $18 a week and a 12-percent commission, the contract setting a standardized price list on which commissions would be paid. Beck denied this was price-fixing.

Beck also fumed at the suggestion that he had raised the cost of living in Seattle. "What kind of damn fool would I be to do that?" he once asked me when I raised the question. "Say we have 500 bakery drivers. Would I penalize the other 29,500 men I have in Seattle to benefit that 500 by raising bakery prices? Sure there has to be regulation. Hell, the day when there was unrestricted competition with no regulation is long gone. You don't think so, you go downtown and buy a plane ticket to Chicago and see how unrestricted competition on plane tickets is. But I don't raise the cost of living and there's no damn truth to saying we pyramid the cost of living.

"Now I ask you, does Dave Beck set the price of Coca-Cola in Seattle? You pay exactly what they pay in Alabama for Coca-Cola. Five cents a Coke. Same with other products. Look at the national magazines. The prices are set nationally on products, nationally; and if they are higher in the West they're higher all over the West, not just up in Seattle. But those people who make Coke, and things, they pay my people more wages; they pay them higher wages but they charge the same price here in Seattle that they do where they pay their workers half as much. Any intelligent person knows Dave Beck can't set prices."

On the other hand, Beck made no bones about the fact that he did everything he legally could to "stabilize conditions" for an industry that did business with him. "Our aim has been to develop better understanding between industry and labor," he said when asked about his Seattle system. "This is our contribution toward good government and better relationship between all classes and elements in the community. We have inculcated the concept that there is a definite understanding between those employed and those who invest capital. We do our part to make the system work. We observe our contracts to the letter."

Employers agreed that when they signed with Beck they could count on their labor force's staying on the job for the duration of the contract. Beck kept his promises to the letter, and he abhorred strikes. The boss could be sure his workers would do a reasonable amount of work. Nor need the employer worry that his men would be indoctrinated with anti-capitalist ideas by the union. Beck didn't believe in "educating" the workers; he held that such talk was "just a lot of CIO-communistic stuff." Anyway, Beck could spread the eagle farther than most patrioteers. He was an all-out anti-Communist who used fear of the Reds as one of his big selling points. "I stand unalterably opposed to the CIO and the sitdown strike," he said in 1937, while courting the bosses. "The seizure of private property by sitdown strikes will breed revolution. The Communists are behind it." Later he assured readers of the *Elks Magazine* that he believed "in a system where a man can be a menial today and own his own business tomorrow; where he and his family can look up at the stars once in a while and laugh and love and learn." As a member of the University of Washington Board of Regents he favored firing faculty members who took the Fifth Amendment.

The businessmen who dealt with Beck could be reasonably sure that Beck's love of free enterprise would not extend to anyone enterprising enough to trim prices. A firm that cut prices in Seattle might find that it had violated some clause of its agreement with the Central Labor Council; a picket could appear on the sidewalk, and the Teamsters could refuse to haul supplies past the picket line. Since the Teamsters control "everything on wheels, everything that moves," the cut-price outfit would either have to fall in line with the rest of the industry or go broke. "We do not want any of our industries to operate without a fair profit," Beck said repeatedly. To keep profits up he was willing to discourage newcomers from entering into competition with industries the Teamsters serviced. He told Richard Neuberger, in the Oregon journalist's pre-Senate period, that Seattle had too many filling stations. "We are going to close some of them," Beck said. "First I advise promoters against starting new stations. If that doesn't work, the Teamsters Union simply will refuse to serve them. They won't last long." The threat was enough to discourage newcomers for some time.

Beck preferred to do business with associations of employers, and his relations with such associations were cordial and close. The Cleaners and Dyers Association, formed in the early thirties, was operated by Beck's good friend William Short, a former president of the State Federation of Labor. The association took in nearly all the plants in Seattle. One of the few holdouts was the little Clean-Well establishment, operated by the Stalin brothers, Max, Sol, and Joe. After the plant had been shaken and smoked and singed by a series of still unexplained explosions and fires, its owners were converted from their primitive belief in unrestricted competition to an understanding of the benefits of the business-association form of collectivism. They joined the Cleaners and Dyers Association, paid dues of one percent on their retail volume, charged standard prices, and lived happily ever after.

The Bakers Association is another typical example. Its members pay dues according to their volume of business. In return they have the right to put a Bakers' union label on their products. Without the label goods cannot be handled by any Teamster.

Beck's definition of a Teamster was wondrously flexible. In Seattle the men who work in breweries are Teamsters. That is the result of a national jurisdictional dispute in which both Teamsters and Brewery Workers claimed jurisdiction over the men who drove beer trucks. The brewers won in the Midwest, so Beck declared that if Teamsters couldn't drive beer trucks in Milwaukee and other "Eastern" beer centers, brewers couldn't make beer in his bailiwick: Teamsters would brew the beer. He quickly organized Northwest breweries, not overlooking the opportunity to avail himself of stock in several of the largest. Employers went along with the shift in organization of their workers; anyone who held out, it was carefully rumored, might have trouble getting hops or bottles or, perhaps, workers in shape to work. After the Teamsters were making beer Beck declared that any beer hauled in the Northwest would have to carry the white label of the Teamster union; Eastern manufacturers might ship their red-labeled products west by train but nobody would truck the cases and kegs to stores and taverns. When Beck heard that the CIO Woodworkers had passed a resolution urging loggers not to drink Teamster-made beer, he said, "They'll either go one hell of a way for a drink or get damn thirsty." For years Northwest brewers were free from the competition of such big-name brewers as Pabst and Schlitz. The Eastern beer men got out injunctions, but the Teamsters got out the pickets: no Eastern beer moved. By the time the dispute was settled, Northwest beer (much of which is good) had secured domination in its home territory. In this industry too Beck kept things stable. When some Northwest breweries lowered their prices Beck told a reporter, "We're going to those men and tell them if they want to go on like that, it's all right, but we won't work for them." He did not have to repeat the suggestion.

When Beck couldn't bring workers directly into the Teamsters, he sometimes wrapped them up in captive locals. The largest of these groups was the Retail Clerks Union. As far as the national AFL structure was concerned, the clerks had a union of their own, but when Beck saw his chance he stepped in and made a quick deal with department-store managers. The managers posted notices telling their employees to join. The Teamsters helped organize the locals, picked the officers, and provided office space in the Teamsters' spacious headquarters. When, some years later, officials from the Clerks national put in an appearance in Seattle and suggested they could handle things, Beck shooed them away.

Of all Beck's union people in Seattle, the clerks were probably the most unhappy: Beck never did win them a good contract. Rival union organizations claimed Brother Dave's clerks received the lowest wages of department-store workers in any West Coast metropolitan area. But since the clerks had been organized by indirection and without struggle, they didn't know how to defend themselves. Turnover among clerks is traditionally high; they have little feeling of labor solidarity and almost no strike experience. So from time to time, when told what their next contract would be, and told to sign it, they signed. After listening to the details of one such sweetheart contract that had been "won" for the clerks by one of Beck's Cadillac-driving subalterns, a girl whose wage was set by it remarked, "Gee, I don't know whether Brother Dave organized the bosses or the bosses organized Brother Dave."

It was a question workers at the Boeing Airplane Company, Seattle's dominant industrial payroll, were to ask themselves shortly after the war. The Machinists had organized Boeing's years before; in 1947 they called a strike. Dave Beck had long coveted some five thousand warehousemen working at Boeing but represented by the Machinists. During the strike he declared limited war and began organizing the warehousemen behind the Machinist picket line. When the Machinists protested that they had been given jurisdiction over all hourly workers at the plant, warehousemen included, Beck blandly said that if that was the way the Machinists felt, the Teamsters would fight them for the whole lot of employees. And he did. Faced with battles against both management and Beck, the Machinists settled their strike on unfavorable terms, then braced themselves for Beck's organizing drive. The National Labor Relations Board called an election to determine which organization Boeing employees wanted to represent them. The Teamsters campaigned on the issues of responsibility and efficiency in unionism. The Machinists were simply anti-Beck; their slogan was "Don't Go Beckwards." The Machinists won, two to one. It was a major defeat for Beck, particularly bitter since it came in his home town.

Brother Dave's willingness to send his Teamsters through picket lines he did not consider legitimate failed to win favor among other unions. The State Federation of Labor roundly condemned his raiding and, in consequence, his local political influence began to decline. But Beck's threat of raids served a long-range purpose: it helped him maintain stability. Rival leaders whose main asset was the militancy of their membership hesitated to call strikes when they knew Beck might move in and start organizing a rival union behind their picket lines. Not being able to strike, they were less effective, and, being less effective, they lost power in relation to Beck.

The Teamsters' deteriorating relations with other unions helped splinter the once solid block of labor votes in Seattle and the state. Beck's endorsement became a questionable political asset. Arthur Langlie, who had begun his vote-catching in 1938 by drubbing Beck's personal mayor, ten years later unseated Beck's friend Monrad C. Wallgren as governor. Langlie's campaign was boldly anti-Beck; his political ads asked, "Do You Want A Beck-

Dominated Governor?" He sent a letter to every union leader in the state, saying he would do business with any representative of organized labor except Beck, who "in his lust for power has attempted to destroy the free trade unions of this state." Langlie won, and Wallgren—who had appointed Beck to the Board of Regents of the University of Washington and had put one of Beck's boys, Paul Ravelle, in as head of the State Board of Transportation—blamed Beck for his defeat. "That man wanted too much," Wallgren complained to a Seattle newspaperman. "He thought he owned me because he gave me some campaign help. I could have won if it hadn't been for him." Since Wallgren's good friend Harry Truman carried the state by a comfortable margin that year, political observers believe that the Beck issue may well have been decisive in Langlie's victory.

Beck's loss of direct political power in his home town did not seem to bother him. He had had it when he needed it. An intensely practical man, he had little interest in politics as social theory. "Our role is confined to protecting the interests of our people," he once said. "When I look at a candidate I ask myself, what would his election do to my relations with the men I do business with?" His relations with those men remained solid. They regarded Beck as a savior, and he gloried in their respect. Though he could no longer elect a personal mayor, he remained firmly in the saddle in Seattle. He didn't have to worry about local politics. His eyes were on more distant horizons.

6.

Like most people who live in Seattle, Dave Beck thinks his home town the most desirable place in the world to live; he has always said he couldn't imagine moving elsewhere. But that did not mean Beck was satisfied to be labor boss of his favorite city: he loved his country too.

By the end of World War II, Seattle was 95 per cent organized. It was only natural that Beck, one of the most efficient labor organizers in America, should be interested in wider fields that those furnished by the remaining 5 per cent. He began looking beyond Seattle as early as 1937, when he organized the Western Conference of Teamsters, a brilliantly improvised answer to the problem posed by the creation of the CIO and by over-the-road trucking.

The International Brotherhood of Teamsters, Chauffeurs, Warehousemen and Helpers of America, like Topsy and most AFL unions, had just growed; its power centered in the scattered urban communities where most trucking was done before the invention of the internal combustion engine. In each city or area the local boss ran things pretty much his own way, though it was advisable for the satraps to make an occasional low bow in direction of Indianapolis, where lived Dan Tobin, president of the Teamsters since 1907. This loose and democratic organization served well until the depression. In the early thirties there was a great spurt in long-distance trucking. And who had jurisdiction over the over-the-road men?

Beck created the Western Conference and was promptly elected its president. The Conference handled intra-Teamster relations in the West with which the national organization was not equipped to deal, but it did much more than that: it partially answered the advantages the CIO gained in vertical unionism. The Conference was divided into trade divisions; each division took in all the specialists in its line. This enabled Beck to apply pressure on a wide front; a baker, say, who bucked him in Sacramento might be hurt in Butte.

The Western Conference had more than 240 locals. They were in every important city in the eleven west-of-the-Rockies states, and in Hawaii and Alaska. The business agents of these locals, plus a staff of organizers at large, numbered nearly a thousand; all were indebted to Beck for their jobs. They were Beck's men and they gave him a loud voice in nearly every Central Labor Council in the West. This increased his national influence in the Teamsters and in the AFL.

In 1947 Beck was named executive vice-president of the Teamsters International. It was a new post, created

just for him, and it let him use his organizational talents
on a nationwide basis. The Teamsters were already the
largest union in the country, claiming more than a million
members and showing a bank balance of $20,000,000.
Beck planned a drive to increase the membership to four
million. First the Teamsters established national conferences on trade lines, designed to net garage workers, cannery workers, laundry workers—any of fifteen categories
of labor to which the Teamsters had laid claim. Beck did
not ask that levies be made on locals or the international
to finance this organizing drive: contributions were volun-
tary. The Western Conference gave most of the money;
men who had proved themselves in the West were put in
charge of the national trade divisions. They were Beck's
men. He set up a national organizing headquarters in
Washington, D.C., safely away from Teamsters International headquarters in Indianapolis, and he hired Burton
K. Wheeler, the former liberal senator, as legal adviser.

For a time labor circles buzzed with talk that Beck
intended to unseat his old benefactor, Dan Tobin. Such
talk made Beck genuinely angry. "Dan took me off a
laundry truck and made me what I am today," he said. "I
won't run until he asks me." Tobin asked Beck to take
over in 1952.

7.

Even Beck's enemies in Seattle saw profit in his elevation. He was the most powerful local man on the national
scene. He could do important favors; for instance he
could, and did, transfer large amounts of Teamster money
from Indianapolis banks to Seattle. Local insurance men
underwrote major Teamster policies. Small wonder that
the Chamber of Commerce wired flowers when Beck became international president, and a civic banquet was
arranged to honor "the first citizen of Seattle."

Accolades from the business community were nothing
new to the rotund Teamster. A Hearst business editor long
since had noted with relief that Beck's attitude on social

experiment paralleled that of the National Association of Manufacturers. The vice-president of the Northern Pacific had described him publicly as "a vigorous opponent of socialism and communist infiltration who is entitled to full and generous credit for his leadership." The president of the Northwest's largest private utility had said, "Beck is absolutely tops. With him around, we've had peace while it might have been hell." But it was Banker Nat S. Rogers, while president of the Seattle Chamber, who pointed up the attribute that made Beck seem to businessmen a pillar of rock amid the shifting sands of economic change. "He has," said the banker, "a sense that it is part of his responsibility to keep the profit motive alive."

Few had ever seen reason to doubt Beck's devotion to the profit motive, but in his postwar phase his observance of the rituals of being rich became more conspicuous. "Beck's attitude toward money," said one of his non-admirers on the University of Washington Board of Regents, "is uxorious." His clothes grew richer and better tailored, his office larger and more deep-toned, his cars longer, his phone conversations curter, his invitations to the annual Round Up Party at the Washington Athletic Club—a must for business and political leaders—more peremptory. It was during this period that Dave Beck moved from the modest frame house which had pinned him to the middle class, into a new Sheridan Beach estate with private pool, private cinema, even sumptuous private quarters for his private bodyguards.

Just as in Beck's early poverty one can see the spark that kindled the flames of both ambition and avarice, so can one see in Beck's fondness for material success a major cause of his success and his downfall. He understood and respected business, wanted to see businesses make money, liked and respected businessmen, and wanted to be liked and respected by them; wanted, indeed, to be one of them. His attitude became that of a businessman who had cornered the market in transportation. He used his monopoly on movement to further other enterprises.

"I'm well paid," Beck told an interviewer who asked

about his luxurious trappings. "The men like to have the fellow who negotiates for them show that he is in every way the equal of those with whom he deals."

If so, the Teamsters and the Clerks and the men who made beer and rolled barrels and all the others Beck had gathered into the fold must have been happy indeed. No businessman in the area was living higher off the hog than Brother Dave.

Among those with whom Beck was dealing at the time was Nathan W. Shefferman, president of Labor Relations Associates of Chicago, Inc., an odd organization with headquarters at 75 East Walker Drive, Chicago, branch offices in Detroit and New York, a number of emissaries at large, and fingers in the strangest of employer-worker pies. A self-styled expert, Shefferman had served briefly with the National Labor Relations Board in the thirties, then found employment as "consultant in employer-employee relations" for Sears Roebuck, and ultimately set himself up as a private enterpreneur in the labor-relations dodge.

For a fee Shefferman would advise employers on how to deal with their workers; he was an expert at finding ways by which his clients could avoid having their men organized, or, failing such perfection, in helping them get their people represented by locals with officials whose lack of militancy was matched by their surplus of pliability. Although Shefferman charged employers for his consultations, he performed helpful services for union leaders free. His speciality was getting things wholesale. A union president or business agent who wanted a television set or power mower or movie camera at cut rates had only to ask and good old reliable Nathan delivered. Sometimes it turned out that the man Shefferman was obliging was the man one of his clients was negotiating with on a union contract, but sometimes not. Some thought they detected in Shefferman's wholesaling the rancid scent of the sweetheart contract, but Nate saw in it only friendship. "This is the only manner in which I had to build good will, and I had no other thing. We don't advertise, and we don't solicit and we don't have any formulas and no

prescriptions or anything of the sort. My business was
being friendly with these men."

In all the labor movement, the records were to show,
Nathan Shefferman's best friend was Dave Beck.

                                8.

On January 6, 1954, a quiet little treasury agent who
had once been a neighbor of Beck's in Seattle received
orders from Washington, D.C., to look into the financial
affairs of the president of the Teamsters International.

Claude J. Watson, the T-man, shared a number of
attributes with Dave Beck. Each loved Seattle, each was
devoted to sports as a spectator, each followed with pride
a son's athletic career. But where Beck was conspicuous to
a fault in Seattle affairs, Watson has been accurately described as "a man who would be inconspicuous in a phone
booth." Few in Seattle today could name the man most
instrumental in bringing Beck down. Yet it was Watson's
sleuthing that turned the Sheridan Beach dream house into
a nightmare for the Teamster leader and remade the nation's conception of Seattle's first citizen.

It did not take Watson long to learn that Beck's boasted
business efficiency did not extend to his own record-
keeping. Where his own financial transactions were concerned, Beck was a back-of-the-envelope businessman.
What records Watson found, however, did not seem to
add up to what was on Beck's income-tax return.

"In three or four months after we started," Watson
quietly recalled later, "I knew we had something. The
question was to prove it. After those first few months
there never was a question in my mind that we would be
going to recommend a case. I just didn't know how good
it was going to be. When you get older, you know too
many things can happen in an investigation and you're
not as optimistic as some of these younger agents are."

Watson shuttled back and forth across the country in
search of statistics. Fifty agents were helping him, but he
did much of the work personally. He flew to Chicago,

New York, Minneapolis, Boston, Washington, Los Angeles, San Francisco. Records would disappear, people would refuse to talk; sometimes they lied. Trail after trail petered out, scents faded and others proved redolent of red herring. But bit by bit the evidence mounted up.

On March 12, 1957, three years and two months after he drew the assignment to investigate Beck, Watson turned in his report. It covered 445 pages of single-spaced typescript, and it warranted presentation to a grand jury. Ten weeks later Beck was indicted in Tacoma for income tax evasion. His friend Nate Shefferman stood charged with conspiracy to help him evade his taxes.

Even before Beck was indicted, the plot of his financial drama had become known to the nation. The Senate's watchdog Select Committee on Improper Activities in the Labor or Management Field—the McClellan Committee—had also traced back the sweet smell of Beck's prosperity as far as 75 East Walker Drive, Chicago. A nationwide television audience followed with fascination and horror the hunt.

Shefferman, driven to corner in the witness seat, painfully talked. He admitted that as an adviser to management he had done much business with Beck. He had once given him a friendly $24,000; he had made him loans without interest; he had gone in partnership with him on real-estate deals; their sons had collaborated in a scheme to sell toy trucks to Teamster locals. Shefferman had, of course, bought things for Beck wholesale. But in addition to doing Beck his standard middleman service, he also served Beck as paymaster in a none too devious arrangement by which Beck foisted his personal bills off onto the Teamster membership.

Beck's arrangement with Shefferman was simple. When the Teamster boss bought something, anything—it might be bow ties or bar-bells, roofing for his house or a Cinemascope screen for his playroom, loveseats or landscaping, knee drawers by the dozen or outboard motors by the pair—he simply sent the bill to Shefferman. And Shefferman paid the bill. Eventually he would be repaid by the Teamsters. Sometimes the money came from the

Seattle local, sometimes from the Western Conference, sometimes from a Teamster public-relations fund in Los Angeles administered by a man involved in the Beck, Junior-Shefferman, Junior, deal to peddle toy trucks with union labels to Teamster locals.

Beck and other Teamster officials claimed that his arrangements for using union funds were legal—a point not disproved—and that his income from the Teamsters was really a loan rather than larceny. He repaid much of the money. To make the repayments and meet Internal Revenue demands Beck was forced to sell his Sheridan Beach house. The hardship was not overwhelming: he sold it to the Teamsters, who granted him the right to keep living in it indefinitely.

There were other ways Beck had made money in bulk or piecemeal. He bought land across the street from various Teamster headquarters and sold the real estate at marvelous markups to the locals when they needed to expand. He bought gas stations near Teamster headquarters in Seattle and directed the boys to gas up at his stations. He established relatives in beer-distributing agencies. He set up relatives in a mortgage company and invested Teamster millions through it. While keeping his eye on the main chance, he did not neglect the little opportunities of economic life. For example, he sold the passes he received to the Seattle Rainiers Coast League baseball park to an elderly ex-Teamster who loved baseball. When the gaffer told Beck that because of ill health he could no longer afford to buy the tickets, Beck generously gave them to him, then paid himself from the Teamster treasury.

Called before the McClellan Committee, Beck repeatedly declined to testify, citing the advice of his attorney. In taking the Fifth Amendment (among others), a maneuver for which, as university regent, he had recommended that professors be fired, Beck said that if only he had the right to confront his accusers in court he would be cleared. But brought to trial in Seattle for having pocketed the receipts from the sale of a used Cadillac belonging to the Teamsters, he declined to take the stand in his own defense, and was found guilty, as was his son. Tried in Tacoma on six counts of income-tax evasion, he again avoided the witness stand and was found guilty on all counts.

One showery afternoon in late February 1959, Dave Beck stood on the worn rose-colored rug in front of the bench in Federal Judge George Boldt's courtroom. Flanked by attorneys who, it was noted, looked more like next of kin than lawyers, the former first citizen of his city reddened slowly as the judge summarized his career.

"No bootblack or newsboy of Horatio Alger's imagination ever rose from a more humble beginning to a greater height than Dave Beck," said the judge. "From the driver's place on a laundry wagon to the seats of the mighty, national and international, is a greater climb than even Alger conceived for any of his heroes. Did we not know what we now do know of Mr. Beck, his success story would be as thrilling and inspirational as almost any in the history of American opportunity, enterprise and ingenuity. The exposure of Mr. Beck's insatiable greed, resulting in his fall from high place, is a sad and shocking story that cannot be contemplated by anyone with the slightest pleasure or satisfaction. A fair appraisal of the evidence shows beyond glimmer of doubt that, as an incident of his tax fraud, Mr. Beck plundered his union, his intimate associates, and in some instances personal friends, most of whom quite readily would have freely given him almost anything he asked. As more than one of the union executive witnesses put it: 'He could have written his own ticket.'"

The Wheel Turns

Dave Beck served his federal time at McNeil Island and returned to Seattle a private citizen, accepted—perhaps more affectionately than before—but no longer dominant. During his lifetime, Seattle has transformed itself from a sawmill town rejuvenated by rubbed-off gold from the Klondike and Alaska, into the area's major financial community, respected and self-respecting, sure of its destiny. The city had remade its topography by casting away the tops of its hills and filling in the swampy salt beaches, an engineering feat that permitted it to expand from a beach-fringed settlement of 80,000 at the turn of the century to a metropolis of more than one-half million.

Seattle's attitude toward labor and politicians changed as greatly as its topography. Beck was peddling papers and the Chamber of Commerce told a committee of United States senators, "We hold that Seattle has no need of the laboring class." Beck was a minor figure in a minor union when Mayor Ole Hanson "saved Seattle from a labor dictatorship." Beck backed the widely-popular *Post-Intelligencer* strike in 1936 and was associated with some of the men whose activities led to James Farley's remark about "the forty-seven states and the Soviet of Washington."

By the fifties, Beck was the leader of a union so powerful that it prided itself on not needing to strike. The man who was called a threat in the thirties was proclaimed a bulwark of stability two decades later. In this, too, he resembled his city.

Seattle at the end of World War II had settled down. The brothels along the Skid Road had long been closed, the box-houses stood empty, the no-limit card games were hard to find, the waterfront was quiet. For years, there wasn't a good riot. The Wobblies maintained an office in the ancient Maynard Building, but no one marched in IWW parades, and Ralph Chapin, who wrote "Solidarity," was featured speaker at Chamber of Commerce dinners. Nor were all the changes among the radicals; Colonel Blethen's old paper, which once tarred dissent with a red brush, won a Pulitzer Prize for clearing a University of Washington professor wrongly accused of being a Communist.

When the Becks were new to Seattle, John Cort closed a high-class box-house he operated north of Yesler Way. "The trouble with Seattle is there's no middle-class," he complained. "There's the Four Hundred and there's the workers and neither of them wants to be caught dead in a place the other goes to." Cort solved his problem by going to New York, and Seattle solved the problem for later entertainers by becoming thoroughly middle-class. In the second decade of its second century, Seattle was a city of high wages (for which Beck was certainly as responsible as anybody) and of pleasant homes, a metropolis which considered itself to be without slums, a city of big wooden houses and wide green lawns, of parks and lakes and hills and trees—but also a city still cultivating a leafless forest of utility poles, still planting its soil to concrete, still convinced that growth was good for its own sake and would create greatness.

Still, Seattle did not consider itself great. It kept an envious eye on San Francisco and, when called on for comparison, tended to talk about the scenery. "To hear you people talk," an Easterner told a Seattle friend, "you'd think you built Mt. Rainier."

"Scenery is their substitute for culture," someone once remarked about Southern Californians, and this might be said of Seattlites, though the town did serve as home base for the leading painters of the North Western school: Mark Toby, Kenneth Callahan, and Morris Graves. Jim Bouton, the dissident knuckle-baller, gravely complimented the community in 1969 for paying more attention to the exhibitions in the lovely Fuller Museum than to the efforts of the Seattle Pilots of the American League during their one-year stand at Sick Stadium. The Seattle Symphony, after decades of delightful turmoil under the batons of such figures as Sir Thomas Beecham (who made no effort to conceal his conviction that he had arrived back of beyond and who, in consequence, was ridden out of town on a newspaper rail, leaving behind the legend that he had described the community as "an aesthetic dustbin"), and Manuel Rosenthal (the brilliant, abrasive Frenchman who was not permitted to return to the United States following an absurd contretemps with the Immigration Service), has stabilized in the high middle-class under Newton Katins. In recent years, Seattle has developed a surprising taste for opera, and the Seattle Repertory Theater, along with the summertime Contemporary Theater, have somehow managed to survive financially and aesthetically.

The Opera House and the Playhouse are residues of one of Seattle's most improbable successes, the World's Fair of 1962. The Fair not only paid its way (by typical Seattle bookkeeping, they counted contributions from the United States Treasury as earnings), but left as legacy a handsome civic center including facilities for music and drama; a coliseum which attracted a major-league basketball team; a multi-purpose arena; a satellite art museum; Minoru Yamasaki's delightful science pavilion; and the big-headed Space Needle which, whatever its limitations as a work of art, has become Seattle's best known artifact. There can be few towns in America of any size that have not dreamed of playing host to the world. Seattle was the first to do so at an apparent profit, a miracle made possible by the legislative skill—pork-barrel power, some say—of Washington's two senators, Warren Magnuson and Henry Jackson. Egged on by city hall politicians, Establishment businessmen, old-timers who recalled the Alaska-Yukon Exposition, and Jim Fabor, a publicist with a streak of the Erastus Brainerd in his makeup, Maggie and Scoop siphoned some 10 million dollars out of the Treasury for the project. Joe Gandy, a lawyer turned Ford dealer, somehow convinced the hard-to-convince Bureau of International Expositions that Seattle indeed was staging a recognizable World's Fair, not just an overblown salmon derby and hydroplane drone.

The Fair left Seattle smugly sure of inevitable success, a euphoria in no way diminished by Boeing's successive tie-ups in the fifties and early sixties with commercial jets. When Seattle captured an American League baseball franchise, floated 40 million dollars for a domed stadium which it felt would surely attract major-league football, while Boeing tooled up to produce the 747 jumbo jet and its design team worked on federally subsidized supersonic transport prototypes, Seattle's cup seemed to be running over. Direct Boeing employment in the Seattle-metropolitan area stood at more than 100,000.

War in the Far East and prospecting discoveries in Alaska, two traditional generators of maritime traffic, helped keep the waterfront busy. New grain elevators and loading equipment lured Inland Empire grain across the mountains and away from the gravity route down the Columbia to Portland. Scoop and Maggie, the only pair of Senate committee chairmen from any state north of the Mason-Dixon Line, dazzlingly re-electable, were household gods of prosperity. A national magazine was sounding out writers for an article to be called, "Will Success Spoil Seattle?": its theme, that with all its dreamings coming true simultaneously, the city was threatened with too rapid growth.

Waking up was painful. The first twinges were on the sports front. The committee to select a site for the domed stadium tried a fast shuffle with the recommendation of a consulting firm, dropped the deck, and in 1971 are still trying to gather up the cards. As a major league team, the Seattle Pilots proved a minor disaster on the field and at the gate, though the franchise itself appears to have been not unprofitable to its owners. Shipments to Southeast Asia slowed as the war went into reverse. Environmental concerns slowed development of the North Slope Oil Fields in Alaska. The airlines, hit by rising costs and slowing demands, cut back on orders for jets. Congress began to talk heresy: Was the SST necessary?

Boeing began to cut back. With the boom still echoing

in the hinterlands where developers were putting split-levels and high-rise apartments for the tens of thousands who had helped build the SSTs, Boeing began cutting back. Employment had fallen by more than 50 percent by the end of 1970, with the company predicting further decline for the coming year.

Smugness had given way to the jitters. Again there were manifestations of discontent in the streets of Seattle: bombings in the central area, anti-war disturbances on the University of Washington campus, marches of protest to City Hall, a demonstration in front of the Federal Courthouse that led to indictment for conspiracy to damage Federal property.

Seattle approaches the 120th anniversary of its founding with Boeing in decline, the SST in doubt, its assurance shaken. The city faces its greatest crisis of confidence since the day, nearly a century before, when the Northern Pacific Commissioners wired Arthur Denny to say, "We have located the terminus on commencement day." There is talk of diversification of industry, of avoiding next time the perils of go-for-broke, boom-or-bust projects, of using the present pause in growth to study priorities and to find ways of making life richer rather than making people rich.

It is a time when new voices are being heard and new ideas given attention. The dreamers of wayward dreams are speaking up again, and perhaps being listened to. Which is all to the good. For Seattle, after all, remains the Queen City of its area, a rank made possible not only by the business like Yeslers, the righteous Ronalds, the proper Burkes, but also the poverty-haunted Becks, the jingo editors and quick-on-the-trigger gamblers, by illiterate showmen and turncoat politicians, by drunken physicians and radical suffragettes, by lonesome Swedes and lonesome Chinese, by whores from San Francisco and virgins from Massachusetts, by every sort of American and almost every sort of people.

The old confidence has been shaken, but for all its disorders the City is handsome on its hills. The salt water that laps the pilings of the waterfront opens onto the oceans of the world. The mountains still catch and hold the rain of the eastering winds. The scenery is better than if it had been planned. And among more than one million people, new dreams are forming, some of which will come strangely true.

FAR CORNER

A Personal View of the Pacific Northwest

Stewart Holbrook

■

From the author of PROMISED LAND comes this fantastic kaleidoscope of the Northwest—the cities, the movements, the mountains, the rivers, the promise, the people.

"The only ex-lumberjack who has lectured at Harvard University on American History." *Lewis Gannett*

$1.50

A COMSTOCK EDITION

A TOUCH OF
OREGON

Ralph Friedman

This is the latest verse in a continuing love song to the state and history of Oregon. It sends you on a pilgrimage along rugged coasts, across desert and wheatfields, through orchards and up majestic mountains.

But more than that, it explores the dimensions of the people—men and women of a unique breed, whose characters have been given special expression by life in a magnificent state—whose destinies have been touched by Oregon.

$1.75

A COMSTOCK EDITION

To order by mail, send price of book plus 25¢ per order for handling to Ballantine Cash Sales, P.O. Box 505, Westminster, Maryland 21157. Please allow three weeks for delivery.

NORTHWEST PASSAGES

A Book of Travel

Ralph Friedman

The author "is an artist with words. You thrill
to magnificent scenery, delight in people, and re-
live history. And you want to pack up and pack
down the roads most people pass by. The book
itself is a vacation."

Medford Mail Tribune

"A 'must' for anyone wanting to travel in Oregon
and the Northwest."

Oregon Journal

$1.50

A COMSTOCK EDITION

To order by mail, send price of book plus
25¢ per order for handling to Ballantine Cash
Sales, P.O. Box 505, Westminster, Maryland
21157. Please allow three weeks for delivery.

BIG SAM

A timberman, his family, and a way of life in
the Pacific Northwest

SAM CHURCHILL

A powerful first-hand chronicle of a real-life Paul Bun-
yan and the raw exciting life of the turn-of-the-century
lumber camps. Against the story of the rise and fall of
the logging industry is set the warm and beautiful story
of a son's admiration for his father.

$1.25

A COMSTOCK EDITION

To order by mail, send price of book plus 25¢
per order for handling to Ballantine Cash
Sales, P.O. Box 505, Westminster, Maryland
21157. Please allow three weeks for delivery.

A Tribute of the Storytellers of the Old West!

ROCKY MOUNTAIN TALES

Levette J. Davidson and Forrester Blake

A collection of yarns and fables from the brave old-timers who first roamed the great frontier. Tales of early Western trails, the pony express, stage drivers, prairie fires, shootings and hangings that perhaps originated around a campfire one dark night and lived to be retold today.

"A book of rare insight."

U.S. Quarterly Booklist

"A lot of fun."

San Francisco Chronicle

$1.50

A COMSTOCK EDITION

To order by mail, send price of book plus 25¢ per order for handling to Ballantine Cash Sales, P.O. Box 505, Westminster, Maryland 21157. Please allow three weeks for delivery.

A lively history of a legendary town

GREEN TIMBER
Thomas Emerson Ripley

Here is Tacoma, Washington in the boom-and-bust days of the early 1890s, when the town was bursting with confidence, and the hills behind were rich in sweeping stands of timber.

"A rich light-hearted memoir, and a valuable fund of joyous historical anecdotes."
— *The Seattle Times*

$1.25

A COMSTOCK EDITION

To order by mail, send price of book plus 25¢ per order for handling to Ballantine Cash Sales, P.O. Box 505, Westminster, Maryland 21157. Please allow three weeks for delivery.

SOURDOUGH SAGAS

Herbert L. Heller

Alaska 1883-1923 . . . Eager, hardy and adventurous, they searched for gold and excitement in the vast white wilderness of the North. They crossed the Yukon into a land that exacted its toll of life and limb from its challengers. The first-hand account of struggle, fun and savage splendor by some of the brotherhood that conquered the last frontier.

$1.25

A COMSTOCK EDITION

To order by mail, send price of book plus 25¢ per order for handling to Ballantine Cash Sales, P.O. Box 505, Westminster, Maryland 21157. Please allow three weeks for delivery.

DONKEYS
OF
THE
WEST

William G. Long

THEY MADE HISTORY—THEY CREATED LORE
AND LEGEND, YET THERE HAS BEEN NO
PRAISE FOR THEM—TILL NOW!

In this unique and witty collection of Western tales about the donkey—the mines
founded and the prospectors saved—the author presents the case of human jackass vs.
manly beast in which the donkey comes off
the better.

$1.50

A COMSTOCK EDITION

To order by mail, send price of book plus
25¢ per order for handling to Ballantine Cash
Sales, P.O. Box 505, Westminster, Maryland
21157. Please allow three weeks for delivery.